JUNIOR

GREAT **WORSHIP** FOR KIDS

HE IS CREATOR

STANDARD PUBLISHING
Cincinnati, Ohio

Writers

Peggy Schlieker, Units 1–3
Nancy Karpenske, Units 4, 5
Sharon K. Johnson, Unit 6

Artists

Dan Grossmann—Pages 8, 13, 14, Activity Pages 1A, 1B, 3B, 9A, 10A, 10B, 12B, 13B
Brenda Mann—Activity Pages 16B, 18A, 21B
Shauna Mooney—Pages 15, 16, Activity Pages 2A, 5A, 6B, 7A, 7B 12A, 15B, 22A, 26A
Debora Weber—Activity Pages 15A, 17B, 25A, 21A, all other inside art
Sandy Wimmer—Title Page, Pages 2, 3, 5–7, 9–11, 121, 175, Activity Pages 2B, 3A, 4A, 4B, 5B, 6A, 8A, 8B, 9B, 11A, 11B, 13A, 14A, 14B, 16A, 17A, 18B, 19A, 19B, 20A, 20B, 21A, 23A, 23B, 24A, 24B, 25B, 26B

Library of Congress Cataloging-in-Publication Data

Great worship for kids. Junior.
p. cm.
ISBN 0-87403-845-6 (v. 1)
1. Worship (Religious education)
BV1522.G66 1991
264'.0083'4—dc20 91-8432
CIP

Table of Contents

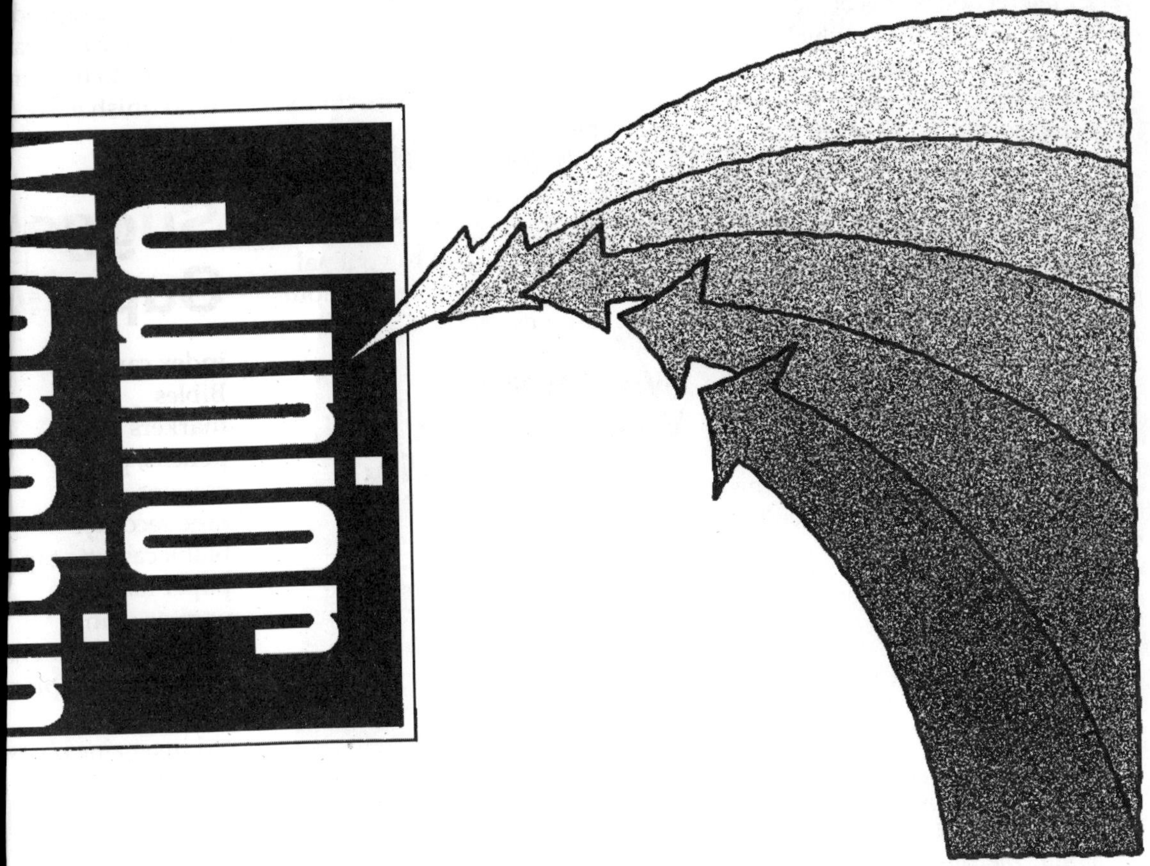

What Is Great Worship for Kids?

Welcome to 26 weeks of great worship sessions for your Juniors. What makes worship a great experience for your kids? What is *Great Worship for Kids*? To determine what great worship is, we must first determine what it is not.

Great Worship for Kids is **not** a second Sunday-school hour. The emphasis in Sunday school is on instruction. The emphasis in worship is on worship.

Great Worship for Kids is **not** a mini-adult worship service. Primaries do not think like adults. Great worship for kids enables them to worship on their level of understanding and development.

Great Worship for Kids is **not** a service designed simply to keep Juniors occupied while adults are in worship. The children's worship is as important and meaningful as the adult worship.

What **is** *Great Worship for Kids*? It is a program in which your Juniors truly worship God with understanding and have the opportunity to actively participate in worship. Juniors take part both in preparation and in actual worship.

Each session provides six small-group activity choices. In the small groups, children prepare to lead the call to worship, Scripture, prayer, special music, devotional, offering, Lord's Supper, or personal praise. As Juniors learn about God—who He is and what He has done, they are given opportunity to respond in praise and thanksgiving. Thus, Juniors are led to worship God.

When Juniors participate in this worship program, they

KNOW Biblical concepts and basic skills of worship.

FEEL positive attitudes toward worship.

DO actively participate in worship.

When Juniors prepare and lead the worship time, they learn the worship is giving, not receiving. Worship is active, not passive. Worship is my responsibility, not the responsibility of the person in front of the church.

Worship cannot be forced on anyone. But when Juniors know who God is and what He has done, they can respond in love, praise, and thanks. Their response is true worship.

How to Use This Material

How Is This Material Organized?

This book contains 26 sessions. The sessions are divided into six units of three, four, or five sessions each. The units explore reasons for worshiping God. Worship God: for His creation, for His promises, for His care, for Jesus, for giving us friends, for being our friend. The sessions are based on Scriptures taken from Standard Publishing's Middler and Junior Sunday-school curriculum.

The sessions are planned so that Juniors work in small groups to prepare the elements of the worship time (call to worship, Scripture, special music, devotional, and so on). The elements the small groups have prepared are then incorporated into the worship time.

Each weekly session is designed to last 80-95 minutes. This includes the time between the end of Sunday school and the beginning of adult worship.

The sessions are organized into six segments.

Worship Focus
Transition Time (10-15 minutes)
Launching the Theme (10 minutes)
Building the Theme (30 minutes)
Sharing in Worship (20-25 minutes)
Closing Moments (10-15 minutes)

What Happens in Each Segment?

Worship Focus

This section gives a reason for worshiping God. Worship God because . . . He created the world; He provides for us; He keeps His promises; He guides us through His Word. Every activity in the session centers on the worship focus.

Transition Time
(10-15 minutes)

Transition Time is the flexible time between Sunday school and Junior worship. This is a casual time for relaxation and conversation. It includes a rest-room and drink break, as well as a game which allows the Juniors to move around freely. This freedom is important after they have been sitting during the Sunday-school hour.

Involving the Juniors in organized activity as soon as they arrive also avoids confusion and eliminates the moments you spend gathering children from the halls when you are ready to begin the worship time.

Launching the Theme
(10 minutes)

During *Launching the Theme*, the leader introduces the theme of the session to the Juniors. The leader may tell a Bible story or modern-day story, present an object lesson, present a skit, or ask Juniors to role-play. Involving Juniors during this section is a priority.

The leader also explains the small-group choices and allows Juniors to choose in which group to participate. The leader guides the children to choose groups they are interested in. Depending upon the maturity level and group dynamics of the children, the leader may assign groups, rather than letting Juniors choose.

Building the Theme
(30 minutes)

During this time, Juniors work in their groups to prepare the elements of the worship time: call to worship, prayer, Scripture, special music, group singing, Lord's Supper, offering, personal praise, or devotional. During *Sharing in Worship*, the Juniors present what they prepared in their groups.

Sharing in worship
(20-25 minutes)

The large group gathers for the worship time. The leader directs this time and integrates the small-group activities into the worship time. Thus, the Juniors participate in worship.

Closing Moments
(10-15 minutes)

Closing Moments is the flexible time between the end of Junior worship and the end of adult worship. This section lists a variety of activities, but each one can be dropped quickly and easily when the adult service is over.

What Other Materials Will I Need?

Activity Pages

Following the worship sessions is a section of fifty-two reproducible activity pages—two pages for each session. The pages are used in a variety of ways—an introductory game, a puzzle, words to a song, a book, and so on.

Worship Songs

The final section of this book contains worship songs which are incorporated into the worship sessions. You may wish to pull out the song section and place it in a loose-leaf notebook for easy reference.

Classroom Supplies

See the Suggested Supplies on this page for a list of supplies you should have available every week. At the beginning of each activity is a list of materials you will need. Read the session early in the week and make a list of any special items or supplies you will need to gather ahead of time.

How Many Leaders Do We Need?

A coordinating leader is responsible to plan *Transition Time, Launching the Theme, Sharing in Worship,* and *Closing Moments.* You will need as many other leaders as you have small groups during *Building the Theme.*

What If We Have Only One Leader?

Shorten *Launching the Theme*, and lengthen *Building the Theme.* Choose two or three small-group activities to complete with your group. The devotional includes a leader talk which can be completed without a group presentation, so you would not need to complete that activity. Some activities can be completed without adult guidance. Write or tape record the instructions for a self-explanatory activity. Choose older or more mature Juniors to complete the activity. Choose an activity th can lead the rest of the group completing at the same time a self-explanatory activity. If yo have time, choose another acti to complete as a large group. During *Sharing in Worship*, om sections if you did not offer the corresponding activity. The Lo Supper, Offering, and Devotion may always be completed with the group presentations.

What If We Worship First And Have an Activity Time Second?

Use the activity in *Launching the Theme* to introduce the worship time. Then proceed with worship, using the leader talk provided wi each section and the devotional talk to tie in the worship to the theme of the day. During the activity time, choose group activities from *Building the Theme* which reinforce the concepts discussed in worship. If you have time, Juniors may share what they have learned in their small groups at the end of the session rather than completing the activity in *Closing Moments.*

What If One Small Group Finishes Early?

If you have not chosen to do the self-explanatory activity for that session, have the materials available. Juniors who finish early can complete that activity. A challenge activity is also included in each section. This activity is for gifted or older Juniors and will take longer to complete. If you have Juniors who are consistently finished early, assign them to this

What Is Great Worship for Kids?

Welcome to 26 weeks of great worship sessions for your Juniors. What makes worship a great experience for your kids? What is *Great Worship for Kids*? To determine what great worship is, we must first determine what it is not.

Great Worship for Kids is **not** a second Sunday-school hour. The emphasis in Sunday school is on instruction. The emphasis in worship is on worship.

Great Worship for Kids is **not** a mini-adult worship service. Primaries do not think like adults. Great worship for kids enables them to worship on their level of understanding and development.

Great Worship for Kids is **not** a service designed simply to keep Juniors occupied while adults are in worship. The children's worship is as important and meaningful as the adult worship.

What **is** *Great Worship for Kids*? It is a program in which your Juniors truly worship God with understanding and have the opportunity to actively participate in worship. Juniors take part both in preparation and in actual worship.

Each session provides six small-group activity choices. In the small groups, children prepare to lead the call to worship, Scripture, prayer, special music, devotional, offering, Lord's Supper, or personal praise. As Juniors learn about God—who He is and what He has done, they are given opportunity to respond in praise and thanksgiving. Thus, Juniors are led to worship God.

When Juniors participate in this worship program, they

KNOW Biblical concepts and basic skills of worship.

FEEL positive attitudes toward worship.

DO actively participate in worship.

When Juniors prepare and lead the worship time, they learn the worship is giving, not receiving. Worship is active, not passive. Worship is my responsibility, not the responsibility of the person in front of the church.

Worship cannot be forced on anyone. But when Juniors know who God is and what He has done, they can respond in love, praise, and thanks. Their response is true worship.

How to Use This Material

How Is This Material Organized?

This book contains 26 sessions. The sessions are divided into six units of three, four, or five sessions each. The units explore reasons for worshiping God. Worship God: for His creation, for His promises, for His care, for Jesus, for giving us friends, for being our friend. The sessions are based on Scriptures taken from Standard Publishing's Middler and Junior Sunday-school curriculum.

The sessions are planned so that Juniors work in small groups to prepare the elements of the worship time (call to worship, Scripture, special music, devotional, and so on). The elements the small groups have prepared are then incorporated into the worship time.

Each weekly session is designed to last 80-95 minutes. This includes the time between the end of Sunday school and the beginning of adult worship.

The sessions are organized into six segments.

Worship Focus
Transition Time (10-15 minutes)
Launching the Theme (10 minutes)
Building the Theme (30 minutes)
Sharing in Worship (20-25 minutes)
Closing Moments (10-15 minutes)

What Happens in Each Segment?

Worship Focus

This section gives a reason for worshiping God. Worship God because . . . He created the world; He provides for us; He keeps His promises; He guides us through His Word. Every activity in the session centers on the worship focus.

Transition Time

(10-15 minutes)

Transition Time is the flexible time between Sunday school and Junior worship. This is a casual time for relaxation and conversation. It includes a rest-room and drink break, as well as a game which allows the Juniors to move around freely. This freedom is important after they have been sitting during the Sunday-school hour.

Involving the Juniors in organized activity as soon as they arrive also avoids confusion and eliminates the moments you spend gathering children from the halls when you are ready to begin the worship time.

Launching the Theme

(10 minutes)

During *Launching the Theme*, the leader introduces the theme of the session to the Juniors. The leader may tell a Bible story or modern-day story, present an object lesson, present a skit, or ask Juniors to role-play. Involving Juniors during this section is a priority.

The leader also explains the small-group choices and allows Juniors to choose in which group to participate. The leader guides the children to choose groups they are interested in. Depending upon the maturity level and group dynamics of the children, the leader may assign groups, rather than letting Juniors choose.

Building the Theme

(30 minutes)

During this time, Juniors work in their groups to prepare the elements of the worship time: call to worship, prayer, Scripture, special music, group singing, Lord's Supper, offering, personal praise, or devotional. During *Sharing in Worship*, the Juniors present what they prepared in their groups.

Sharing in worship

(20-25 minutes)

The large group gathers for the worship time. The leader directs this time and integrates the small-group activities into the worship time. Thus, the Juniors participate in worship.

Closing Moments

(10-15 minutes)

Closing Moments is the flexible time between the end of Junior worship and the end of adult worship. This section lists a variety of activities, but each one can be dropped quickly and easily when the adult service is over.

What Other Materials Will I Need?

Activity Pages

Following the worship sessions is a section of fifty-two reproducible activity pages—two pages for each session. The pages are used in a variety of ways—an introductory game, a puzzle, words to a song, a book, and so on.

Worship Songs

The final section of this book contains worship songs which are incorporated into the worship sessions. You may wish to pull out the song section and place it in a loose-leaf notebook for easy reference.

Classroom Supplies

See the Suggested Supplies on this page for a list of supplies you should have available every week. At the beginning of each activity is a list of materials you will need. Read the session early in the week and make a list of any special items or supplies you will need to gather ahead of time.

How Many Leaders Do We Need?

A coordinating leader is responsible to plan *Transition Time, Launching the Theme, Sharing in Worship,* and *Closing Moments.* You will need as many other leaders as you have small groups during *Building the Theme.*

What If We Have Only One Leader?

Shorten *Launching the Theme,* and lengthen *Building the Theme.* Choose two or three small-group activities to complete with your group. The devotional includes a leader talk which can be completed without a group presentation, so you would not need to complete that activity. Some activities can be completed without adult guidance. Write or tape record the instructions for a self-explanatory activity. Choose older or more mature Juniors to complete the activity. Choose an activity that you can lead the rest of the group in completing at the same time as the self-explanatory activity. If you have time, choose another activity to complete as a large group. During *Sharing in Worship,* omit sections if you did not offer the corresponding activity. The Lord's Supper, Offering, and Devotional may always be completed without the group presentations.

What If We Worship First And Have an Activity Time Second?

Use the activity in *Launching the Theme* to introduce the worship time. Then proceed with worship, using the leader talk provided with each section and the devotional talk to tie in the worship to the theme of the day. During the activity time, choose group activities from *Building the Theme* which reinforce the concepts discussed in worship. If you have time, Juniors may share what they have learned in their small groups at the end of the session rather than completing the activity in *Closing Moments.*

What If One Small Group Finishes Early?

If you have not chosen to do the self-explanatory activity for that session, have the materials available. Juniors who finish early can complete that activity. A challenge activity is also included in each section. This activity is for gifted or older Juniors and will take longer to complete. If you have Juniors who are consistently finished early, assign them to this activity. You may also wish to use one of the reproducible activity pages in each session as an optional activity to be completed by Juniors who finish early.

Suggested Supplies

index cards
Bibles
markers
pencils, pens
crayons
tape recorder
blank cassette tape
paper fasteners
yarn or string
chalkboard and chalk
stapler and staples
push pins
old magazines/newspapers
scissors
glue
cellophane tape
Plasti-Tak
paper hole punch
plain paper
writing paper
construction paper
newsprint paper
poster board
paper towels/tissues

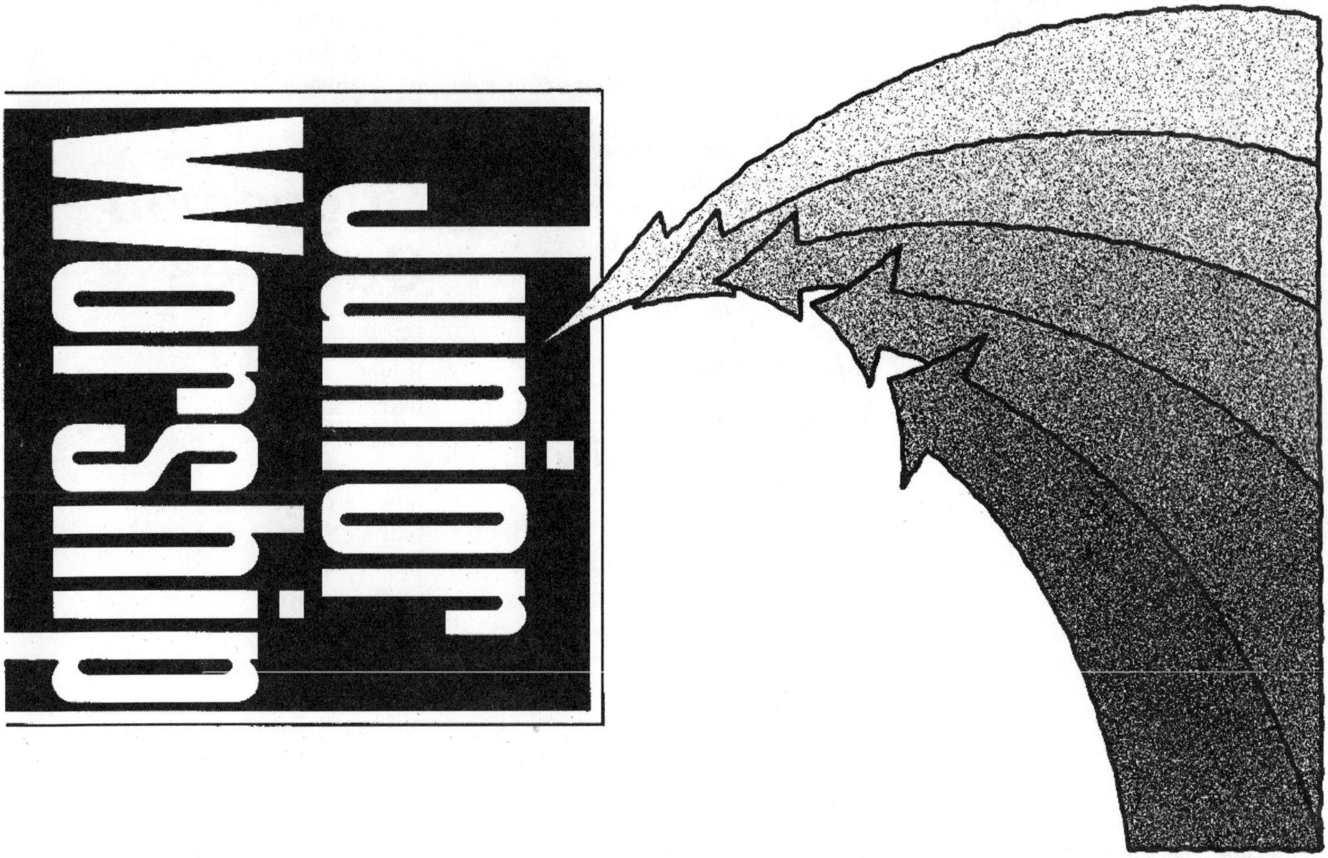
Junior
Worship

Worship
God

Worship Plan Sheet

Session ______ Date __________

Unit Title ______________________________

Session Title ______________________________

Worship Focus ______________________________

Transition Time

Leader ______________________________

Materials: ______________________________

Preparation: ______________________________

Procedure: ______________________________

Launching the Theme

Leader ______________________________

Materials: ______________________________

Preparation: ______________________________

Procedure: ______________________________

Building the Theme

Group 1. ______________________________ Leader ______________________________

Materials: ______________________________

Preparation: ______________________________

Procedure: ______________________________

Group 2. ______________________________ Leader ______________________________

Materials: ______________________________

Preparation: ______________________________

Procedure: ______________________________

Group 3. ______________________________ Leader ______________________________

Materials: ______________________________

Preparation: ______________________________

Procedure: ______

Group 4. ______ Leader ______
Materials: ______

Preparation: ______

Procedure: ______

Group 5. ______ Leader ______
Materials: ______

Preparation: ______

Procedure: ______

Group 6. ______ Leader ______
Materials: ______

Preparation: ______

Procedure: ______

Sharing in Worship

Leader ______

Closing Moments

Leader ______
Materials: ______

Preparation: ______

Procedure: ______

Activities for Special Days

Autumn Bookmark

Materials: A copy of page 15 for each child, yarn (32″ long), construction paper, scissors, glue, crayons or markers.

Distribute copies of page 15. Give the children the following instructions.

1. Choose two autumn patterns from this page.
2. On one pattern, write something God made. On the other pattern, write a thank-you prayer to God for that thing.
3. Decorate the patterns.
4. Cut out the patterns.
5. Glue the patterns to construction paper. Put another piece of construction paper behind the piece you glued the patterns on.
6. Cut around the patterns through both pieces of construction paper.
7. Spread glue on the back of two matching patterns.
8. Put one end of the yarn between the two patterns and stick them together.
9. Do the same thing with the other end of the yarn and the other two patterns.

Christmas Wreath

Materials: A strip from a brown paper bag (2 1/2″ x 36″) for each child; scissors; glue; pencils; a stapler; chenille wire; construction paper, fabric scraps, wallpaper scraps, narrow ribbon, glitter, crayons or markers, or Christmas stickers to decorate the wreaths.

Distribute the materials to the children. Give them the following instructions.

1. Crush and twist the brown strips into a small circle (approximately 3″ across).
2. Ask a leader to staple the ends of the wreath together for you.
3. Wrap a piece of chenille wire around the wreath and twist it into a bow.
4. Decorate your wreath. You can cut objects out of construction paper, fabric, or wallpaper and glue them to the wreath. You can put stickers or glitter on your wreath. You can wrap ribbon around your wreath.

Option: If your time is limited, you may wish to make the undecorated wreaths yourself before the session.

Winter Pop-up Card

Materials: A copy of pages 13 and 14 made on white construction paper for each child, construction paper, crayons or markers, scissors, glue.

Distribute copies of pages 13 and 14. Ask the children to color and cut out the snowman. Then read the instructions on activity page 14 with them. You may wish to demonstrate each step as you read it.

1. Cut out Piece A. Fold it in half. Cut on the solid lines.
2. Fold back the small tab you cut out.
3. Open the paper and push the tab through to the other side.
4. Cut out Piece B. Cut on the solid line in the middle.
5. Fold on the dotted lines.
6. Open the paper and push the folds inside.
7. Fold a piece of construction paper in half.
8. Spread glue around the outside edge of Piece A. Glue Piece A inside the folded construction paper.
9. Spread glue around the outside of Piece B. Glue over Piece A, making sure the tab on piece A can be seen.
10. Spread glue on the front of the tab. Glue the snowman to the tab.

Valentine Place Mat

Materials: A copy of page 15 made on white construction paper for each child, A copy of page 16 made on pink construction paper for each child, scissors, glue, markers or crayons, clear adhesive paper (optional).

Distribute the activity pages. Give the children the following instructions.

1. Cut on the solid lines on activity page 16 to make slits.
2. Cut the heart strips from activity page 15.
3. Weave the heart strips in and out of the slits on activity page 16.
4. On each heart, write something you could say to show God's love. Examples follow: God loves you. You are special. God sent Jesus for you. I love you. I will help you.
5. Decorate your place mat with construction-paper scraps or crayons and markers.
6. Cover your place mat with clear adhesive paper.

Let's Talk About Salvation

by Barbara Bolton

One of the greatest joys of teaching Juniors is the opportunity to participate with a child as he or she reaches the point of salvation. Actually, many individuals may be a part of this life-changing decision. Some will be seed planters. Some will be encouragers. Some will model the love of God. And some will be involved in the conversation that precedes the acceptance of God's great gift.

Juniors may ask questions, opening opportunities to discuss their need to accept God's gift of eternal life. These suggestions will help you discuss salvation with your Juniors.

• *Use concrete terms.* Children are not symbolic thinkers. They are easily confused by symbolism and often hear and understand in a literal way. "Let Jesus come into your heart" may produce a mental image of Jesus literally walking into a heart! Select vocabulary that is accurate, comfortable for you, and appropriate for your pupils' age; for example, "Let Jesus become a part of your life."

• *Use words consistently.* Prepare a list of words with simple definitions and always use those words with those meanings. As you begin a conversation with a Junior, for example, you would use the words **sin**, thinking or acting in ways that do not please God; **forgiveness,** being pardoned by God and not punished for our sins; and **eternal life**, living forever with new help from God.

• *Talk and listen.* Talking, questioning, listening, thinking, and praying together enable you to determine a young person's readiness and desire to take this important step.

• *Seek direction from the Holy Spirit.* He knows the heart of every person. Continually pray that the Spirit will give you sensitivity to the needs of each Junior. Do not rush ahead or lag behind His leading.

• *Know your Juniors.* Invest time in building the kind of relationships that communicate unconditional love and acceptance. Juniors will seek you out with their questions if you do. Become acquainted with each Junior's family. Attend special events in which they are involved. Talk with them as they arrive on Sunday, call them on the phone, or visit them at home.

• *Avoid situations in which peer pressure or adult pressure will unduly influence this vital decision.* Salvation decisions must not be group decisions. In a group setting, questions may be answered in a general way, but the actual discussion of individual salvation should occur in one-to-one conversation. Conclude times of group discussion by assuring Juniors that you will talk individually with anyone who has questions.

Individual conversation enables you to discover the Junior's level of understanding, extend your teaching, and correct any wrong information. And it will help you know how best to involve parents (another good reasons for having made calls and visits to the home earlier in the year!).

• *Select Bible references to share with the young person who is ready for salvation.* There are many from which to choose. Select those you think are most appropriate and highlight them in your Bible. Encourage the young person to read the verses from his or her own Bible. Consider these verses. (Always use an easy-to-understand translation. The *International Children's Bible* , a direct translation, is easily understood.)

Romans 3:23—Everyone has sinned ("is a sinner").

Romans 6:23—We *earn* the penalty for sin (death). God *gives* us the gift of life forever in Christ Jesus.

1 Corinthians 15:3, 4—Christ died for our sins (took our punishment). He was buried and raised to life on the third day.

After discussing these Scriptures, study together one or more of the following conversion stories from the New Testament: the crowd on Pentecost (Acts 2:36-41); the Ethiopian eunuch (Acts 8:26-39); Cornelius (Acts 10:24-48); Lydia (Acts 16:12-15); the Philippian jailer (Acts 16:22-34); the Corinthians (Acts 18:1-8); Saul of Tarsus (Acts 22:3-16).

• *Encourage growth in a Junior who makes a salvation decision.* Help him or her consider some of the wonderful promises made to believers by God. Provide direction for establishing habits that will encourage continual growth. Discuss Scriptures that talk about growth, and develop a plan for accountability.

Scripture provides a wonderful promise for those who are involved in ministry. Claim this promise as you have continued opportunity to share God's Word with Juniors: "Using the Scriptures, the person who serves God will be ready and will have everything he needs to do every good work" (2 Timothy 3:17, *ICB*).

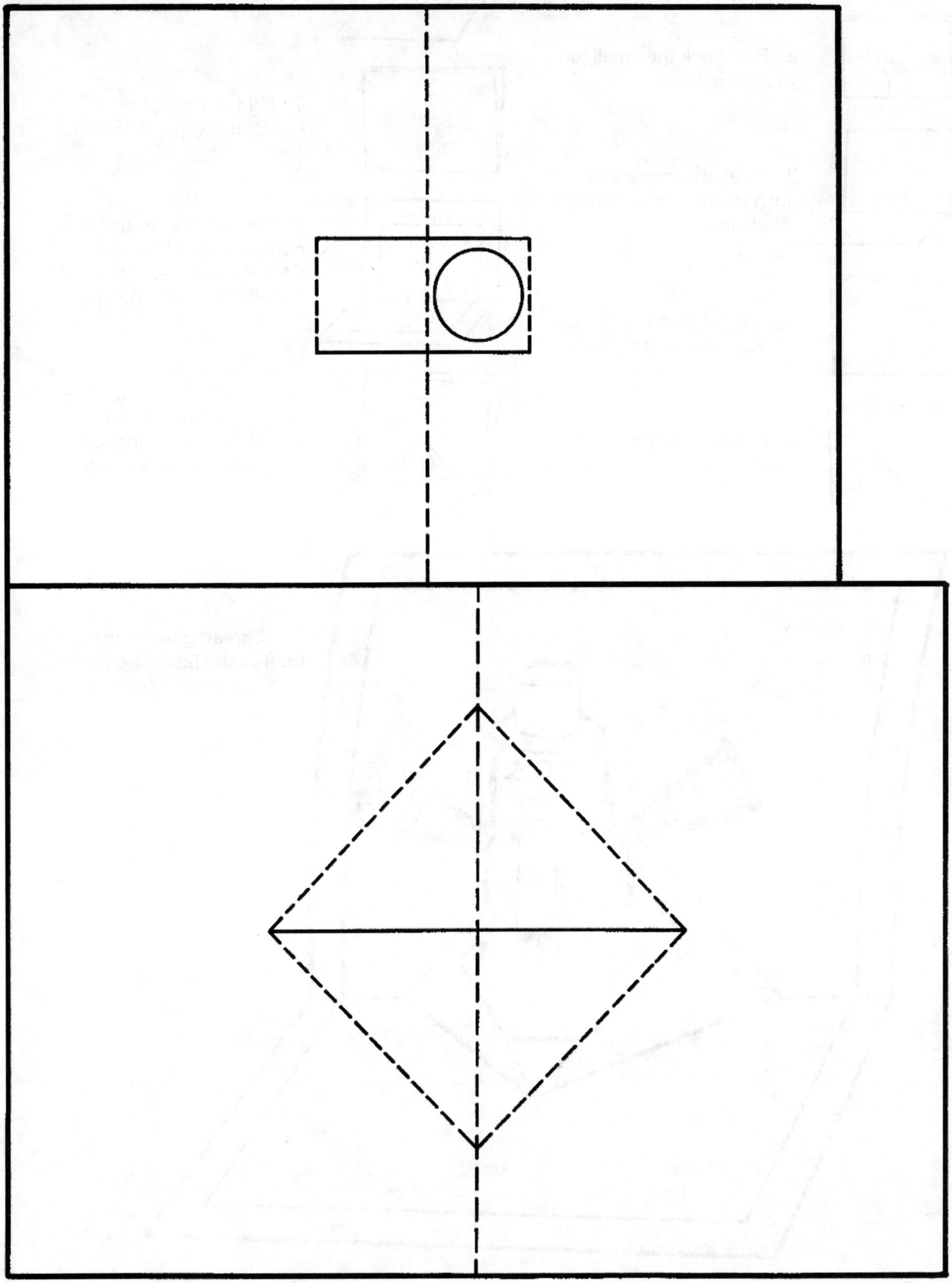

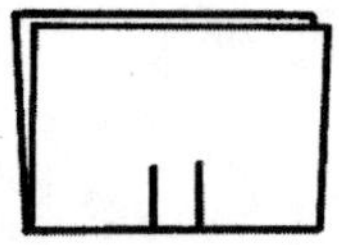

1. Cut out Piece A. Fold it in half. Cut on the solid lines.

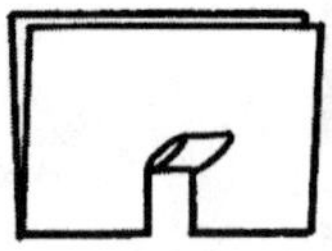

2. Fold back the small tab you cut out.

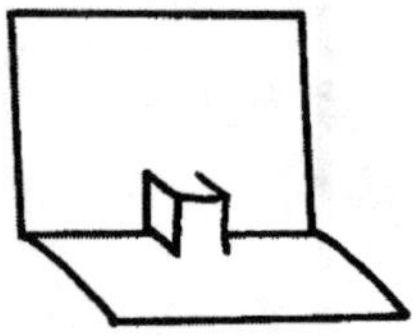

3. Open the paper and push the tab through to the other side.

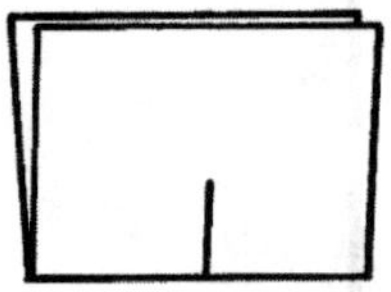

4. Cut out Piece B. Cut on the solid line in the middle.

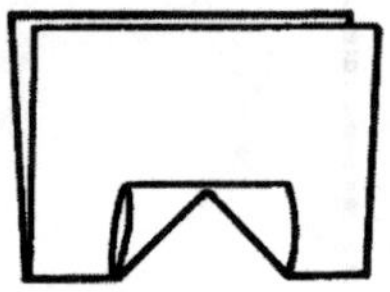

5. Fold on the dotted lines.

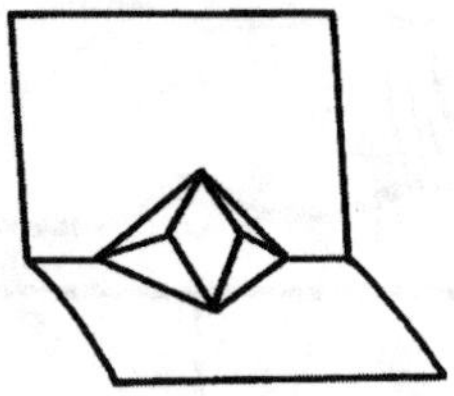

6. Open the paper and push the folds inside.

7. Fold a piece of construction paper in half.

8. Spread glue around the outside edge of Piece A. Glue Piece A inside the folded construction paper.

9. Spread glue around the outside of Piece B. Glue over Piece A, making sure the tab on piece A can be seen.

10. Spread glue on the front of the tab. Glue the snowman to the tab.

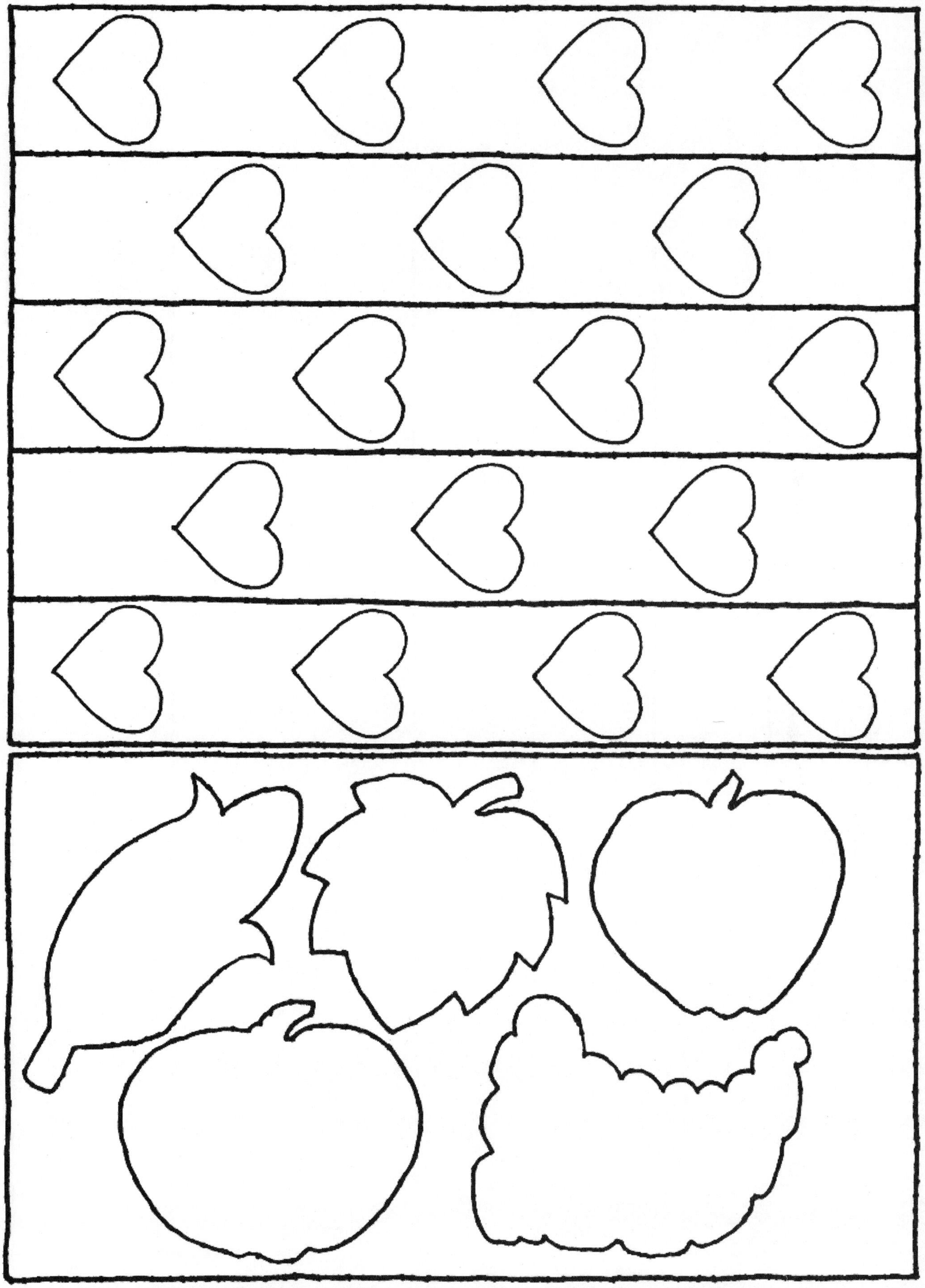

Unit 1
Worship God for His Power

Session 1

God's Power Created the World

Worship Focus

Worship God because only He has the power to create.

Transition Time

(10-15 minutes)

Name Game. Probably your Juniors have recently promoted into this worship group. This game will help them get better acquainted with each other. Ask Juniors to sit in a circle. Give one Junior a sack of marbles. He will take a marble, tell his or her name and a fact about himself or herself. He or she then gives the sack to the person on his or her left. This person repeats the first person's name and information, then takes a marble, and says his or her name and a fact about himself or herself. He or she then passes the sack to the person on his left. Each subsequent person must repeat all the information given previously before saying his or her information. If you have a large group, divide the class into groups of ten or less. Variation: Use an edible treat instead of marbles.

Launching the Theme

(10 minutes)

Before class ask several parents to loan you items that their children have made. **These articles were made by some of you. As I show these things, please come forward if you made it.** (Show items and acknowledge the artists)

Variation: Collect magazine or newspaper pictures of great things people have made. Pass out the pictures to the Juniors and have them tell about them.

People make many great things. What great things have you seen? (Mt. Rushmore sculpture, airplanes, monuments, paintings, and so on.) **Even though people make wonderful things, we don't compare with God. He made the world and everything in it. What kind of materials did you use to make your projects?** (Pupils answer.) **You used different raw materials, but God made the world by simply speaking. Can any of us make something by just talking? No. We worship a special God! Today we will worship Him because only He has the power to create the world.**

Explain choices of *Building the Theme* activities.

You may need to help your Juniors form groups for *Building the Theme*. These suggestions will also keep the groups at manageable numbers. 1) Group them alphabetically by the first letter of their middle names. For example, if you want six Juniors per activity, assign the first six Juniors to activity 1. 2) Post one list for each activity that you are offering. At the top of each paper write a brief description of the activity. Number the papers down the left side to indicate the maximum number of Juniors allowed at that activity. As Juniors enter the classroom, ask them to write their names beside a number on the paper for the activity they want to do. Juniors must choose another group if a group has reached its maximum number.

Building the Theme

(30 minutes)

1. Call to Worship. Juniors will illustrate Bible verses that tell of God's power. Juniors may complete this activity without adult guidance. Provide NIV Bibles, paper, and markers. Write or record on a casette tape the following instructions. **We see God's power in His creation. Creation also shows how special God is, because no person can do what God did. Select one verse from the following to read aloud: Nehemiah 9:6; Psalm 95:4 or Psalm 147:8, 16, 17. Tell the rest of the group how God shows His power in your verse. Take a piece of paper and copy your verse on one side. On the other side, draw a picture to illustrate the verse.** During *Sharing in Worship,* the Juniors will show their pictures, as they read their verses.

2. Scripture. Juniors will discover and scramble words that tell of God's power. Provide Bibles, blank transparency, markers, overhead projector, poster board, and marker. Before the session, write the following Scripture references on the poster board: Psalm 29:10; 66:3; 78:4; 89:8; 97:9; 105:2. **Who is the most powerful person you know?** (Juniors answer.) **Why is that person powerful?** (Juniors will name things the people do.) **What makes a person powerful?** (Does things most people can't.) **What**

makes a person special? (When they are different from others.) **God is both powerful and special. When God made the world, He showed how special and powerful He is. The Bible tells more about God's power.** (Display the verses on posterboard.) **You will read these verses today. Then you'll make a scrambled word game for the large group to solve.** Ask the Juniors to read the verses and list the words that tell about our powerful God. Write the words on the poster board. (Suggested words follow: king, awesome, great, praiseworthy, mighty, most high, exalted, wonderful.) After the Juniors have completed the list, discuss any unfamiliar words. You may provide a dictionary. Then assign each Junior one answer. If you have more than eight Juniors, they may work in pairs. **Each of you will scramble the letters of your word and copy the scrambled word on the transparency.** The Juniors from this group will read the corresponding Scriptures. If the large group is unable to unscramble a word, a Junior may read the verse to give them the answer.

3. Devotional. This group will tell how God planned each animal to fit its environment. This is a good activity for older or gifted Juniors. For these Juniors, you may furnish encyclopedias or other books, so they can read more about these animals and plants. Provide crayons, tape, paper, and pencils. Make one copy of the following information for each Junior.

1. Albatrosses have hollow bones. 2. Bats have large, sensitive ears. 3. The lungfish can hibernate for four years. 4. The musk ox has very thick fur. 5. Flamingos have special bills to filter their food from the water. 6. Over half of a cacti's weight is water. 7. Owls have huge eyes. 8. Lamprey cling to rocks with their large, suckerlike mouths. 9. Some snakes can sense the heat given off by other animals. 10. Some fish have special blood that does not freeze easily. 11. The ptarmigan turns white in winter.

God showed His power and wisdom when He made the world. One way God is special is in His wisdom. He was so intelligent that He made each animal or plant especially for its environment, or habitat. A habitat is where an animal or plant lives. Just like God said, this world is very good. Ask Juniors to make five large pictures, one illustrating each of these habitats—the air, the dark, the desert, the cold, and the stream. Distribute the fact sheets you prepared. Show the five habitat drawings. **How are each of these animals or plants especially designed for one of these environments?** (Answers #1—air; #2, #7, #9—dark; #3, #6—desert; #4, #10, #11—cold, #5, #8—stream.) **How do these creations show God's wisdom and power? Tell how other animals and plants are suited for their environments.** As time permits, allow the group to do further research from the reference materials you provide.

During *Sharing in Worship,* this group will tape the five environment pictures on the wall. They will say that God made each animal to fit its surroundings. They will read the sentences about each animal or plant, one at a time. This large group will decide in which environment that animal or plant lives. Then the Juniors will explain how the characteristics of the animal or plant help it survive.

4. Personal Praise. This group will make a picture booklet to enable them to praise God for their parts of creation. Provide copies of Activity pages 1A and 1B, scissors, pencils, Bibles, and a stapler. **How did God show His power when He made the world? How did God show that He is special when He made the world?** (He had more power than any person has. We can't do what God did.) **We should always remember to praise God for the world He made. Name one thing God made that you are especially thankful for today.** (Allow response.) **As we do this activity, we'll remember specific things we like about our world.**

Distribute activity pages and scissors. Juniors will cut out the booklet pieces. They will assemble them according to the numbers, matching the staple lines. Guide the pieces together to form one picture. Distribute Bibles and pencils. **Turn to Genesis 1. On what day did God make lakes and seas?** (v. 10, 13, Day 3) **What one lake or ocean are you thankful for? Write the name of it on page 2. Be sure to write it under page 1, so you can't see it when the booklet is closed. On what day did God make dogs?** (vs. 24, 31, Day 6) **What one animal are you thankful for? Write the name of it on page 3, where it won't show when the booklet is closed.** Continue in the same manner for the remaining pages. If time is limited, omit the questions where the Juniors find the day of creation.

During *Sharing in Worship,* this group will show their picture booklets, and take turns praising God for the specific things they wrote. One Junior will praise God for his favorite lake. The next Junior will praise God for an animal. Continue until every person in this group has praised God.

5. Special Music. Juniors will write words to the tune, "He's Got the Whole World in His Hands" from page 177. Provide Bibles, paper, markers, and pushpins. **Option**: Provide taped piano accompaniment and a tape player.

God made a wonderful world for us. We see God's power in His creation. Where in the Bible do we find the story of the creation? (Genesis 1.) **From Genesis 1, name some things, other than people, that God made.** Using these answers, the Juniors will write words to the tune. They may work as one large group, or several small groups. One suggestion:

He's got the fish and the birds in His hands,
He's got the oceans and the heavens in His hands,
He's got the mammals and the reptiles in His hands,
He's got the whole world in His hands.

Ask Juniors to write one large copy of the verses. Practice singing the song with the new words. Juniors may illustrate the verses beside the words, on separate paper. During *Sharing in Worship,* this group will post the words and the illustrations and sing the song.

6. Prayer. Juniors will write thank-you notes to God. Provide construction paper, scissors, pencils, and markers. Option if time is short: Use purchased thank-you notes instead of construction paper.

God showed His great power when He made the world. He also showed His special wisdom, because it is just right for us. God made the world for us, for people everywhere. God made the dry ground, oceans, and plants on the third day. How do these things help you? God made the sun, moon, and stars on the fourth day. How do they help you? God made the birds and fish on the fifth day. How do they help you? God made animals on the sixth day. How do they help you? (Allow Juniors to answer each question.) **Today we will write thank-you notes to God.** Distribute construction paper, scissors, pencils, and markers. **You may cut out your note as you decide. Choose one or two things God made, and tell Him why you are thankful for them.**

An example: Thank You, God, for making trees. Our maple trees shade my house in the summer, so we are cooler. I like to jump in the leaves in the fall. Trees make oxygen for me to breathe. Thanks, God. Love, ________ (Junior's name)

When you are finished, you may decorate your note. During *Sharing in Worship,* this group will read their notes as prayers to God.

Sharing in Worship
(20-25 minutes)

Omit any of the following sections if you did not offer the corresponding activity. The devotional may be given without the presentation of Group 3.

Call to Worship (Group 1): **The Bible tells us about God's power in creation. Look at the pictures as you listen to these verses that tell the powerful things our special God can do.** Group 1 presents their pictures and verses.

Song: Let's sing about our great Creator. Listen as I sing this song. Sing with me the second time. Lead Juniors in "God Is the Great Creator" from page 178. **Option**: Provide taped accompaniment to help the pupils sing better.

Scripture Reading (Group 2): **Group 2 discovered Bible words that describe our powerful God. They scrambled the letters on this transparency. Try to unscramble these words about God.** Group 2 will project their transparency and continue their presentation.

Offering: When I think of our mighty, exalted, praise-worthy, awesome, great, wonderful, Most-High God, I want to thank Him. One way we thank God is by giving Him some of our money. As you give, silently thank God for being so special. Choose volunteers to pray and collect the offering.

Lord's Supper: We know that God showed His great power when He made the world. Jesus showed His power when He came alive after death. No one but God and Jesus can make dead people come alive! They are special and powerful. As we take the Lord's Supper, thank Jesus that He is alive now and forever. Pray and serve the Lord's Supper.

Devotional (Group 3): You will need a picture of a spider's web or a spider in a jar, and one ear of corn per pupil.

When you want to know about God, where do you look? (In the Bible, ask a parent or teacher, in Sunday school.) **Those are all good places. Another place where we can learn about God is in nature. That might seem like a strange place, but the Bible says, "God has clearly shown them everything that may be known about Him. There are things about God that people cannot see – his eternal power and all things that make him God. But since the beginning of the world those things have been easy to understand. They are made clear by what God has made."** (Romans 1:19, 20, ICB.) **David said, "The heavens declare the glory of God; the skies proclaim the work of his hands"** (Psalm 19:1, NIV). **Nature tells us about God!**

What can we learn about God by looking at His creation? (Juniors answer.) **We see that God is very smart. We also learn that He is powerful. He made huge things. What big things did God make?** (Juniors respond.) **God also made tiny things. What very small things did God make?** (Juniors respond.) **God made the world with a marvelous plan. When we look at all the creatures, we know that a great**

intelligence planned these things. Group 3 learned how God made each animal and the plant exactly right for its environment. They'll share their presentation now. If you did not offer Activity 3, ask **How did God make the fish perfect for its habitat? How did God make the cactus perfect for its habitat?** Continue with well-known animals, such as polar bear, bird, snakes. **Wildlife did not happen accidentally.**

The Bible tells us God started everything by speaking the words, "Let there be," and the world took shape. It was a perfect world. Nature is so special that people over the whole earth can know God exists by looking at His creation. This week notice the things around you that God has made. Think about a spider's web. Show a picture of a spider's web or a spider in a jar. **How can a spider make such a perfect design with its web?** (Juniors answer.) **The spider was made by a great God.**

One ear of corn (show corn) **when planted, can produce bushels of corn to feed a family. Do you know that every ear of corn has an even number of rows?** Distribute ears of corn. Have each Junior count the number of rows on his or her ear of corn. **How many rows did your ear have?** (Juniors answer.)

When we look at a painting, we notice the artist's signature at the bottom. We give credit to the person who made the picture. When we look at God's creation, let's remember to notice the artist—God.

If time allows, take Juniors for a nature walk to examine things God created. If so, divide the class into small groups and provide an adult leader for each group. Give each group a small jar and sack, so they can bring back to the class some plants or insects. These could be used during *Closing Moments.*

Personal Praise (Group 4)**: I know we all have favorite parts of God's creation. I especially like ______** (name your favorite plant or animal). **Group 4 made booklets that help them remember their favorite creations. They will praise God for these specific parts of creation.** Group 4 shows picture booklets and praises God.

Special Music (Group 5)**: Group 5 wrote a song that tells about God's power in creation. They will sing it for us now.** Group 5 sings. The class may sing along the second time.

Prayer (Group 6)**: God made this beautiful world especially for us, for people! Do you remember to thank God for the gift of our world? Group 6 wrote thank-You notes to God. How can we send Him a thank-You note?** (Juniors respond.) **We can read them to Him, because we know He hears our prayers. Let's pray as we listen to their letters to God.** Group 6 reads their notes as prayers.

Closing Moments
(10-15 minutes)

Provide several small animals in jars (such as fish, insects, spiders, or worms) and magnifying glasses. (**Option**: Borrow a microscope and examine a drop of water or a human hair.) Let Juniors look closely at these items through a magnifying glass. **What amazes you about God's creation? Some people think that all these things came into being by chance and luck. What would you say to them? How do these things tell about God's special power?**

Suggested Resources

The Amazing Story of Creation from Science and the Bible by Duane T. Gish, Institute for Creation Research, 1990.

God's Power Created Man

Worship Focus
Worship God because only He has the power to create man.

Transition Time
(10-15 minutes)
Talent Show. This activity will help the Juniors appreciate God's great job in creating them and their friends. Ask Juniors to "show off" some of their talents. Give them a few minutes to think about what they would like to do. They may look through any materials you provide: math problems to solve, poems or Scriptures to read, art materials for drawing a picture, a song book for singing and so on. Make suggestions to them for physical talents: wiggling ears, doing push-ups, or a ballet dance. Then ask for volunteers to show their talents to the class. Following the presentations, say, **God showed His special power when He created men and women. He did an excellent job on each of you.**

Launching the Theme
(10 minutes)
Ask a doctor or nurse to speak to the pupils on the topic: "The Amazing Human Body—God's Best Creation." Ask him or her to tell specific things that the body and mind can do. **Today** (name of speaker) **will share with us about God's best creation—our bodies. Think about how powerful God must be to create such a wonderful thing. Thank the speaker following the presentation.**

If you are unable to locate a speaker, use this alternate activity. Read these questions and ask pupils to identify the body parts. What is the bag that squeezes our food for about six hours? (Stomach.) **What pumps more than 100,000 times a day?** (The heart.) **What do we call the detectives in the blood that protect you against germs?** (White blood cells.) **What is the control center of the body?** (The brain.) **What small organs filter and clean your blood everyday?** (Kidneys.) **What holds up your body, stores fat, makes blood cells, and can even heal itself?** (Bones.) **What chemicals in the body control when and how much you grow?** (Hormones.)

God showed His special power when He created Adam and Eve. Today we will worship God for His power in the creation of man.

Explain choices of *Building the Theme* Activities.

Building the Theme
(30 minutes)
1. Call to Worship. Juniors will complete a worksheet to help them learn that people are a unique creation. Provide copies of activity page 2A, pencils, and Bibles.

What did God make last? (Adam and Eve.) **Read Genesis 1:27. God made people different than animals. What is different about the way God made people?** (Made in God's image.) **People are made like God. We're not exactly like God, but more like God than animals. Let's discover how people are a unique or special creation.** Distribute copies of the activity sheet and pencils. All these sentences describe qualities that God gave people. Some of the things are also found in animals; some are not. Draw a stick figure person beside the sentences that only describe people, not animals. (Answers: Sentences 3, 5, 7, 10, 12, 13 describe people.) You may need to clarify sentence 5. Explain that although animals appear to think, they can only do what comes naturally to them, by instinct, or what they have been trained to do. For sentence 10, say that while animals can communicate with each other, they cannot speak a language about things they have not seen. **We are a very unique creation. People are God's most special creation.**

During *Sharing in Worship,* this group will read the six sentences that only describe people. Then they will read Genesis 1:27 together.

2. Special Music. Juniors will write words to the tune, "He's Got the Whole World In His Hands" from page 177. Provide taped piano accompaniment and a tape player.

Read Genesis 2:7, 22. **What was God's last creation?** (Man and woman.) **What different kinds of people has God made?** Juniors may name people of different ages, nationalities, occupations, or physical characteristics. Using these answers, the Juniors will write words to the tune. They may write several verses. They may work as one large group, or several small groups. One suggestion follows:

He's got the Whites and the Blacks in His hands.
He's got the babies and the grandmas in His hands.
He's got the brown-eyed and the blue-eyed in His hands,
He's got the whole world in His hands.

Ask Juniors to make one large copy of the verses. Practice singing the song with the new words. Juniors may illustrate the verses beside the words, or on separate paper. During *Sharing in Worship,* this group will post the words and the illustrations and sing the song.

3. Devotional. Juniors will demonstrate the five senses. Provide paper cups, water, salt, sugar, lemon juice, peppermint gum, two crayons (taped together), and a clock (with a loud tick). Keep supplies hidden until used. Put a small amount of salty water, sugar water, or lemon water in each cup.

God showed His special power in the creation of people. In His great wisdom, He gave us five senses. Can you name them? (Smell, taste, touch, hearing, sight.) **We will do experiments to illustrate these senses.**

Smell and Taste: Give each Junior one cup. Ask half of the Juniors to pinch their noses closed while they taste the liquid The other half will taste without holding their noses. **How does it taste?** (Sweet, salty, or sour.) **Do you need to smell to taste these?** (No.) **God created our tongues to taste salty, sweet, and sour.** Give each Junior a piece of gum, with the outside label removed. Ask half of the pupils to hold their noses while they chew the gum. The other half will chew the gum without holding their noses. **What flavor is the gum? Do you need to smell to taste this?** (Yes.) **How does your food taste when you have a bad cold?** (Not as good.) **Our sense of smell helps our tasting.**

Touch: Ask the Juniors to close their eyes as you touch the points of the crayons to their necks. **How many crayons did you feel?** (One.) Now touch the crayons to their fingers. **How many points did you feel?** (Two.) **Why did you feel a difference?** (Juniors respond.) **God gave our fingers more nerves for feeling than our necks. Why?** (We need our fingers to be more sensitive than our necks. We do more touching with our fingers.)

Hearing: Stand a few feet away from the Juniors. **Shut your eyes and listen.** Allow the clock to tick. **Stand only when you hear the clock ticking.** Slowly move toward them, and then away. **You heard the sound better when the clock was close. How does sound reach our ears?** (The sound makes the air vibrate, which makes our eardrums vibrate. Tiny nerves send the message to our brains: "A clock is ticking.")

Sight: **Choose an object across the room that you would like to look at. Now cover one eye. Hold up a finger on your other hand to block out your object. Hold your finger still and cover your other eye. What happened to your object?** (Juniors answer.) **It seemed to move. You can see it now. Why?** (Each eye takes a picture from a different side. The brain uses both pictures to tell us how big and how far away the object is.) **How do the senses show God's unique power?**

During *Sharing in Worship,* you will do these demonstrations with Juniors from the large group. You will explain God's wonderful creation—our bodies. Help Juniors prepare and decide on the part of the presentation they will each do.

4. Offering. Juniors will illustrate how their bodies help them earn money. Juniors may complete this activity without adult guidance. Write or tape record the instructions and teacher comments. Provide paper, pencils, and crayons or markers.

God saved His best work until last. Your body is a marvelous creation. How does your body help you make money? (Juniors share.) **Each of you may take a piece of paper and draw a picture to show how you earn money. Along the bottom of the paper, write the parts of your body that help you do your job.** Suggestions follow: cleaning their rooms, delivering newspapers, washing dishes, pulling weeds, taking care of a pet. Ask Juniors to share their pictures with each other. **How many body parts did your jobs need?** Juniors will soon realize that they use their whole bodies for many tasks. How do you feel about this creation—your body? (Juniors respond.) **One way we show thankfulness to God is by giving some of the money God helps us earn. We should always share our money with God.**

During *Sharing in Worship,* the Juniors in this group will show their pictures, express their gratitude in prayers, and pass the offering baskets.

5. Scripture. Juniors will make and present an acrostic. Provide overhead projector, transparency, markers, Bibles, pencils, and paper.

Read Genesis 2:7, 22. **What did God make last?** (Man and woman.) **What do you think is great about the human body?** (Juniors answer.) **When you think about this creation God made, how do you feel?** (Juniors answer.) **David praised God for making him. We'll read some of David's words.** From these verses, Juniors write the words that tell what we should do because God made us. (Psalm 100:1-4—shout for joy, serve, thank; 139:14—praise; 145:6, 7—tell of God's power, proclaim God's great deeds, celebrate.) Next ask Juniors to write the word, *CREATOR*, vertically on their papers. Guide them as they plan the acrostic, fitting the answers with the letters in *creator.*

A suggestion follows:

Celebrate
se**R**ve
prais**E**
th**A**nk
Tell of God's power
sh**O**ut out for joy
p**R**oclaim God's great deeds

Ask one Junior to write *CREATOR* down the center of the transparency. During *Sharing in Worship,* this group will project the transparency on the wall. They will ask the other Juniors to listen for words that answer this question: **What should we do because God is our creator?** A Junior will read one Scripture. Juniors from the large group will name words they hear that answer the question. Juniors from this group may take turns writing the answers on the transparency, fitting them into the acrostic. They can repeat the verses as necessary. Continue until all the Scriptures have been read, and the acrostic is complete.

6. Personal Praise. Juniors will make name plaques as reminders that they are special creations. Provide copies of activity page 2B, pens, Bibles, clear adhesive paper, scissors, paper hole punch, colored pencils, and gold cord. To adapt this activity for older or gifted pupils, furnish a Bible concordance.

Read Genesis 2:7, 22; 3:20. **Who were the first people God made?** (Adam and Eve.) **From Genesis 1:31, what did God say about them?** (They were very good.) **All people are very special creations of God. Today you will make name plaques to remind you that you are a wonderful creation.** Distribute materials. Ask each Junior to write his or her name on the first blank. **Adam and Eve's names had special meanings. Look in your Bibles at Genesis 2:7. Perhaps your footnote tells you what the name Adam means.** (Man, maybe taken from the word for ground.) **Why do you think that Adam was a good name for the first man?** (God made him from the ground.) **Read Genesis 3:20. Why did Adam name his wife Eve?** (Because she would be the mother of all living. *Eve* means *living.*) **Many Bible people were named for special qualities they had. You have special qualities, too. Some good characteristics that you might have are listed in Galatians 5:22, 23.** Ask Juniors to read this passage and choose qualities they have. To help each Junior choose a quality that he or she has, ask these questions. **Has someone complimented you for one of these things? Are you usually happy? Is it easy for you to wait for people? Are you a good friend? Do you like to do things for others?** Ask each Junior to write the quality in the second blank. Assist as necessary as they cut out the plaque, cover it on both sides with clear adhesive paper, punch holes in the top, and make a hanger from the gold cord. As time allows, they may color the border.

For older or gifted Juniors make these changes. Before copying the activity page, tape white paper over the Bible verse at the bottom. After the Juniors have filled in their names and characteristics, instruct them to find Bible verses in the concordance that talk about the characteristics in Galatians. Each Junior will copy one verse on his plaque that goes with his good quality. Suggestions follow:
Joy—Isaiah 12:6a;
Patience—Proverbs 19:11a.

During *Sharing in Worship,* this group will show and read their plaques. Then they will pray, thanking God that He made them.

Sharing in Worship
(20-25 minutes)

Omit any of the following sections if you did not offer the corresponding activity. The devotional may be given without the presentation of Group 3.

Call to Worship (Group 1)**: Last week we worshiped God for His power to create the world. This group will begin our worship time by telling us about God's most special creation—people.** Group 1 reads sentences and verse.

Special Music (Group 2)**: Every person on the earth was made in God's image. Group 2 will remind us of some of the different people God made.** Group 2 sings. The class may sing along the second time.

Group Singing: Let's praise our Creator by singing. Lead pupils in "God Is the Great Creator" from page 178. **Option**: Provide tape accompaniment.

Devotional (Group 3): You will need a picture of a human fetus, ink pad, paper, paper towels.

God is powerful! How does His creation of human beings show His power? (Juniors respond.) **People have studied the human body for centuries, and they still are making discoveries every day. Our bodies are very complex, yet they are just right for us. We see God's power in the development of a baby.** Show picture. **This baby is still ____ months from being born. It is only ____ inches long. What parts of this baby can you see?** (Juniors answer.) If you have more than one picture, show them in chronological order. Ask Juniors to tell when certain body parts develop. **Babies are true miracles from God.**

God showed great wisdom when He gave us our five senses.

Group 3 will help us appreciate them. Group 3 presents their demonstrations.

It is impossible to talk about all the marvelous parts of our bodies. We will discuss only one more. When we look at each other, the organ that we see the most is skin. One person called skin, the miracle wrapping. An adult has about two square yards of skin. On the wall show Juniors two square yards. **What does skin do for us?** (Juniors respond.) **Your skin keeps your body fluids inside. It protects your insides from injury. It protects your body from harmful radiation from the sun. It protects you from germs, hot, and cold. It stretches. It is very sensitive to touch, cold, heat, or pain. What do the sweat glands on your skin do?** (Keep you cool by releasing water.) **How did God design the skin to perform when it is cut?** (Juniors respond.) **When a cut bleeds, the blood helps clean the wound. Usually the blood clots soon, and then a scab forms to protect the skin while it heals. After a few days, it is hard to tell where the cut was. The skin healed itself.**

What is special about the skin on your fingertips? (Juniors answer.) **Each of us has a unique pattern of folds on our fingertips. Your fingerprints are different than other people's. Let's examine our fingerprints.** Allow each Junior to touch the ink pad with a finger, and press the fingerprint on the paper. **What differences in these fingerprints can you see?** (Juniors answer.) **Each of us was made in God's image, yet each of us is different and special.**

Let's thank God for the marvelous creation of our bodies. Would one of you like to thank God for us? Junior volunteer prays.

Offering (Group 4)**: One way our bodies serve us is by helping us do things to earn money. We can show God that we are thankful for our bodies by sharing our money with Him. Group 4 will show us ways that their bodies help them earn money.** Group 4 presents pictures, prays, and collects the offering.

Lord's Supper: God had a great plan when He created people. He planned our bodies to serve us well for many years. He also had a plan for when we sin. God planned to send Jesus to die for us, so that we could be forgiven. As we eat the Lord's Supper, let's thank God for His wonderful plan. Pray and serve the Lord's Supper.

Scripture (Group 5)**: The book of Psalms tells us what we should do because God is our Creator. As Group 5 reads verses, listen for ways we can praise God for creating us.** Group 5 reads verses and presents activity.

Personal Praise (Group 6)**: You are special! You have a special name and special abilities. Group 6 made plaques to remind them that God made them in a wonderful way.** Group 6 shares plaques and prays.

Closing Moments
(10-15 minutes)

Read the following facts about the human body. As you read each sentence, have Juniors vote whether it is true or false. Then tell them if they are right.

There are 206 bones in the body. (True.)

Your joints are equipped with oil, so they'll move easily. (True.)

Some muscles can be controlled, others can't. (True.)

Your brain weighs about thirty pounds (False. It weighs about three pounds.)

Your eyes are constantly moving. (True.)

Our big toe is our main organ of balance. (False. The inner ear is the main organ of balance.)

You have three different kinds of teeth, each with its own job. (True.)

More than two-thirds of your body is water. (True.)

Your brain only works when you are awake. (False. Your brain is always working.)

Different parts of your tongue can taste different foods. (True.)

Suggested Resources

These materials may be used to further teach your pupils to appreciate God's creation of people.

Books—

The Amazing Story of Creation from Science and the Bible by Duane T. Gish, Institute for Creation Research, 1990.

For Next Week

You will need 200 wooden matches for each pupil. The matches should be struck and promptly blown out. Enlist your youth group or other workers to help strike the matches. See Group 5 in Session 3 for more information.

God Has Power to Deal With Sin

Worship Focus

Worship God because only He has the power to deal with sin.

Transition Time
(10-15 minutes)

Yes/No Game. This game will help pupils realize that there is always a punishment when they disobey. Give each pupil ten dried beans. **We will play a game as you walk around and talk to each other. These are the rules. Try not to say the words "yes" or "no." Each time you say "yes" or "no" you must give one bean to the person to whom you are talking. Of course, you'll try to get other pupils to say the words, so that you'll get more beans. Nodding, shaking your head or saying "uh-huh" are not allowed. The winner is the person with the most beans at the end of the game.** When it is time to begin the lesson, stop the game. Ask them to count their beans and declare a winner. **When you broke the rules, you had to pay the price. In this game, the price was one bean. That's a very small punishment. Sometimes punishments are bigger. But there is always a punishment when we disobey.**

Launching the Theme
(10 minutes)

In your school, what happens when a pupil disobeys the rules? (Allow several pupils to share.) **Are these good consequences?** (Pupils share.) **What might happen if a child hit another child and didn't get punished?** (Pupils share.) **Do you think it is good or bad for teachers to punish children who break the rules?** (Pupils share.) **When teachers set rules and punishments, they are doing what God does. God tells us what He wants us to do. He told Adam and Eve the rules. Read Genesis 2:16, 17. What rule did God give them?** (Could not eat from one tree.) **Did they break God's rule? Read Genesis 3:6 and find out.** (Yes.) **When we don't obey God, He punishes or disciplines us because He wants us to do what is right. If you know you'll get disciplined for breaking a rule, do you still break it?** (Pupils respond.) **Sometimes we still do, but many times, we don't. God wants s to learn to obey. He always deals with our sin to help us. Today we will worship God for His power to deal with sin.**

Explain choices of *Building the Theme* activities.

Building the Theme
(30 minutes)

1. Call to Worship. Pupils will draw a rebus for the Bible verses. This activity may be done without adult supervision. Write or record on tape the instructions and teacher comments. Provide the *International Children's Bible,* poster paper, white construction paper, scissors, clear tape, markers, and push pins. If you do not have several *ICB* Bibles, make copies of Proverbs 3:11, 12, *ICB.* Before class draw pencil lines on the poster board, so the pupils can write in straight lines. **God punished Adam and Eve for disobeying His rule. Tell about a time when you were punished for breaking a rule.** (Pupils share.) **Did the punishment help you learn to obey?** (Pupils answer.) **If it did, then you learned what God wanted. Read Proverbs 3:11, 12. Does God punish us because He hates us and likes to see us suffer? Why does God punish us?** (Because He loves us and wants to correct us.) This group will draw a rebus of these verses. **First, one of you will write the verse on the poster board with a marker. Write large and use the whole poster board. Now decide which words could be illustrated by a picture. Decide who will draw which pictures. Make your pictures big enough to cover the words you are replacing. Cut out the pictures and tape them over the words they will replace. Draw as many of the words as you can. When you are finished, read the rebus.** Suggestions for drawings: *son*—boy, *not*—knot, *think*—brain, *nothing*—O, *Lord*—gold cloud, *punishes*—crying child or pointing hand, *you*—U, *loves*—heart.

During *Sharing in Worship* this group will post their rebus on the wall and read it for the class. Then the large group will read it with them.

2. Scripture. Pupils will identify and present people who God punished. Provide Bibles, copies of Activity page 3A, pencils, heavy paper, and markers. **Why**

does God punish people? (To help them learn to do right.) Distribute activity pages and pencils. Assign each pupil, or small group of pupils, one of the Bible passages listed. **Read your Bible verses, and write on the charts the name of the people punished, the reason they were punished, and their punishment.**

Answers follow:

1. Adam and Eve: ate forbidden fruit; have pain in childbirth, work hard for living, must leave garden.

2. Israelites: worshiped a golden calf; God sent a plague (sickness).

3. Moses and Aaron: struck the rock for water, didn't trust God; were not allowed to take the people into the promised land.

4. Saul: didn't kill all the animals and people; God rejected him as king.

5. Jonah: ran away to Tarshish; swallowed by a fish.

6. Peter: said that he didn't know Jesus; Jesus looked at him.

7. Paul: harmed Christians; became blind.

Give each pupil (or small group) a piece of heavy paper and a marker. They will make name cards for their people. Then assist them as they prepare their presentation. Notice that one or two verses are underlined in each Scripture on the activity page. During *Sharing in Worship* each pupil (pupil group) will read the underlined verse. The large group will identify the person who was punished. If the group is unable to guess the person, the pupil may give additional clues. After the person is named, the pupil will hold up that name card and tell why the person was punished. Continue for the other six people. **God punished these people because He wanted them to do right.**

Older or gifted pupils can do further research on each of the people. They may read the entire chapters listed. Also, ask them to find out if the people changed their sinful ways after God punished them. Give them these Scriptures to help their study. 1. Genesis 4:1, 2, 25, 26. (We know little about Adam and Eve. They did acknowledge God's gifts of sons.) 2. Psalm 78:9-37. 3. Deuteronomy 34:10-12. 4. 1 Samuel 28:5-20. 5. Jonah 3:1-3. 6. John 21:15-17. 7. Acts 9:10-30.

3. Special Music. Pupils will write words to the tune, "He's Got the Whole World in His Hands," p. 177. Provide Bibles, paper, markers, and pushpins. Option: Provide taped piano accompaniment and a tape player. **Who were the first people who sinned?** (Adam and Eve.) **What did they do?** (Ate from the tree they were told not to.) **Read Genesis 3:1-6. Why did they disobey God?** (Satan tempted them, it looked good, wanted to be wise.) From these verses, ask pupils to tell what God calls people who sin. Psalms 32:10—wicked; 78:8a—stubborn, rebellious; 78:32a—sinning; 78:57—disloyal, faithless, unreliable; Proverbs 10:23—fool, evil; Zephaniah 2:1—shameful; Romans 1:31—senseless, heartless, ruthless. Take the time to explain any unfamiliar words. **Did God quit loving Adam and Eve because they sinned?** (No.) **He continued to help them and their children. God holds even the sinning person in His hands.** Using the descriptions of sinners, the pupils will write words to the tune. They may work as one large group, or several small groups. As time allows, they may write more than one verse. A suggestion follows:

He's got the stubborn boy in His hands,
He's got the rebellious mother in His hands,
He's got the foolish girl in His hands,
He's got the whole world in His hands.

Ask pupils to write one large copy of the verses. Practice singing the song together with the new words. Pupils may illustrate the verses beside the words, or on separate paper. During *Sharing in Worship* this group will post the words and the illustrations and sing the song.

4. Devotional. Pupils will illustrate sins and their consequences. Provide Bibles, construction paper, pencils, scissors, yarn, paper, paper punch, and pushpins. **What happened when Adam and Eve sinned?** (Were punished; thrown out of garden to work the ground.) **What always happens when we sin? You will find the answer in Proverbs 11:21a.** (Will be punished.) **Today you will make pictures to show that sin always has a consequence, or a punishment. Draw a picture of someone doing something wrong.** Encourage each pupil to illustrate a different sin. Ask them to show and explain their pictures. **What might be the consequence, or punishment if you did this?** (Allow pupils to share several possible punishments.) **Now you will cut a shape from construction paper to illustrate a punishment that could go with the sin you pictured.** Suggestions: stealing/a broom to represent working to pay back the money; cheating on a test/an F; lying to mother/hand to represent a spanking; gossiping about a friend/one child alone to represent no friends; sassing teacher/ a sign that says "Principal's Office"; fighting at school/desk to represent no recess. **When you are finished, punch a hole in the picture and the shape. Tie them together with yarn.** Ask pupils to pin their pictures and shapes to the wall, close to the large group area. The shapes should be hidden behind the pictures. During *Sharing in Worship*, one pupil will point at his or her picture and say, "I think I'll ____________." (fill in with the pictured sin). Then the pupil will lift up the picture and reveal the consequence. He or she will explain the punishment for the sin, saying, "But if I did it, _________ (the punishment) might happen." Continue for each picture.

5. Lord's Supper. Pupils will make crosses as a reminder that Jesus paid for our sin. Provide Bibles, copies of Activity page 3B, scissors, pencils, glue, 200 wooden matches per pupil, and cardboard (9" x 6", one per pupil). Before class, strike each match and promptly blow it out. This will make the matches black on one end. To save time, enlist members of your youth group to help strike the matches. **What did God do to Adam and Eve because they sinned?** (Punished them.) **What does God do to us when we sin?** (Punishes us.) **What should be our biggest punishment because we sin? Find the answer in Romans 6:23.** (Death.) **This doesn't mean dying physically, like everybody does, but dying forever in hell. God didn't want that to happen to us, so He and Jesus did a wonderful thing. Read Isaiah 53:5 and tell what Jesus did.** (Jesus was punished for us.) **When was Jesus punished for us?** (When He died on the cross.) **We'll make crosses today to remind us that Jesus was punished so we could go to heaven. Jesus took our punishment.** Distribute materials. Pupils will cut out the cross pattern from the activity page. Using the pattern, they will cut the cardboard into a cross shape. They will copy the first line of Isaiah 53:5 on one side of their cross. On the other side, they will glue the matches, burned side pointing out, as indicated on the pattern. They need to begin with the four matches in the center, then work out from those.

During *Sharing in Worship* this group will answer the same questions that are listed above. Ask a pupil volunteer to ask the questions. Then they will show their crosses (if dry enough to handle) and read Isaiah 53:5. Volunteers from this group will pray and serve the Lord's Supper.

6. Prayer. Pupils will tape record prayers, thanking God for His discipline. Provide an *International Children's Bible*, tape recorder, and blank tape. **Why did God punish Adam and Eve?** (They broke God's rules.) **Read Hebrews 12:7-11 aloud. Why does God punish us?** (He loves us just like a father. He wants us to learn to do right.) **Why should we thank God for punishing us?** (The more we obey God, the better our lives will be. God knows best, and He wants what is best for us.) **We'll thank God in our prayers today for helping us do right. We'll tape record these prayers. You will say, "Thank You, God, that I was _____ (punishment) for _____ (sin). I learned to _____ (right behavior)."** Encourage the pupils to name general sins. You do not want them to be embarrassed when the tape is played. One example: Thank You, God, that I had to stay in recess for talking during school. I learned to do my work and not talk to my friend. Other ideas: stealing, sassing, lying, swearing. Help pupils word their prayers. Then record the prayers on the blank tape. Be sure to record your prayer too.

During *Sharing in Worship* one pupil will explain why God's punishment is good. With the large group in a prayerful mood, play the recording.

Sharing in Worship
(20-25 minutes)

Omit any of the following sections if you did not offer the corresponding activity. The devotional may be given without the presentation of Group 4.

Call to Worship (Group 1): **God is so powerful. He not only made us, He also takes care of us. One way He does this is by punishing us when we do wrong. Group 1 will help us begin our worship time by sharing with us the reason that God punishes us.** Group 1 presents rebus.

Group Singing: Let's praise our Creator. Lead pupils in "God Is the Great Creator" from p. 178. Option: Provide taped accompaniment to help the pupils sing better.

Scripture (Group 2): **The Bible tells us about people who God punished. This group will give you clues as they read Bible verses. You will guess who God punished. Then they'll share more facts about these people.** Group 2 presents.

Special Music (Group 3): **When I sin, I sometimes think that God doesn't love me anymore. That's easy to think, but it isn't true. God always loves us, no matter what we do. He punishes us so that we'll love and obey Him more. Group 3 will sing us a song to remind us that God loves us, even when we sin.** Group 3 posts words and sings. The large group may join in the second time.

Devotional (Group 4): You will need a rubber snake or picture of a snake. **God disciplines us in love. Sometimes when we know what might happen to us if we disobey, we decide to obey. Group 4 drew pictures of sins you might be tempted to do. They'll share their feelings about doing them now.** Group 4 shows pictures of sins and consequences.

We have talked today about God's punishment of Adam and Eve. However, there was someone else in today's story. Can you guess who that was? (Pupils respond.) **Hold up the snake. It was the snake. The snake tempted Eve to eat the**

fruit. He tried to get her to sin. Do you think that the snake in the Garden of Eden was just like a snake we see today? (No.) **Actually the snake was Satan. Satan made himself look like a snake, so Eve would think he was just a harmless animal. Satan was successful. Adam and Eve both disobeyed God. God didn't just punish Adam and Eve. He also punished the snake and Satan. In Genesis 3:14 it says that God punished the snake by making him crawl around on his belly and eat dust the rest of his life. We know that snakes still do that. God is also strong enough to punish Satan. He is omnipotent—He has all power. Satan's punishment was that someday a descendant of Eve would crush the head of Satan. That descendant of Eve was Jesus. Jesus crushed Satan's head by coming alive after He died. Also, Satan never got Jesus to sin. Jesus always won!**

God is still stronger than Satan. Satan knows that God will win someday, but he keeps trying to get us to sin . When we do sin, we should remember that God still loves us. God will do what we need to help us to obey. He's a great God and always does what is best.

Lord's Supper (Group 5): **Because we have sinned, God could be angry with us. Instead, He loves us. He sent Jesus to die, so that we can be forgiven of our sins. Group 5 will help us appreciate what Jesus did.** Group 5 answers questions and shows crosses. They also pray and serve the Lord's Supper.

Offering: God gave His best for us. He gave His only Son to die for us. What are some of God's other gifts to us? (Pupils answer.) **As we give our money to Him, let's thank Him for His great gifts.** Pupils pray and collect the offering.

Prayer (Group 6): **It is hard to thank God for His punishments. We have learned today that God punishes us for our good. Group 6 tape recorded their prayers. They thanked God for the times when they learned to obey after being punished. Let's bow our heads and listen as they play their tape.** Group 6 presents. If time allows, other pupils may pray aloud in the same manner as the taped prayers.

Closing Moments
(10-15 minutes)

Before class, write many silly and easy consequences on slips of paper. Place them in a bowl or box. Examples: turn around 3 times like a ballerina, touch your toes, show us your scariest face, say "kookie cookie critters" as fast as you can, try to wiggle your ears, curtsy to the class, imitate your pet, sing like an opera star.

Use a game to illustrate the principle of consequences. "Simon Says" is a familiar game to play. You or a pupil can be Simon. Give the pupils various commands, alternating between those that Simon does and does not say. When a pupil makes a mistake, he or she must draw a consequence card from a bowl. After the pupil does the consequence, he or she can continue to play the game.

God Has Power to Keep His Promises

Worship Focus

Worship God because only He can keep all His promises.

Transition Time
(10-15 minutes)

Pictionary. Think of a promise that someone made to you. It can be either a promise that you are still waiting for them to do or a promise that they have done. Give the pupils ideas such as: someplace a person will take you, a gift he or she will give you, or something he will do for you. Encourage them to think of promises their teachers, friends, brothers, sisters, or parents have made. Ask a pupil to draw a picture of this promised thing on the chalkboard. The other pupils will guess what the picture is. Permit as many pupils to draw their promises as time allows. **When someone keeps his or her promise, we feel great!**

Launching the Theme
(10 minutes)

Before class write promises on the chalkboard. Write some promises that you could keep, others that would be impossible for you to keep. Suggestions: I promise: to take you out for lunch; that it won't rain tomorrow; to give you a present; to teach a great lesson today; to give you a million dollars; that no one will ever beat you up; to give you a hug; that you will get all A's on your next report card; that you'll marry when you are 25 years old.

Which promises would you like for me to make to you? Why? (Pupils respond.) **If I made this promise (**point to an impossible promise), **could I keep it?** (Pupils discuss.) **Which promises on this list could I keep? Which promises could I not keep, even if I tried?** (Pupils discuss.) **Those promises would not be good promises for you. Promises are only good when they are kept. God keeps all His promises. Today we'll worship God because only He has the power to keep all His promises.**

Explain choices of *Building the Theme* activities.

Building the Theme
(30 minutes)

1. Call to Worship. Pupils will make bookmarks to remind them that God keeps His promises. Provide copies of the *International Children's Bible* fine-point permanent pens or markers, 2" wide plain-colored stiff craft ribbon, and scissors. If ICB Bibles are not available, make several copies of Numbers 23:19, ICB. "God is not a man. He will not lie. God is not a human being. He does not change his mind. What he says he will do, he does. What he promises, he keeps." Before class cut the ribbon into 6" strips. Iron the strips flat. Make several copies of this sentence, "What God promises, He keeps."

Have you ever made a promise that you didn't keep? How did you feel? (Pupils respond.) **Tell about a time when someone broke a promise they gave to you. How did you feel?** (Pupils share.) **Read Numbers 23:19. How is God not like men?** (He will not lie or change His mind.) **Does God break His promise?** (No.) **How does this make you feel?** (Pupils share.) **People can't always keep their promises, even if they try. Sometimes they get sick, or things happen so they can't keep the promise. God can always keep His promises. Is He more powerful than we are?** (Yes.) **We know that when God gives us a promise in the Bible, He'll do it. We'll make bookmarks to remind us that we can trust God to keep His promises.** Distribute the materials. Pupils will cut the ribbon as shown. Then they will print vertically on their bookmarks, "What God promises, He keeps." They may copy it from the copies you provide. They may decorate their bookmarks with

different-colored markers. When the ink is dry, they may place them in their Bibles with a copy of Numbers 23:19.

During *Sharing in Worship* this group will stand, holding their Bibles open. They will read together Numbers 23:19 from the copies. Then they will show their bookmarks and recite the words on them.

2. Special Music. Pupils will write words to the tune, "He's Got the Whole World In His Hands," p. 177. Provide Bibles, paper, markers, and pushpins. Option: Provide taped piano accompaniment and a tape player. **Tell about a promise you made this week.** (Juniors share.) **Did you keep it? Have you ever made a promise that you were unable to keep?** (Pupils respond.) **Suppose you promised your music teacher that you would sing in the school program. On the day of the program you got very sick and couldn't keep your promise. People can't always keep their promises, even if they try their best. We can't control the future. God always keeps His promises, because He has the power to control what will happen. From these verses tell what God knows about the future.** Assign one verse to each pupil to read aloud and explain. Genesis 18:10 and Luke 1:13 — when babies will be born; 2 Samuel 7:19, Daniel 2:45, and Psalm 139:16 — what will happen to us; Jeremiah 29:11 — what God will do for us. God keeps all His promises. Using future dates and times the pupils will write new words to the tune. Encourage the pupils to think of close dates, things that are a few years away, and events that are ten or more years away. They may work as one large group, or several small groups. As time allows, they may write more than one verse. One suggestion:

He's got tomorrow night in His hands,
He's got the year 2,000 in His hands,
He's got my teen-age years in His hands,
He's got the whole world in His hands.

Ask pupils to write one large copy of the verses. Practice singing the song together with the new words. Pupils may illustrate the verses beside the words, or on separate paper. During *Sharing in Worship* this group will post the words and sing the song.

3. Scripture. Pupils will make a word search puzzle of God's promises. Provide Bibles, paper, large-ruled graph paper, one blank transparency, marker, overhead projector, and pencils. **God made many promises to people in the Bible. Can you name some of them?** (Pupils answer. Suggestions: Noah/safety from flood: Abraham/land and son; Moses and Israelites/freedom and protection; Paul/safety from shipwreck.) **God has made many promises to us, too. Where do we read about these promises?** (In the Bible.) **Assign each pupil one of the following verses. From the verses, they will write on paper the words that tell what God has promised.** Psalm 62:12 — rewards; John 3:16 — eternal life; Philippians 4:19 — needs; 2 Thessalonians 1:6, 8 — trouble, relief; 2 Thessalonians 3:3 — faithful, strengthen, protect; 1 Timothy 6:17 — provides; James 1:5, 12 — wisdom, crown; 1 Peter 5:7 — cares; 1 John 5:14 — hears. Take time to explain the words as needed. Ask pupils to write all the answers in the graph paper squares in any direction (forward, backward, horizontal, vertical, or diagonal). Then they will fill in the blank squares with any letters. One pupil will lay the transparency over the graph paper and copy the letters onto the transparency. While he or she is copying the puzzle, the other pupils can choose the verses they want to read during the presentation. Options: to make the puzzle easier to solve, the pupils may list the answers on the transparency beside the puzzle. If the group is small or time is limited, they do not need to use all the verses given. If you have a large group of pupils, furnish two transparencies and markers. Divide the pupils into two groups. Divide the Scriptures between the groups, to enable them to make two puzzles. In this way more pupils can participate.

During *Sharing in Worship*, the pupils will project the puzzle on the wall. The large group will find the words in the puzzle. As they find each word, one pupil will circle the word while another reads the corresponding Scripture. After all the words have been found and the Scriptures have been read, one pupil will read the list of things God has promised to us.

4. Lord's Supper. Pupils will draw a mural of the promises God kept through Jesus. This activity may be done without adult supervision. Write or record on tape the instructions and teacher comments. Provide copies of activity page 4A, a roll of paper, markers, scissors, pencils, pushpins, and Bibles. **God made many promises in the Bible. Many promises tell what Jesus would do and be. God could keep all these promises because He has the power to control and know the future. How does this make God more powerful than people?** (People do not know what will happen and cannot control what will happen.) **Each of you may choose one of the verses on your activity page. Read your verses. What promise about Jesus did God make in each verse? How did He keep the promise?** Answers: 1. Micah 5:2 (birth place); 2. Matthew 2:14, 15 (would go to Egypt and return); 3. Matthew 8:16, 17 (heal people); 4.

Matthew 13:34, 35 (would teach with parables); 5. John 12:12-15 (triumphal entry into Jerusalem); 6. Isaiah 53:5, 9 (death); 7. Matthew 1:21 (save from sins). **The Bible often says that Jesus fulfilled something that the Old Testament said. This means that He kept the promise God made during the Old Testament. The word, *fulfilled*, is a good clue that Jesus kept a promise. You will each draw a picture of the way God kept the promise in the verses you read. These pictures will make a mural of Jesus' life. You will want to draw the pictures in the order that they happened. They were given in the correct order when the verses were assigned. If you need to, refer to that list. Lay the paper on the floor or table and position yourselves in the correct order. Give each person enough room for a picture. Now you can draw.** When everyone is finished, cut the paper and hang the mural on the wall. Option: Pupils may make their drawings on blank transparencies. They may project them with an overhead projector onto the wall.

During *Sharing in Worship* this group will show their mural as they tell how God kept the promises. Then they will pray and serve the Lord's Supper to the group.

5. Devotional. Pupils will present skits to illustrate how we should behave because God keeps His promises. You will need copies of activity page 4B.

When God promised Sarah and Abraham that they would have a son, they did. When He promises you that He'll be with you and answer your prayers, He will. Knowing that God is dependable should change the way we act. Distribute activity page 4B. Divide pupils into groups with two or three pupils. Give each group one situation, or let them choose. Guide pupils to plan skits to illustrate the situation with the correct response. One way they may do it is to act out the problem, then give the correct response as a prayer to God. Use these questions to help the pupils decide on the ending to their problems. What is the person's problem? What has God promised that would help the person? Since God always keeps His promises, how does that help the person make the right decision? Option: Younger or less mature pupils may work out a few skits as a group. Older or gifted pupils may want to use props, or write dialogue for the skits.

Suggested endings for the skits: 1. God promised to hear our prayer and to help us. Child prays for mother's health, and that God would help him while she is away. 2. God promised to punish sin and to help us not to sin. Child tells friend that she cannot cheat and prays that God will help her to do her best honestly. 3. God promised to reward us for doing right. Child prays that he will continue to have the courage to do what is right, even if other people don't like it. He trusts God to reward him. 4. God promised to take care of us and give us courage. Child doesn't get even, because God takes care of sin. Child prays that God will give him courage, and then tells the boy how he feels. 5. God promised to take Christians to heaven when they die. The child thanks God for taking care of his grandpa. He asks God to take care of him and his family. 6. God promised to always be fair and to give us courage. Child thanks God that He is fair, because sometimes people aren't. He asks God for the courage to explain the situation to his teacher

During *Sharing in Worship* the pupils will present their skits.

6. Personal Praise. Pupils will make a bulletin-board or wall display to illustrate how God has kept His promises to them. Provide Bibles, paper, pencils, markers, pushpins, construction paper, letter stencils, and scissors. **We make promises almost everyday. Tell us one promise that you made today.** (Pupils share. Remind them that saying "I will" is the same as making a promise.) **God makes many promises, too. Read Genesis 18:10 and tell the promise God made to Abraham and Sarah.** (A son.) **Genesis 21:1, 2 tells how God kept the promise. Let's read it together.** Do so. **God makes promises to us too. Name some of these promises.** (To forgive us, to take care of us, to hear our prayers, to help us when we want to do wrong, to take us to heaven, to love us, to reward us when we do right, to protect us, to be with us always.) You may need to help the pupils by asking questions. **What does God promise to do when we are sorry that we have sinned? When we pray? When we need things to live?** As pupils answer, write God's promises on paper. **The big difference between us and God is that we *usually* keep our promises, but God *always* keeps His. How has God kept His promises to you and your family?** (Pupils can refer to the list you made previously. Suggestions: helped Father find a job, provided clothing, healed someone, gave them a friend when they prayed, protected them in an accident, gave courage, helped them do right.) Distribute materials. **We'll make a bulletin board (wall display) to praise God for keeping His promises to us.** Pupils will write their names on the construction paper and draw pictures or write sentences to tell how God kept one promise to them. As pupils finish the activity, they may make the heading for the display. They should trace and cut out letters from construction paper for the words, "God Keeps His

Promises." They will pin the letters to the bulletin board or the wall and pin their pictures under it. As time allows they may add a border. Option: To save time, you may partially prepare the heading before class. You may trace and/or cut out the letters. Also, you may purchase a border for the pupils to use.

Sharing in Worship
(20-25 minutes)

Omit any of the following sections if you did not offer the corresponding activity. The devotional may be given without the presentation of Group 4.

Call to Worship (Group 1): **God is so powerful that He can keep all His promises. Group 1 will read a verse that describes God.** Group 1 reads verse and shows bookmarks.

Special Music (Group 2): **God can keep His promises because He knows the future. He also is in control of the whole world. We can trust Him. Group 2 will sing a song that reminds us of God's power.** Group 2 sings. The large group can join them the second time.

Scripture (Group 3): **God made many promises to people in the Bible. He also makes promises to us. As we solve Group 3's word search, we will discover some of God's many promises that He'll keep.** Group 3 present their word search.

Group Singing: As you listen to me sing this song, remember that God keeps His promises. Sing "God's Promise Is a Promise" from p. 179. Then ask pupils to join you as you sing it two more times. Option: Provide taped accompaniment to encourage the pupils to sing better.

Lord's Supper (Group 4): **I'm very thankful that God kept the promises He mad about Jesus. Group 4 researched some of these promises. As they show their mural, they will explain how God kept many promises when He sent Jesus.** Group 4 will present their mural, pray, and serve the Lord's Supper.

Offering: When we give God our money, we are telling Him that He is powerful. He deserves our worship and our money. He has kept all His promises to us. Pupils collect the offering.

Devotional (Group 5): **Do you trust me to keep my promises? I hope you do, because I try to keep them. If I promised that I would give you $100 tomorrow morning, what would you do or think about today?** (Allow several pupils to answer.) **If I promised that I would put honey in your bed at midnight, what would you do tonight?** (Pupils answer.) **Your answers told me that you trust me to keep my promises. When we trust someone to keep their promises, we act certain ways. When we trust God to keep His promises, we act in certain ways, too. When God promised Abraham and Sarah that they would have a son, Sarah laughed. She thought that God couldn't keep His promise because she was too old to have children. A year later Sarah held her own baby boy. She praised God for keeping His promise.**

Sometimes it's hard to believe that God will keep His promises. Listen to Isaiah 46:9-11. "I am God. There is no one like me. From the beginning I told you what would happen in the end. A long time ago I told you things that have not yet happened. When I plan something, it happens. I do the things I want to do . . . I will make what I have said come true. I will do what I have planned." The Bible also says, "What he promises, he keeps." (Numbers 23:19 *ICB.*) God said that He loves us. When we think, "God can't love me, or He wouldn't have let my friend move away," we need to remember "what He promises, He keeps." God said that He will take care of us. When we think, "God can't forgive me because what I did was too bad," we need to remember "what He promises, He keeps." Encourage pupils to say these words with you each time. **God said that He will help us do right. When we think, "No one can help me. I have to do the wrong thing," we need to remember "What He promises, He keeps." Group 5 will present skits to show how we should act because we know that God keeps His promises.** Group 5 presents skits.

Personal Praise (Group 6): **We worship God today for keeping His promises to us. Group 6 made a display to illustrate how God kept His promises to them. They'll show it to us now.** Group 6 presents bulletin board/wall display.

Prayer: Ask for four volunteers. Assign each pupil one of the following topics for prayer. They are: Praise God for His special power shown in creation, creation of man, punishment of sin, keeping His promises.

Closing Moments
(10-15 minutes)

Read a short story to the pupils in which one character does or does not keep his promise. After reading, ask the pupils to identify the character that did or did not keep his promise. **How was this person like or not like God?** Suggested books which are available in most public libraries: Horton Hatches An Egg by Dr. Seuss—a story about an elephant who keeps his promise to a bird. Pinocchio by Collodi—the familiar story about a disobedient wooden boy. This is a long story, so read only one part where Pinocchio breaks a promise, such as chapters 8 and 9. Option: You may tell a story about a person who did or did not keep a promise.

God Is Faithful to Protect Us

Worship Focus

Worship God because He is faithful to protect us.

Transition Time

(10-15 minutes)

Hangman. This game will focus the pupils attention on the subject of protection. Copy these words on slips of paper—seat belt, suntan lotion, vitamins, parachute, helmet, boots, oven mitt, knee pads, and railing. One pupil will take a slip of paper and draw on the chalkboard the same number of blanks as letters in the answer. The other pupils will take turns guessing letters. When a correct letter is guessed, the pupil will fill in the corresponding blank(s) with the letter. When an incorrect letter is guessed, he or she draws one part of a stick-man. They will continue guessing letters until the word or the stick-man is complete. The pupil may tell the answer if the group cannot guess it. Repeat the game with other words until it is time to start class. **What do all of these things or people do for us?** (Protect us.)

Launching the Theme

(10 minutes)

Provide newspapers and scissors. Check to see that they contain many articles or ads that are appropriate for this activity. **Look through these newspapers and cut out articles or advertisements that deal with protection. The article may be about a person who saved or protected someone from injury or death. You may find an advertisement for a product to protect yourself from burglars or high blood pressure. There may be an ad about someone who wants to protect your house against termites.** Assist pupils as they find the articles. Options: Pupils may work in groups of two. If time is limited or pupils are young, you may clip the articles before class and proceed with the activity. **Read your article and be ready to tell us two things: Who or what protected (or will protect) someone? What did (or will) they protect against?** When pupils are ready, ask for their reports. **We all need to be protected. None of us can take care of ourselves all the time. People and things can protect us sometimes, but the best protector is God. Why can God protect us better than other things?** (He has more power, knows, and controls everything.) **Today we will worship God because He protects us.**

Explain choices of *Building the Theme* activities.

Use these suggestions if you need to help your pupils form groups for the *Building the Theme* activities. 1) Make slips of paper for each activity you will offer. Make the same number of slips per activity as pupils that may participate in it. For example: If five pupils can do activity 1, mark five slips 1. Do the same with each activity. Make approximately the same number of slips as expected attendance. Place all the slips in a box. Place numbered signs on each table to identify the activities. Pupils will choose a paper and go to the correct center. 2) Group the pupils by the main color of the clothes they are wearing. Place a different colored piece of construction paper on each activity table. Use popular clothing colors. Pupils will go to the table with the color that most closely matches their clothes. If you have too many pupils at one activity, have the pupils wearing the most of that color remain, while the others go to another table.

Building the Theme

(30 minutes)

1. Call to Worship. Pupils will make a wall hanging illustrating a Bible verse about God's protection. Provide Bibles, one International Children's Bible, paper, burlap (2′ x 3′), dowel (28″ long), materials for letters and illustrations (wallpaper or felt), letter stencils, pencils, white craft glue, gold cord for hanging, scissors, and a pushpin. Before class sew a narrow hem at the top of the burlap for the dowel. Hem or fringe the bottom and side edges. **God protected many people in the Bible. How did God protect Lot and his family?** (Saved them when God destroyed the city he was living in.) If pupils are unfamiliar with the story, ask them to read it in Genesis 19:12, 13, 15, 16. **How did God protect Noah and his family?** (Saved them when God destroyed the world by a flood.) If pupils are unfamiliar with the story, ask them to read it in Genesis 6:13, 14, 18. **God also protects us.**

Proverbs 18:10 tells us about God's protection. Let's read it. Also read the verse from the International Children's Bible to clarify the meaning. **We will make a banner to illustrate this verse. You will cut out letters and/or pictures to show the verse.** Guide pupils as they plan the banner on paper, then cut out the figures. They'll glue them on the burlap. When the pupils are finished, ask them to put the dowel in the top hem. They will tie the gold cord around the ends of the dowel to make a hanger.

During *Sharing in Worship* this group will hang the banner and recite the verse.

2. Special Music. Pupils will identify words from hymns that describe God's protection. This activity is good for older or gifted pupils. It requires more reading than most activities. Provide copies of activity page 5A, and pencils. Also provide copies of "Anywhere with Jesus" from p. 180. Option: Provide recorded accompaniment to enable the pupils to sing better. **Tell about a time when God protected you from something bad.** (Pupils share.) **How did you feel about God?** (Pupils share.) **Sometimes it helps us appreciate God to describe mental pictures about Him. A mental picture is the picture in our minds when we think about how God protects us. We might picture a big, strong house because God keeps us safe. We might picture our father carrying us through a bad storm. Share with us some of your mental pictures about God's protection.** (Pupils share. Suggestions follow: mother, snuggling before a warm fire at home, soldier's armour.) **Often song writers use similar word pictures to describe God. On your activity page, you will find the words to six hymns and some pictures. Read the words and underline the part that tells about God's protection. Then draw a line from the words to the picture that the hymn puts in your mind.** Be prepared to explain these archaic words: ancient of days—has lived a long time; pavilioned—housed; girded—clothed; balm—medicine. Answers follow: "O Worship the King"—soldier; "Safely Through Another Week"—calendar; "Wonderful Peace"—sleeping peacefully; "Tis the Blessed Hour of Prayer"—praying for protection; "I Never Walk Alone"—storm; "Anywhere with Jesus"—together with Jesus at school. When the pupils are finished, learn together the song, "Anywhere with Jesus." Option: Older or gifted pupils may want to make their own words for the chorus of this song. The group can use their words for the presentation.

During *Sharing in Worship* this group will describe how the pictures show God's protection. Then they will sing "Anywhere with Jesus."

3. Scripture. Pupils will portray Bible people who were protected by God. Provide Bibles, pencils, and six pieces of paper. Before class copy one of the following six Scriptures on each piece of paper. The answers are in parentheses. 1. Genesis 6:7-10, 7:6, 7 (Noah by ark); 2. Genesis 19:1, 12, 13, 15, 16 (Lot by escape); 3. Genesis 16:15; 21:14-20 (Hagar and Ishmael by giving water); 4. Genesis 37:2-4, 23-28; 39:1, 2 (Joseph by making his master pleased with him); 5. 2 Kings 4:1-7 (widow's sons by giving oil for money; 6. 2 Kings 6:14-20 (Elisha by making enemies blind). Write the following on each paper. **Whom did God protect? Write two sentences that tell about that person Write one sentence that tells how God protected that person.** Examples follow: I had three sons. I was a good man. God protected me by telling me to build an ark. OR, I was Abraham's nephew. I lived in Sodom. God protected me by helping me escape from the city.

We know that God will protect us because He protected many Bible people. Give each pupil or pair one paper. **Read the Scriptures on your paper and follow the instructions. Choose one or two verses from your Scriptures that tell how God protected the person. Now we will practice this presentation for *Sharing in Worship.*** One pupil from each group will portray the Bible person. He or she will read the three sentences. The large group will guess the person's identity. Then another pupil will read the Bible verses that describe how God protected the person. Do the same for each Bible person. Option: If you have young pupils, do the activity as a large group. Use as many of the Scriptures as time allows.

During *Sharing in Worship* the pupils will do the presentation as given above.

4. Devotional. Pupils will present a play about trusting in God's protection Provide copies of Activity page 5B, light-colored markers, Bibles, and props for the play. **Read Psalm 91:14. What will God do for us?** (Rescue and protect.) **When do you need to be protected or rescued?** (Pupils share.) If needed, suggest possible places or situations, such as in a new school, in a storm, when we are sick, in a car on icy roads, when a stranger talks to you, when children tease you. **God is the best protector. He protected us before we were born, and He'll still be protecting us after we die. You will present a play today that tells that we should trust God to protect us.** Distribute copies of the activity page and markers. Read through the play, then help pupils choose parts. Pupils will highlight their lines with the markers. Options: The play is written for seven characters, but can be done with only five. Holly, David, and Justin's parts can be grouped together into two parts. The mother and father parts can be done by one pupil. Some of the boy and girl parts can be changed by simply changing the names. If you have more than seven pupils, some children can be in the classroom scene, but not have a speaking part. Some pupils can help gather props and introduce the play. Pupils can gather props from the classroom. Practice the play at least two times. As time allows, discuss these questions: **How does this play show that God's protection is best? Can we always protect ourselves? How did Carl need God's protection?**

During *Sharing in Worship* pupils will present the play.

5. Personal Praise. Pupils will write accounts of times when God protected them. Provide Bibles, pencils, and paper. **When God sent the flood, the world was in danger. Yet God protected Noah. How did He do it?** (In the ark.) If pupils are unfamiliar with the story, they may read Genesis 6:13, 14, 17, 18. **When God decided to destroy Sodom, those people were in danger. Yet God protected Lot. How did He do it?** (By warning him to escape.) If pupils are unfamiliar with the story, they may read Genesis 19:15, 16. **When have you been in danger? How did God protect you?** (Pupils respond.) **God protects in many ways. Sometimes He gives us courage and wisdom. Sometime He sends someone to help. Even when a person dies, God takes care of him or her in heaven. God always protects us. You will write stories (5-6 sentences) of what happened to you. Be sure to include how God protected you and how you felt. These stories will praise God for protecting us.** If pupils have trouble thinking of a time God protected them, provide opening sentences to help them. "One time I was afraid." "One time I was alone." "One time I was in trouble." If time allows, pupils may illustrate their stories.

During *Sharing in Worship* pupils will read their stories.

6. Prayer. Pupils will write a litany prayer to thank God for His protection. The pupils may do this activity without teacher supervision. Write or tape record the instructions and teacher comments. Provide paper, pencils, and Bibles. **Read Proverbs 29:25b. Who is kept safe?** (Whoever trusts in God.) **Did Noah trust in God? Was he kept safe? Read 2 Peter 2:5 for the answers.** (Yes.) **Did Lot trust in God? Was he kept safe? Read 2 Peter 2:7 for the answers.** (Yes. Yes.) **God is faithful to protect us. When did God keep you safe? How did you feel? Write a prayer, telling God how you feel because He kept you safe. When you read your prayers in the large group, the whole group will say "Whoever trusts in the Lord is kept safe" after each prayer.**

During *Sharing in Worship,* pupils will read their prayers, quoting Proverbs 29:25b following each prayer.

Sharing in Worship
(20-25 minutes)

Omit any of the following sections, if you did not offer the corresponding activity. The devotional may be given without the presentation of Group 6.

Call to Worship (Group 1): **David describes God's protection in this verse.** Ask Group 1 to hang their banner and read the verse.

Special Music (Group 2): **David pictured a strong tower when he thought of God's protection. Hymn writers often use words to make pictures in our minds. Group 2 will share word pictures from songs that describe God's protection. Then they'll sing a song about the way we feel when God protects us.** Group 2 presents word pictures and hymn.

Scripture (Group 3): **Many Bible people knew how it felt to be protected by God. The Bible tells us their stories. We will guess the Bible people that Group 3 studied.** Group 3 reads clues and verses.

Lord's Supper: God protects us from the punishment of our sins. He sent Jesus to die for us, so that we could be forgiven. Ask a pupil to pray and serve the Lord's Supper.

Offering: When we love someone, we want to give him or her gifts. One way we show God that we appreciate Him is by giving our money to Him. Pupils collect offering.

Devotional (Group 4): You will need pictures of a U.S. President, soldier, mother, father, doctor, policeman, scientist, a child, and teacher. Before class place the pictures in a box.

Everyone needs protection because everyone has times when they can't help themselves. Group 4 prepared a play. Watch it and decide how Carl needed protection. Group 4 presents their play. **Why did Carl need protection?** (Other people were embarrassing him.) **Why was it impossible for Carl to protect himself?** (Needed glasses, couldn't do everything the kids wanted him to do.)

Sometimes we need protection from people who want to embarrass us. Sometimes we need protection from the weather or germs. In this box are pictures of people we depend on to protect us. Call on a pupil to take a picture from the box. Ask him or her to tell how we depend upon that person to protect us. (Suggested answers: president, soldier, police—protection from bad people; mother and father—protection from hunger, cold, loneliness, bad people; doctor and scientist—protection from disease and pollution; child—protection from loneliness; teacher—protection from other children, ignorance.) **Can God protect us better than him/her? How?** (All people have limitations—they can only do their best. God has no limits. He can do anything.) Continue until all the pictures have been used.

God cares about us. He cared about Noah so much that He protected him from a flood that destroyed all living things on the earth. God told Noah how to build a huge boat. That boat was home to Noah, his family, and many animals for a whole year! God cared about Lot. God sent angels to lead Lot and his family out of the city that God would destroy. God protected Lot from the destruction of Sodom. Because God loves us, He protects us.

Before Jesus died, He prayed that God would protect us from Satan. God is faithful to do it! Even when our situation looks hopeless, like no one can help, God can protect. We should praise God everyday for protecting us from Satan and his plans for us.

Personal Praise (Group 5): **God protects us everyday. Sometimes we say that we were lucky, but many times it was God's protection. He is always with us. Group 5 wrote stories about times when God protected them.** Group 5 reads stories.

Prayer (Group 6): **I want to worship God when He protects me.** (Tell a personal story of a time when God protected you.) **Group 6 will lead us in worship as they read prayers to God.** Group 6 reads prayers.

Closing Moments
(10-15 minutes)

Play this game to reinforce the concept of protection. Provide 20 blown-up balloons. Divide pupils into two teams. Place 10 balloons at each end of the room. Assign each team one pile of balloons to defend. The object of the game is to burst all the opposing team's balloons before your balloons are burst. The team members must protect their own balloons, while trying to break the other team's balloons. You may play the game several times, if you have more balloons.

Suggested Resources

Use these resources to supplement the pupils' appreciation and understanding of God's protection.

Video Cassettes—

Twister and Shout from the *McGee and Me* Series. Focus on the Family Publishing, 30 minutes.

For Next Week

Collect empty oatmeal boxes, foil pie pans, empty baby food jars or pill bottles, 2 large nails, wood blocks, and sandpaper. See Group 5 of Session 6 for more information.

God Is Faithful to All Generations

Worship Focus
Worship God because He is faithful to all generations.

Transition Time
(10-15 minutes)

Families. This activity will introduce the theme of families and generations. Provide copies of Activity page 6A and pencils. Distribute the materials. **Write your name on your paper. Various facts about people are written in each square. Draw an *X* in one square that describe one of your relatives. Think of the people who live in your house, as well as great-grandparents, grandparents, aunts, uncles, and cousins. Now you may ask other pupils to draw an X on your paper for sentences that describe a relative of theirs. You may find several facts that describe your relatives. You don't have to put the X in the same place on each paper, but you can only write one X per paper. The first pupil to get four X's in a row wins the game.** Option: If you have a large class, ask pupils to get two rows of *X's* to win.

Launching the Theme
(10 minutes)

Before class borrow pictures of several generations of one family. **What is a generation of people?** (People that are closer to the same age.) **The people that are close to your age are one generation. The people that are close to your parents ages are another generation. The people close to your grandparents ages are another generation. Here are pictures of ______ (how many) generations of one family.** Show pictures and point out the generations. If known, tell their approximate year of birth. **How many generations of your family have you met?** (Pupils answer.) **It is good to know that God takes care of all these people. He also took care of their parents, grandparents, great-grandparents, and so on. God has been faithful to people since He created Adam and Eve. Today we will worship Him because He is faithful to all generations.**

Explain choices of *Building the Theme* activities.

Building the Theme
(30 minutes)

1. Call to Worship. Pupils will make a wall hanging illustrating a Bible verse about God's faithfulness to all generations. Provide Bibles, paper, burlap (2′ x 3′), dowel (28″ long), materials for letters and illustrations (wallpaper or felt), letter stencils, pencils, white craft glue, gold cord for hanging, scissors, and a pushpin. Before class sew a narrow hem at the top of the burlap for the dowel. Hem or fringe the bottom and side edges. **Read Genesis 17:7, 8. What promises did God make to Abraham?** (To be his and his children's God; to give him the land.) **What did God do for Abraham's son, Isaac? Read Genesis 25:11 for the answer.** (Blessed him.) **What promise did God make to Jacob, Abraham's grandson and Isaac's son? Read Genesis 35:12.** (Give him the land.) **We just read that God was faithful to three generations. *Faithful* means that God does what He says. God continues to be faithful even up to ______ (present date). Read Deuteronomy 7:9. What does God do for all the people who love Him?** (Keeps His promise to love them.) **God is faithful even to a thousand generations of people. If a generation is 20 years, how many years is a thousand generations?** (Twenty thousand years.) **We will make a banner to illustrate this verse. You will cut out letters and/or pictures to illustrate the verse, beginning with "He is the faithful God."** Guide pupils as they plan the banner on paper, then cut out the figures. They'll glue them on the burlap. When the pupils are finished, ask them to put the dowel in the top hem. They will tie the gold cord around the ends of the dowel to make a hanger.

During *Sharing in Worship* this group will hang the banner and recite the verse.

2. Scripture. Pupils will make a coded puzzle to tell how God remains faithful. Provide Bibles, paper, one blank transparency, overhead projector, marker, and pencils. Before class write a code at the top of the transparency. Use shapes, numbers, or symbols for the letters, such as A=8, B=#, C=$. **Read Malachi 3:6a. What does this verse say about God?** (He does not change.) **God remains**

faithful through the years. We worship the same God that Jacob worshiped. The God that saw what you did this morning is the same God that watched the people build the tower of Babel. If pupils are unfamiliar with these Bible stories, they may read Genesis 35:11-14; 11:3-5. Scriptures and answers: Genesis 9:12-15 – rainbow reminds us God will not flood the whole earth; Psalm 33:11 – plans; Psalm 102:24 – years; Psalm 105:8 – word; Psalm 111:3 – righteousness; Psalm 119:91 – laws; Psalm 135:13 – name; Psalm 145:13 – kingdom, dominion; Psalm 146:10 – reign.) Distribute paper and pencils. Divide the following verses among the pupils. **Write your verse(s) on your paper and read it (them). Write the way(s) God remains the same through the generations. Below each answer use the code to write your answer in code.** When pupils have finished, each pupil will write his or her coded answers on the transparency.

During *Sharing in Worship* the pupils will project the transparency on the wall. As the other pupils decode the words, the pupils from this group will take turns writing the decoded words on the transparency. Other pupils will read the corresponding verses and tell how God remains faithful through all generations.

3. Devotional. Pupils will prepare a time line to show the generations to whom God was faithful. This is a good activity for older or gifted pupils. Provide Bibles, paper, pencils, newsprint paper (or sheets of paper taped together), yardstick, pushpins, and markers. Also provide reference materials for the dates of Bible people and Church History. (Suggestions follow: Bible dictionaries, *Eerdman's Handbook to the Bible, Eerdman's Handbook to Christianity in America.* or *Dictionary of Christianity in America,*by InterVarsity Press.) Make copies of these Scripture references and A.D. Christians for the pupils. The names and dates in parentheses are for your use to check pupils answers. Genesis 12:1-3 (Abraham, 2100 B.C.); Genesis 28:10, 13-15 (Jacob, 2000 B.C.); Exodus 3:15 (Moses, 1500 B.C.); 1 Samuel 16:1, 12-13 (David, 1000 B.C.); Daniel 6:20, 21 (Daniel, 600 B.C.): Acts 9:15-20 (Paul, A.D. 35); Constantine (300); St. Francis of Assisi (1200); Martin Luther (1500); George Whitefield (1700); Alexander Campbell (1800); Billy Graham (1900). If the reference books named above are unavailable, also write the dates given on the pupils' papers.

Who is the oldest Christian you know? (Pupils share.) **Millions of people love God today. People on earth have served God for thousands of years. Read Psalms 100:5. What does God promise everyone who loves Him?** (To be good, loving, and faithful.) **People throughout centuries have counted on God to do what He said. We can count on God, too. We will make a time line to show the people to whom God was faithful** Distribute papers and divide the Scriptures among the pupils. Pupils may work in small groups. **Read your verses and decide to whom God was faithful. In these reference books, find the approximate dates when the people lived. Write your answers on your papers.** Show pupils the pages in the books that give the dates. Help younger children with this research.

To make the time line, pupils will spread the newsprint paper on the floor or table. With the yardstick they will draw a straight line horizontally down the center of the paper. They will position themselves in chronological order, based on the dates of their people. Be ready to explain that B.C. dates are measured backwards from Christ's birth. The larger the number, the earlier the date. The pupil who studied the earliest person to live (Abraham) should be at the left end. Each Junior will put a mark on the time line for the person he or she studied. They will write the names and dates by the marks. Since Abraham was not the first person to live, they should leave a small amount of line to the left of Abraham's mark. Ask a pupil to draw a cross before Paul's mark, to signify the death and resurrection of Christ. All the dates after the cross are A.D. (in the year of our Lord) years.

God has been faithful to people since Bible times. We'll add the names of some A.D. believers. These people all lived after Christ died. Divide the names among the pupils. Show pupils how to use the books to find the dates for these people. Instruct pupils to mark the time line, writing in the names and dates for these Christians. The dates after Christ go from small to large. Constantine (A.D. 35). **Now, let's add our names to the line.** Ask all to write their names by a mark labeled with the current year. Hang the time line on the wall. It is not necessary for the time line to be in proportion. The dates just need to be in chronological order. Option: Older or gifted pupils may want to make their time line in proportion. They may make a scale for it, such as 6" = 100 years.

During *Sharing in Worship* the Juniors will read the names and dates. **Option:** Juniors may tell how God was faithful to each of these people.

4. Personal Praise. Pupils will make booklets to show God's faithfulness through the generations. Provide copies of Activity page 6B, colored pencils or crayons, pencils, scissors, and Bibles. **Who taught you about God?** (Pupils share.) **Was he or she from a different generation**

than you? (Probably yes.) **God was faithful to that person. He kept His word. How has God kept His word to you?** (Pupils share.) **God is faithful to you in this generation. God wants you to tell others about Him. He will be faithful to those people, too. Distribute materials. You'll make booklets to show God's faithfulness. Cut out the page on the solid lines. Fold on the dotted lines to make a book. Let's read the cover verse together.** (Do so.) **Open the book to page 2. Read Psalm 44:1 and fill in the blank.** (Pupils may read from the *International Children's Bible* or *NIV.* Answer: "have told us") **Draw on this page a picture of the person who told you about God. Draw a way that God helped that person or how he or she taught you about God. Look at page 3. Read Psalm 33:4 and fill in the blank.** ("faithful") **On this page you will draw a way that God has helped you. Turn to page 4. Read Psalm 89:1 and fill in the blank.** ("generations") **On page 4, draw a picture of yourself telling someone else about God. You could draw a picture of when you are older, telling your children about God..**

During *Sharing in Worship,* these pupils will read together the verse on page 1. Then ask one third of the group to explain their page 2 pictures and read the verses. Continue for the next two pages.

5. Special Music. Pupils will make rhythm instruments to accompany their praise of God for His faithfulness. Provide Bibles and copies of "I Will Sing of the Mercies of the Lord" from p. 181. Option: Taped accompaniment of the song will help pupils sing better. Also provide materials for several rhythm instruments. Suggestions:

Put a small amount of dried beans in an empty baby food jar or pill bottle and use it as a shaker.

Cover empty oatmeal boxes with construction paper and use for drums.

Use two foil pie pans as cymbals.

Tie a string around a large nail. As a pupil holds the string, he or she hits the nail with another nail.

Staple or nail sandpaper to small wood blocks.

What does God promise us in Deuteronomy 7:9? (To show love to a thousand generations.) **God is faithful forever. Name times from Bible stories when God was faithful, or did what He promised.** (Pupils may give answers from their knowledge. Suggestions: gave Jacob the land, protected David, Daniel, and Paul, sent Jesus.) **When we know that God was faithful to people long ago, and is faithful to us, and will be faithful to people living a hundred years from now, we want to worship him. Read Psalm 89:1. What did David do to worship God's faithfulness?** (Sing and told others.) **The song we will sing today has some of the same words as this verse, We'll learn the song, then make rhythm instruments to help us praise God.** Sing the song two times with the pupils, then explain the choices of rhythm instruments. Guide them as they make the instruments. If you have a tape of the song, play it while they are working. After the instruments are made, practice singing and playing the instruments.

During *Sharing in Worship* Juniors will present the song in the same manner.

6. Prayer. Pupils will make a montage of people to whom God was faithful. This activity may be done without adult supervision, if you provide written or tape recorded instructions. Provide Bibles, glue, posterboard, marker, scissors, pushpins, and pictures of people of all ages, all nationalities, and from many centuries. **God is faithful. That means that He'll do what He says. Read 1 Chronicles 16:15. How long is God faithful to His promises (covenants)?** (For a thousand generations.) **If one generation is twenty years, how long is a thousand generations?** (twenty thousand years.) **Read Galatians 3:28. What kinds of people does God love?** (All races, backgrounds, and sexes.) **God is faithful to every person in every country in every century. He was faithful to Adam and Eve, and He'll be faithful to the people who are not born yet. We'll make a montage of the people to whom God is faithful.** First one pupil should copy 1 Chronicles 16:15 across the bottom of the poster. Option: Shorten the verse to "He remembers the word he commanded for a thousand generations." **Cut out pictures of different kinds of people—different races, ages, sexes, and from different centuries. You'll overlap the pictures as you glue them to the poster. During *Sharing in Worship* each of you will pray, thanking God that He is faithful. Each prayer will be about one specific kind of person. Choose now the group of people for whom you will pray. You might say, "Thank You, God, for being faithful to the Indians."**

During *Sharing in Worship* this group will display their poster and pray.

Sharing in Worship
(20-25 minutes)

Omit any of the following sections if you did not offer the corresponding activity. The devotional can be given without the presentation of Group 3.

Call to Worship (Group 1): Group 1 hangs banner and says the verse.

Scripture (Group 2): **We'll remember the many ways that God is faithful as we solve this word puzzle that Group 2 made.**

Group 2 projects puzzle and leads group.

Lord's Supper: Read 1 Corinthians 11:23-26. **We should remember Jesus' death as we eat the Lord's Supper. Until Jesus comes, every generation will remember the great act Jesus did for us.** Pray and serve the Lord's Supper.

Offering: God was faithful to the people who are older than you. They shared their money with God and helped furnish this building. When you share your money with God, you are helping the next generation—your children. Ask pupils to pray and collect the offering.

Devotional (Group 3): You will need a match and several old, worn-out items. **What is the oldest thing you have?** (Pupils share.) **Does it still work? Has it changed over the years? I brought some old things to show you today.** Show items. For each item tell how old it is and approximately how long it worked. Tell how the items have changed over the years. Some of them may have been damaged by rust or water. Some may have worn parts. Others are broken. **Almost everything gets worse with age. That's a fact of life. How long will this match last after I light it?** Ask pupils to guess, then strike the match and time it. **It only lasted ____ seconds. Now I'll throw it away. What happens to toys as they get old? What does an old car look like? Even our bodies get old and quit working like they should. There's only one thing I know that doesn't change through the years. That's God. He is always the same. He is faithful. God said, "I the Lord do not change" (Malachi 3:6). My great-grandparents lived in the 1800's. Most things of their time have been thrown away, because they wore out. When I die, very few of the things I have now will be good enough to give to my children. It is great to know that the same God that was faithful to my great-grandparents has promised to be faithful to my great-grandchildren. God is faithful through the generations. He never changes or wears out.**

There have been people who loved God through the centuries. We can read about some of these people in the Bible. One Bible family is the family of Abraham. God promised Abraham that He would be with him and take care of him. God also took care of Isaac, Abraham's son. God took care of Jacob, Abraham's grandson. And God took care of Abraham's great-grandchildren. The family tree goes on and on. Let's look at Abraham's family tree in Matthew 1. Whose name is first on the list? (Abraham.) **What other names do you recognize?** Let pupils read the familiar names. **Whose name is last in verse 16?** (Jesus.) **Mary and Joseph were both relatives of Abraham. God was faithful to all the people on this list and millions more. God has also been faithful to people since the Bible was written. Group 3 prepared a time line to show us people who lived in Bible times and later.** Group 3 stands and presents time line. If you did not offer this activity, make the time line before class and present it now. **We worship God, who stays the same through thousands of years.**

Personal Praise (Group 4): **God was faithful to the person who told you about Him. He's also faithful to you. He will be faithful to the people that you tell about Him. Group 4 will tell you more about this.** Group 4 shares.

Special Music (Group 5): **Group 5 will sing a song taken from the last verse Group 4 read—Psalm 89:1. "I will sing of the love of the Lord forever; with my mouth I will make your faithfulness known through all generations."** Group 5 sings.

Prayer (Group 6): **Group 6's project will remind us that God is faithful to all people. They'll thank God for His faithfulness to different people.** Group 6 hangs poster and prays.

Closing Moments
(10-15 minutes)

Provide paper, pencils, tape, scissors, crayons, and copies of a doll pattern. See the illustration. Juniors will cut out paperdoll chains to represent their family. To make the chains, fold a piece of paper, accordion style, into thirds. Then trace the pattern on the top sheet. The hands should reach to the sides of the paper. Cut out the doll, not cutting around the hands. One piece of paper will make three dolls. Pupils should make as many dolls as the number of people in their family. They may tape the dolls together to make one chain. Ask pupils to label the dolls with the people's names.

Unit 2
Worship God Because He Is Faithful

Session 7

God Is Faithful to Provide for Us

Worship Session

Worship God because He is faithful to Provide for us.

Transition Time
(10-15 minutes)

Relay. This game will focus the pupils' minds on different food that God provides. Place Scrabble letters on a table at one end of the room. Divide pupils into teams. Ask the teams to stand at the other end of the room, relay style. The pupils will take turns running to the table, picking up a letter, saying the name of a food that begins with that letter, and running back to tag the next person in their line. The pupils will take the letters back to the line with them. The first team to finish wins. Play the game several times. Options: 1) Write letters on the chalkboard. Pupils erase the letters as they choose them. 2) Pupils must name a food that ends with the chosen letter. **God has provided a wide assortment of food for us. Food is just one of many things that God provides.**

Launching the Theme
(10 minutes)

Before class gather many items that would be important to take on a camping trip. (Suggestions: food, matches, first aid supplies, blanket, tent, water, map, compass, comb, clothes, soap.) Display them in front of the class. Divide the pupils into small groups. **If you were leaving today on a camping trip, you would need to take some things. Pretend that you can only take four of these items. In your groups, choose the most important four things to pack.** Ask groups to share their choices and tell why. **It is hard to choose only a few things, because we need more. God knows what we need, and He promises to give it to us. Today we will worship God because He is faithful to provide for us.**

Explain choices of *Building the Theme* activities.

Building the Theme
(30 minutes)

1. **Call to Worship.** Pupils will make a wall hanging illustrating a Bible verse about God's provision for us. Provide Bibles, paper, burlap (2′ x 3′), dowel (28″ long), materials for letters and illustrations (wallpaper or felt), letter stencils, pencils, white craft glue, gold cord for hanging, scissors, and a pushpin. Before class sew a narrow hem at the top of the burlap for the dowel. Hem or fringe the bottom and side edges. Read Genesis 41:47, 48, 53-57; 45:6, 7. **What did the people need during the famine? How did God provide it?** (Food, by letting Joseph be in charge.) Read Genesis 12:1, 2. **What did Abraham need for his long journey? What did God promise?** (Guidance, help, to show him the land, and bless him.) **God gave Joseph, Abraham and the people around them the things they needed. What do you need?** (Pupils answer.) If necessary, help them understand the difference between *needs* and *wants*. **What will God do according to Philippians 4:19?** (Give us what we need.) **God is faithful to provide for our needs. We will make a banner to illustrate this verse.** They may picture various ways God provides for their needs. Guide pupils as they plan the banner on paper, then cut out the figures. They'll glue them on the burlap. When the pupils are finished, ask them to put the dowel in the top hem. They will tie the gold cord around the ends of the dowel to make a hanger.

During *Sharing in Worship* this group will hang the banner and recite the verse.

2. **Scripture.** Pupils will make Bible-verse matching cards to identify what God provides. This activity may be completed without adult supervision, if instructions are written or tape recorded. Provide Bibles, white construction paper, markers, and scissors. Write each of the following references on a piece of paper. The answers are for your use. Psalm 29:11a (strength); Psalm 111:5a (food); Psalm 127:2b (sleep); Psalm 127:3 (children); Psalm 147:8 (rain); Psalm 147:14 (peace); Proverbs 2:6a (wisdom); Proverbs 29:13b (sight); Ecclesiastes 5:19 (wealth, possessions, happiness in work); Matthew 7:11b (good gifts); John 10:28a (eternal life); 1 Timothy 6:17b (everything). **God is faithful to give us what we need. What do you need to live? Think about things to keep your body alive and healthy, as well as**

things to make you feel good about your life. (Pupils answer.) **God will provide for all our needs. He provided for the needs of Abraham on his long journey. He provided for the needs of the Egyptian people and Joseph's family during the famine. The Bible tells us many things that God gives to us. As we obey God, He provides for us. Choose a partner. Each team will take one paper with a Scripture on it. Read the verse and tell what God provides. Now take a piece of construction paper. Cut the paper into two pieces, like two jigsaw puzzle pieces. Write one-half of your verse on each piece. If your reference says to read only the a or b part, divide that part of the verse in half for each piece. On the back of one puzzle piece write what the verse says that God provides. If you have extra Scriptures and time, your team may make another verse-puzzle.**

During the *Sharing in Worship*, one pupil from each team will hold the first of the verses and stand on one side of the room. If a team did two verses, they may hold the first half of both verses, one in each hand. The partners will hold the second-half pieces on the other side of the room. The large group will match the two halves of the verses. Then the pupils will read their verses aloud, telling what God provides.

3. Lord's Supper. Pupils will complete an activity page to show that God provided Jesus for them. Provide copies of activity page 7A, Bibles, and pencils. **Read Philippians 4:19. What will God do?** (Meet all our needs.) **How does God meet your need to have blood circulating?** (Gave us hearts and arteries.) **How does God meet your need to talk to others?** (Provided people on earth, gave us mouths.) **How does God meet your need to have vitamins and minerals?** (Made plants and animals that have the right nutrition for us.) **God knows what we need and provides it. On the activity page, you see three pictures of things that you cannot do for yourself. You need someone to help you. Beside the pictures, write the name of the person who God provided to meet these needs.** (Answers: person to scratch your back, person to drive you places, person to pay your bills.) **Draw a picture in the box of one more thing that you cannot do for yourself. If you wish, you can write a sentence instead of drawing a picture. Beside the picture, write the name of the person that does this for you. God has given you many people to take care of your needs. God knows all our needs. He knew that we need help because we sin. The Scriptures printed tell you why you needed Jesus to die for you. Read the passage. Then write in your own words several endings to this sentence: "I need Jesus because . . ." The underlined words will help you.** (Suggested answers: I was weak; I was living against God; I was a sinner; I was God's enemy.) **In the second column you will write several endings to the sentence, "God provided Jesus to . . ." The circled words tell the answers.** (Suggested answers: die for me; show God's love; make me right with God; save me from God's anger; make me God's friend; save me; make me happy.) **When God sent Jesus, He gave us just what we needed.** When the pupils have finished, ask each pupil to read one of their sentences for *Sharing in Worship*. Choose the best sentence from each pupil's page, remembering to include some from each list.

During *Sharing in Worship*, the pupils will read their sentences. Then they will pray and serve the Lord's Supper.

4. Offering. Pupils will make clay models of things that God has provided. Provide Bibles, clay or salt dough, knives, wax paper, and 6 trays or cookie sheets. Copy this sentence on paper before class: "When God gives us money, He wants us to share it with Him and others." **What has God given you to provide for your needs?** (Pupils respond.) **Have you ever asked God for a specific need?** (Pupils share.) **How did God meet the need?** (Pupils respond.) **Often God provides someone to help you. Sometimes He helps you understand that you don't really need what you wanted. Sometimes He asks us to wait. However He answers, He always provides for our needs. Today you will make from clay (salt dough) one thing that God has provided for you** (Suggestions: house, clothes, food, talents and abilities, parents, bicycle, friends, money, joy, sister or brother.) Give each pupil a piece of wax paper and a portion of clay or dough. Juniors may use knives to shape their clay and toothpicks to mark designs in the clay. When the objects are completed, transfer them on the wax paper to a tray or cookie sheet. **Read 2 Corinthians 9:11a. Why has God given us these things?** (So we can share them with others.) **Look at the model you made. How can you share the real thing with someone?** (Suggestions: share food with local food bank or friends, give extra clothes to people in need, share your talents and abilities with others without bragging, be willing to let others play with your friends, invite people to your house and share your toys, give your money to God and needy people.) **I need one volunteer to read a sentence.** Give the volunteer the sentence you wrote on paper. **I also need volunteers to read the Bible verse, pray, and collect the offering during the large group time. Who wants to do one of these tasks?** Pupils volunteer for the jobs.

During *Sharing in Worship*

pupils will show their clay objects. They will tell how God has provided for their needs, and how they can share with someone. One pupil will read the sentence. Then pupils will read the Bible verse, pray, and collect the offering.

5. Devotional. Pupils will draw movie advertisement posters to illustrate how God or Jesus provided for Bible people's needs. This activity is suitable for older or gifted pupils. Provide Bibles, large paper, pencils, pushpins, and markers. Copy each of these Scripture references on a piece of paper. Matthew 8:5-10, 13 (centurion needed healing for his servant); Matthew 8:23-27 (disciples needed the storm to quit); Matthew 9:18, 19, 23-25 (girl needed life); Matthew 14:15-21 (people needed food); Luke 19:2-10 (Zacchaeus needed to change his way of living and be saved); John 2:1-10 (wedding host needed wine); John 20:24-29 (Thomas needed proof that Jesus was alive). **God asked Abraham to go to a different country. God provided for Abraham's needs in this new place. Joseph was sent to Egypt as a slave, yet God provided for his needs. God gave the Egyptians and Joseph's family enough food during the famine. There are many more stories in the Bible about God and Jesus giving people what they need.** Give each pupil one Scripture reference. **Read your verses and decide what the person needed and how Jesus gave it to him or her. How did the person feel before and after? You have seen posters in movie theaters advertising films they are showing. Pretend that a movie was made about the story you read. You will draw a poster to advertise the movie. Decide on a title for your movie. Your poster won't tell the whole story, but it should tell what the person needed. It should make people want to see the movie and discover how Jesus provided for the person.**

During *Sharing in Worship* pupils will display their posters and briefly describe the stories they read. They'll tell what the person needed and how Jesus or God provided for the need.

6. Prayer. Pupils will thank God for providing the materials needed for their houses. Provide copies of activity page 7B, Bibles, several dictionaries, and pencils. **Read 1 Timothy 6:17b. What does God provide for us?** (Everything.) **Why does He give it to us?** (For our enjoyment.) **God is happy to provide things we need. What has God provided for you?** (Pupils share.) **Tell us about a time when you had a special need. How did God provide for you?** (Pupils share.) **Do you have a need now? Are you asking God to provide it?** (Pupils share.) **Distribute materials. God has given us places to live. On this page, draw a simple picture of the house, apartment, or mobile home where you live.** When pupils have finished, continue. **In the first box write the name of one part of your house.** (Examples: walls, floors, roof, insulation, foundation.) **In the second box, write what it is made of.** (Examples: walls/plaster; floors/wood, linoleum, carpet; roof/wood, shingles; insulation/fiberglass; foundation/concrete.) **In the third box, write the raw materials that make that part. You will probably need to use the dictionary to find this answer.** (Examples: plaster/lime, water, sand; wood/trees; linoleum/cork, wood, gums, pigments, oil.) **In the last box write what God provided to furnish these materials.** (Examples: lime/limestone; water/ocean; sand/rocks; cork/trees; gums/trees and plants.) As time allows, pupils may trace more products back to their "roots".

During *Sharing in Worship* these pupils will pray, thanking God for providing the things we need to make houses that they listed on the activity page.

Sharing in Worship
(20-25 minutes)

Omit any of the following sections if you did not offer the corresponding activity. The Lord's Supper, offering, and devotional may be given without the group presentations.

Call to Worship (Group 1): **Paul wrote a verse telling about God.** Group 1 hangs banner and recites verse.

Scripture (Group 2): **As we match the verses that Group 2 studied, we will discover some of the many things that God provides for us.** Group 2 presents activity.

Lord's Supper (Group 3): **God provides things that we can't get ourselves. God provided food for Joseph's family during the famine. God took care of Abraham's family in the new land. When we eat the Lord's Supper, we remember that God provided Jesus. Group 3 will share reasons why we needed God to send Jesus.** Group 3 reads their sentences. If you did not offer this activity, say, **"We cannot save ourselves. God provided Jesus to be our Saviour. The Lord's Supper helps us remember His death."**

Offering (Group 4): **It's wonderful that God gives to us. Should we thank Him and just keep taking from Him? Does He want us to do anything special with the things He gives us? Group 4 will help us answer these questions.** Group 4 presents their clay models and collects the offering.

Song: Sing "I Will Sing of the Mercies of the Lord Forever," p. 181.

Devotional (Group 5): Before class, make a poster of your pupils' favorite TV programs. Include at least one "Superhero" program, such as Flash, Teenage Mutant Ninja Turtles, or Batman. If available, glue pictures of the actors on the poster. Display it in front of the class.

When I woke up this morning, I needed many things. I needed water with which to wash. I needed clothes and food. I needed a house to keep me warm and a car to drive. Those are just a few of the things I needed. Everyone needs things. Sometimes we can get what we need by ourselves. Many times we need someone to help us. In these TV shows, what do the people do when they need help? (Pupils answer. Suggestions: ask a parent, friend, lawyer, policeman, doctor, superhero, do something wrong, such as steal or lie.) **Most of these things are good to do, but there is one thing we should always do when we are in need. What is that?** (Ask God to help.) **God will provide what we need. Matthew 6:8 says that God knows what we need before we even ask Him. We should always trust God to provide our needs, and then decide what we should do.**

On TV we see many examples of policemen, doctors, and others giving people what they need. In the Bible we see many examples of God giving people what they need. Group 5 studied some of these stories. They'll show you the posters they made and tell you about the stories. Group 5 presents. **If you did not offer this activity, ask pupils to tell about Bible stories they know where God or Jesus provided for a person's needs.**

Our God is a strong God. He can give us everything we need. Maybe your dad needs a job. Knowing that God will give you everything you need, how do you feel—scared, worried, or safe? (Pupils respond—safe.) **Maybe you were sick a long time and now have piles of homework to do. Knowing that God will give you everything you need, how do you feel—depressed, angry, stupid, or confident that you can do it?** (Confident.) **Maybe your friend keeps getting you in trouble. You need to stand up to him and do what is right. Here he comes now. Knowing that God will give you everything you need, how do you feel—nervous, scared, or brave?** (Brave.) **We can have peace and be confident because God provides for us.**

Prayer (Group 6): **Everything we have comes from God. He created the world and continually provides for our needs. Group 6 will thank God for making the materials that are used in making our homes.** Group 6 prays.

Closing Moments
(10-15 minutes)

Provide catalogs and scissors. Give each small group of pupils one catalog. Ask them to cut out pictures of things that we need to live. When they are finished, ask them to share their pictures with the group. Discuss these questions: **What is the difference between something we need and something we want? Do we need more things, or want more things? Does God give us what we want or what we need? Sometimes God gives us both. He promises to give us what we need.**

Suggested Resources
Use these materials to further teach your pupils about God's provision.

Activity Books—
Becoming Kingdom Kids, Book 3 pp. 28, 37 by Oyer, Cannon, Torjussen, Harvest House Publishing.

For Next Week
Make a tape of different sounds. See *Transition Time* in Session 8.

Unit 2
Worship God Because He Is Faithful

Session 8

God Is Faithful to Hear Us

Worship Focus

Pupils will worship God because He is faithful to hear us.

Transition Time

(10-15 minutes)

Sounds. This activity will focus the pupils' attention on listening. Before class tape record many different sounds. Place a five second silent space between sounds. Suggestions: alarm clock ticking and ringing, car noises, ambulance siren, various animal sounds, shower running, walking through leaves. You may include a few harder sounds, such as unlocking a door, filing or clipping fingernails. As you play each sound, ask pupils to identify it. Option: Make two copies of the tape. Divide the pupils into two groups. Each group will listen to the tape and write the answers. When the groups have finished, reward the group that correctly identified the most sounds. **You need to listen carefully to play this game well. God listens carefully to us when we talk to Him.**

Launching the Theme.

(10 minutes)

Before class, ask a pupil to tell about his or her favorite sport or hobby during this portion of the class. Ask a confident Junior who can participate in the following activity without hurt feelings. At the beginning of the lesson, send the pupil out of the room on an errand, so that you may give these instructions to the other pupils. **We are going to play a joke on ______ (pupil who is out of the room). When he or she returns, he or she will tell us about a favorite hobby. I want you not to listen. You may look around the room, go to sleep, read, or doodle on paper. Don't give away our joke by laughing.** When the pupil returns, ask him or her to share. After a few minutes, interrupt the pupil and explain the plan. **How did you feel when no one listened? What did you want to do?** After the pupil has shared, ask him or her to start again? We'll listen this time. Allow the pupil to talk again, while everyone listens. **It's frustrating to talk when no one hears us. We don't have that problem with God. Today we will worship God because He is faithful to hear us when we talk to Him.**

Explain choices of *Building the Theme* activities.

Building the Theme

(30 minutes)

1. **Call to Worship.** Pupils will make a wall hanging illustrating a Bible verse about God's faithfulness to hear us. Provide Bibles, paper, burlap (2' x 3'), dowel (28" long), materials for letters and illustrations (wallpaper or felt), letter stencils, pencils, white craft glue, gold cord for hanging, scissors, and a pushpin. Before class sew a narrow hem at the top of the burlap for the dowel. Hem or fringe the bottom and side edges. **Read Exodus 1:11-14. If you were an Israelite person, what would you say to God?** (I'm tired; I don't like being a slave; help me.) **Did God hear the Israelites? Read Exodus 3:7, 8 to find out. What did God plan to do?** (God heard them and planned to rescue them.) **Today you will make a wall hanging to illustrate Psalm 4:3b. Let's read it together. We know that God will hear us when we talk to Him.** Pupils may write the words to the verse or illustrate people talking to God. Guide pupils as they plan the banner on paper, then cut out the figures. They'll glue them on the burlap. When the pupils are finished, ask them to put the dowel in the top hem. They will tie the gold cord around the ends of the dowel to make a hanger.

During *Sharing in Worship* this group will hang the banner and recite the verse.

2. **Scripture.** Pupils will make a mobile that matches Bible people and their prayers. Provide copies of activity page 8A, Bibles, paper, markers, a 10" cardboard circle, paper punch, scissors, pencils, yarn, and a stapler. Before class punch eight holes around the edge of the cardboard circle. Option: use plastic needlework canvas instead of cardboard. Use the holes that are in the canvas instead of punching holes. Decide how to hang the mobile from the ceiling and prepare the base for hanging. Cut lengths of yarn to hang the mobile pieces. **Read Proverbs 15:29b. What does this verse say about God?** (He hears prayers.) **God is always faithful to hear us. Many Bible people prayed to God, and He heard**

them. Distribute the materials. Assign each pupil one passage from the list on page 8A. If you have less than eight pupils, omit some passages. Pupil may work as teams if you have more pupils. **You will each read your verses and decide who God heard and what the person wanted. For some of the passages, the Bible doesn't tell us exactly what the person wanted. You can make an intelligent guess about it. Draw a line from your Scripture verse to the person. Then draw a line to what the person wanted.** (Answers: Exodus 3:7—Israelites, freedom from suffering; Numbers 11:18—Israelites, meat; Judges 13:8, 9—Manoah, how to raise the boy; 1 Kings 17:17-22—Elijah, life for the boy; Psalm 18:6—David, safety from Saul [see footnote in Bible]; Luke 1:13—Zechariah, son; John 11:41-44—Jesus, probably someone to teach Him about God.) When pupils are finished, ask them to share their answers. Then, ask each pupil to trace one hand on a sheet of paper. Pupils will place another sheet of plain paper behind the one they traced on. As they cut out the hand they will cut through both papers, making two hands. On one they will print with marker the name of the person God heard. On the other hand, they will print what the person wanted. Be sure they print on the *outside* of the hands. When the hands are matched together, the printing will be seen on each side. Ask pupils to hold the hands together and punch one hole at the top. **The hands look like praying hands. These people prayed to God, and He heard them.** Assist pupils as they practice the following presentation for *Sharing in Worship*.

During *Sharing in Worship* they will distribute the hands with the names of various pupils in the large group. Then one pupil will read his or her verses. (For the longer passages, they may choose which verses to read.) The pupil should *not* read the person's name. When the name is given, the pupils should say, "the person," or "these people." After the verses are read the pupil will hold up the hand that says what the person wanted and say, "Who wanted ______?" (Fill in blank by reading the writing on the other hand.) The pupil in the large group who has the matching hand will identify the person. Other pupils may help as needed. The pupil will see if the two hands match. If they do they will know if the answer is correct. He or she will staple the hands together, tie a yarn through the hole, and tie the hand to the cardboard circle. Continue with each Bible passage. When all the hands are tied to the circle, hang the mobile from the ceiling.

3. Special Music. Pupils will read songs about prayer. This activity is appropriate for older and gifted pupils. Provide hymn and chorus books, paper, pencils, and Bibles. **Look at Psalm 4. What does it say right below "Psalm 4?"** (Many Bibles have "For the director of music. With stringed instruments.") **Psalms is called the hymn book of the Bible. Many of the Psalms were sung, not just read. We don't know the tunes the people used, but we know the words. David wrote many of these songs about prayer. Let's read some of them.** Ask volunteers to read Psalm 4:3b; 5:2, 3; 69:13, 33a. **What do the notes in y our Bibles say about the music to Psalms 5 and 69?** (Psalm 5—for flutes, Psalm 69—to the tune of "Lilies.") **When we sing, we often praise God for hearing our prayers. We'll look through these chorus books and read the words to songs about prayer.** Show pupils how to use the topical index. As you find songs about prayer, write down the page number. When pupils are finished, or have found at least one song each, ask them to read the words aloud to the group. **What does this song say about God's faithfulness to hear our prayers? How do these songs make you feel? If your song was a prayer, what did it say to God?** Choose at least one song that the group knows and sing it together several times. Suggestions: "What a Friend," "Whisper a Prayer," "God Is so Good." If the pupils do not know the words well, ask pupils to make copies of the words.

During *Sharing in Worship* pupils will share words from the hymns that best describe God's faithfulness to hear our prayers. Then the group will sing the songs(s) they have practiced. Option: Before class ask a musician from your class to play a song about prayer on his or her instrument. He or she may present it following the group song.

4. Devotional. Pupils will tell how they should act in various situations. Provide paper, pencils, and a bowl. Before class, write these sentences on papers and place in the bowl. Begin each sentence with "Because God hears me . . ." I will keep praying. I will not worry. I will tell others that God will help. I will not sin. I will keep trying. **The Israelites asked God to help them. They were slaves in a foreign country. We are not in their situation, but we still ask God for many things. What do you ask God?** (Pupils share.) Guide pupils to think of serious requests, as opposed to winning games or getting toys. Write these specific requests on paper. **It is easy to do the wrong thing when we need something very much. The Israelites might have quit believing in God because they were slaves. They might have fought with each other because they were overworked. Because God hears us, we can do the right thing.**

Guide pupils as they practice the following presentation for *Sharing in Worship*. Practice more than once, since pupils will draw a different paper each time.

During *Sharing In Worship* a pupil will read his or her request. Then, he or she will draw a paper from the bowl. He or she will read it and tell how he can show that feeling or action. (For example: I prayed that God would give me a Christian friend. Draws: Because God hears me, I will keep trying. I'll keep trying to be friends with others, even if they are not Christians.) These questions will help pupils with their responses: **Why is it hard to keep praying when God doesn't answer your prayer? What might you worry about in this situation? How could you tell others that God will help you? How might you sin and do the wrong things in this situation? How can you keep trying in this situation?** After answering, the pupil will return the paper to the bowl. Continue for each pupil's prayer.

5. Prayer. Pupils will make prayer posters. This activity may be done without adult supervision. Write or tape record the instructions. Provide copies of activity page 8B, crayons, pencils, and Bibles. Option: Provide star-shaped stickers. **I need five volunteers to read verses from Psalms. These are the verses: Psalms 4:3b; 5:3; 66:19, 20; 69:33a; 145:18, 19. Read them aloud now. What do these verses teach us about God?** (He hears our prayers.) **Since God always hears our prayers, we should remember to pray. Do you pray? For what do you pray?** (Pupils answer.) **Today we'll make posters to remind us that God hears our prayers. Read the verse at the top of your activity page. For whom do you pray? Do you pray for your family? friends? yourself? teachers? missionaries? others? In the three boxes under the verse, write three kinds of people for whom you often pray. This week when you pray, write what you ask on this paper. If you pray for your sister to get well, write that under the "family" title. If you pray that you'll do a good job in school, write that under the "me" title. When God answers your prayer, color the star beside it.** (If you provide stickers, change it to "stick a star beside it.") **God promises to hear our prayers. Sometimes we don't get what we want because God knows what's best for us. You can use any extra time to decorate your posters. When you get home, put them by the place you pray.** Option: Pupils may start their posters by praying for one thing now. They can record their prayers in the appropriate place on the poster.

During *Sharing in Worship,* pupils will show their prayer posters. Volunteers will thank God for hearing our prayers.

6. Personal Praise. Pupils will pantomime ways God answered their prayers. Provide Bibles, paper, and pencils. **In Deuteronomy 26:7, Moses is talking. He is reminding the Israelites about when they were slaves in Egypt. What did God do when they cried out to Him?** (Heard them.) **What should we do when we have troubles?** (Pray to God.) **When we pray, God is faithful to hear us. Sometimes God doesn't give us what we want, but He always hears us. Tell about one of God's answers to your prayers.** (Pupils share.) You may prompt the pupils by asking questions. Did you need something? Did you pray for someone to get well? Did you pray when you were afraid? Suggestion: Prayers for safety, for friends, for health, for help in making choices, for bravery, for leaders of our country, for jobs. **We will pantomime (act out without speaking) the different ways God answered our prayers.** With the pupils' help, make a list of the answered prayers they will use. If your group is small, use one prayer from each pupil. Assist the pupils as they plan the parts they will play in each pantomime. They may write this information on paper. **Now we'll practice the pantomimes.** Pupils may use props from the classroom.

During *Sharing in Worship* this group will present their pantomimes. The large group pupils will guess how God answered their prayers. Following the pantomimes, at least two pupils will thank God for hearing their prayers.

Sharing in Worship
(20-25 minutes)

Omit any of the following sections if you did not offer the corresponding activity. The devotional may be given without the group presentation.

Call to Worship (Group 1): **This is a good verse to remember everyday.** Group 1 hangs banner and recites verse.

Song: "I Will Sing of the Mercies of the Lord Forever," p. 181.

Scripture (Group 2): **God showed His faithfulness to many Bible people. He heard their prayers. Group 2 will help us learn about them.** Group 2 presents activity.

Lord's Supper: Read John 3:16. God loved the Israelites enough to send Moses to rescue them. God loved us enough to send Jesus to rescue us from going to hell. Pray and serve the Lord's Supper.

Offering: God continually gives to us. He gives us His time and attention when He hears and answers each of our prayers. We can never give God more than He gives us. He appreciates our thankful gifts. Pupil says a prayer and collects the offering.

Special Music (Group 3): **David wrote many songs**

praising God for hearing his prayers. We can read them in the book of Psalms. Group 3 studied modern songs about prayer. They'll read some of the words and sing one song. Group 3 presents activity.

Devotional (Group 4): Before class cut a dime-size hole in a piece of paper. Provide a dime and a quarter. Practice the object lesson with a different paper than you use for class.

I need two pupils to help me. Give each of them one coin. **You see that one pupil has a dime and one has a quarter. They each have the same job: to fit their coins through this hole without tearing the paper.** Show paper. **There is one small problem, though. This hole is the size of a dime. How many people think that the dime will go through the hole?** (Pupils vote.) **Let's try it.** Hold the paper flat, as pupils drop their coins on the hole. The dime will slip through, the quarter will not. **You were right, the quarter didn't go through. It seems impossible for a quarter to go through a dime-size hole. It seemed impossible to the Egyptians that the Israelites would ever escape their slavery. The Egyptians thought that they were in control. They worked the Israelites hard and kept them poor. It seemed impossible to me when** ______ (share an impossible situation from your life that God solved.) **Even though it looks impossible for a quarter to go through this hole, I know a way to do it. All you need to do is ask me for help. Do you want help?** (After pupils have asked, fold the paper through the center of the hole. Unfold the paper and hold it in a V shape, with the fold along the bottom. While holding it in a V, bend up the two ends. Now ask your helper to drop in the quarter. It will easily slip through the hole.) **This was an easy trick, and God can do much more. When things are impossible for you, ask God for help. God heard the Israelites call for help. He rescued them. God heard my prayers and solved my impossible problem by** __________ (share God's answer to the situation told earlier). **He is faithful to hear our prayers.**

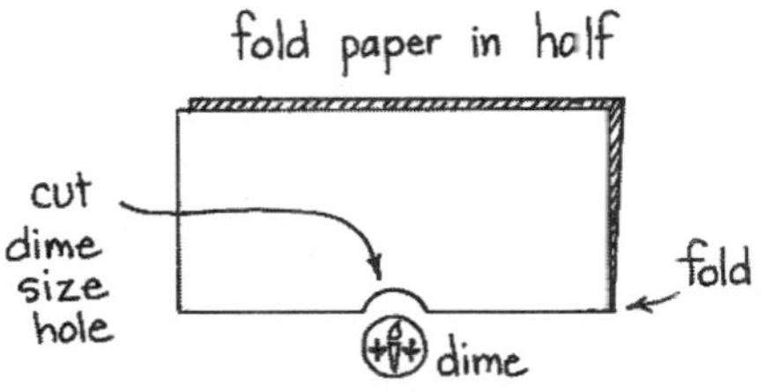

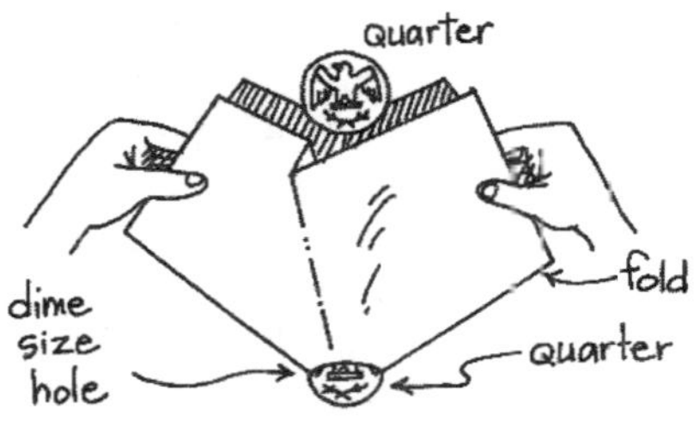

It's easy to be discouraged and grumpy when we really need something. However, when we remember that God hears our prayers, we can trust Him to do what's right. Nothing is too hard for Him. Group 4 will share some of their prayers. Then they'll tell us how they can still do right because they know that God has heard them. Group 4 makes presentation.

Prayer (Group 5): **God answers our prayers everyday. Sometimes we forget about them. The Israelites had to be reminded over and over how God saved them from slavery. Group 5 made prayer posters that will help them remember God's answers.** Group 5 shows posters.

Personal Praise (Group 6): **Group 6 will pantomime some of God's answers to their prayers.** After each pantomime, you can guess God's answer. Group 6 pantomimes and prays.

Closing Moments
(10-15 minutes)

The pupils will find and read Bible verses about God's faithfulness to hear people. Before class use a New International Version Bible concordance and write many Scripture references that refer to God hearing people. You will find them under "hear," "hears," and "heard." Also use the appropriate verses from today's worship session. **We'll play a game to help us learn more about God's faithfulness to hear. You'll also get practice in finding Bible verses.** Divide pupils into groups of three. Each group needs one NIV Bible. To make the game even, mix fast and slow pupils in each group. You will say the verse to find. One pupil in each group finds the book, then passes the Bible to the next pupil, who finds the chapter. The last pupil finds the verse. Then the entire group stands up. After all your pupils find the verse, the group who stood first may read it. To encourage them to listen to the verse, ask a question following the reading, such as, **"Who did God listen to in this verse?"** or **"What does this verse say about God?"** Continue as time allows.

Suggested Resources

These materials will further help your pupils understand about God's willingness to hear their prayers.

Activity Books—

Becoming Kingdom Kids, Book 3, pp. 21, 22 by Oyer, Canon, Torjussen, Harvest House Pub.

Unit 3
Worship God by Obeying Him

Session 9

God Gives Us Rules to Obey

Worship Focus

Worship God because He gives us rules to obey.

Transition Time

(10-15 minutes)

Relay. As pupils play this game, they will learn what it means to trust others. Divide the pupils into two teams. Within their teams, the pupils should each find a partner. If there is an odd number of pupils on a team, one pupil may do the game twice. The pupils should line up for the relay at one end of the room. The partners will stand beside each other, placing their inside hands on each other's shoulders. Then they will hop on their *outside* feet to the opposite end of the room and back. When the first pair returns to the line, the next pair does the same thing. The first team to finish wins. If a pupil touches his or her inside foot to the floor, the team must go back to the starting line. **When you played this game, you depended upon each other. You trusted your partner to do his part, and not let you fall down. When we lean on God, He does His part. We can always trust God.**

Launching the Theme

(10 minutes)

Provide copies of activity page 9A. Distribute papers. **Everyday we trust people and things to do what they are supposed to do. Look at this picture. Who is trusting something or someone? What are they trusting them to do?** (Pupils answer. Suggestions: Pop company and restaurant to supply good food; street workers, tree trimmers, carpenter, airplane pilot, policemen, paramedics to do good job; tools to work right; driver to be alert; roof to be sturdy, and newspaper reporters to be honest.) **Do any of these people or things ever fail us? Yes, because people make mistakes and things break. Sometimes we can't even trust ourselves! Only God is always trustworthy. Today we will worship God because He deserves our trust.**

Explain choices of *Building the Theme* activities.

Use these suggestions if you need to help your pupils form groups for the *Building the Theme* activities. 1) As pupils arrive, ask them to write the numbers of their addresses on the chalkboard. Assign them to the activities in numerical order. For example, if five pupils need to be in activity 1, the five pupils with the lowest house numbers will go to that activity. 2) As pupils arrive, ask them to write their birthdays on the chalkboard. Assign them to the activities according to their birthdates. Pupils with the earliest birthdays in the year will go to activity 1.

Building the Theme

(30 minutes)

1. Call to Worship. Pupils will make plaques of a Bible verse that emphasizes God's trustworthiness. Provide Bibles, round toothpicks (colored, if available, approximately 30 per pupil), glue, pencils, scissors, index cards (white or colored), gold thread, and fine tip markers. Make one plaque before class as a model for the pupils. Option: If your pupils are young, write on the index cards before class, "God never leaves those who trust Him." **God deserves our trust because He has never failed anyone. How did God prove worthy of trust when He helped the Israelites escape from Egypt?** (If needed, ask pupils to read Exodus 11:1-6; 12:1, 2, 7, 12, 13, 29, 31. God did not kill any Israelites and helped the people escape.) **How did God prove worthy of trust when He asked Abraham to kill his son, Isaac?** (If needed, ask pupils to read Genesis 22:1-12. God stopped Abraham from doing it.) **Why would it be hard to trust God in these situations?** (It seemed that God would not be able to make things right.) **God is always right. He is worthy of our trust. Abraham and the Israelites could have said the words of Psalm 9:10 (*ICB*.) "Those who know the Lord trust him. He will not leave those who come to him." The plaque we make today**

will remind us that God always deserves our trust Distribute materials. Pupils will write on their index cards, "God never leaves those who trust Him." (See illustration.) Then they will form a frame for it from the toothpicks, as illustrated. The frames do not have to be exactly like the illustration. They should not glue the toothpicks yet, just lay them where they want them to be. Ask the pupils to draw around the toothpick frame and cut the index card in the shape of the frame. Give each pupil six inches of gold thread. They'll glue this at the top of the index card. Then they'll glue one layer of toothpicks around their cards. The points of the toothpicks should overlap. Very little glue is needed. After the first layer is set, they'll glue a second and third layer of toothpicks over the first layer. This will give the plaque a three-dimensional look. While the frames are drying, practice quoting Psalm 9:10.

During *Sharing in Worship* this group will show their plaques and quote the verse.

2. Scripture. Pupils will draw pictures of times when God showed that He is worthy of trust. Provide paper, pencils, markers, Bibles, and tape. **Have you ever trusted someone or something that disappointed you?** (Pupils share.) **Everything disappoints us at times. We trust that we'll be healthy, but we get sick. We trust that our teachers will be fair, but they make mistakes. It is good to trust people, but we have to remember that only God deserves our trust all the time. We only have to read the Bible to learn that God is always trustworthy.** Give each pupil one of the following Scriptures. Exodus 14:31 (Israelites, save them from Egypt); 2 Kings 18:5 (Hezekiah, to take care of him); 1 Chronicles 5:20 (Israelites, defeat enemies); Daniel 3:28 (Shadrach, Meshach, and Abednego, take care of them in the fire); Daniel 6:23 (Daniel, take care of him in the lions' cage); Matthew 27:37, 43a (Jesus, to take care of Him on the cross). If you have more than six pupils, they may work in pairs. **Read your Scriptures. Decide who trusted God to take care of him.** When the pupils have read their passages, discuss the Bible stories. **For what did they trust God? Why was it hard to trust God? Did God deserve their trust?** (See answers above. Yes.) After the discussion, ask pupils to draw a picture of their person in the situation. When the pupils have finished, ask them to take the picture under six chairs in the large group area. Explain the presentation for *Sharing in worship.*

During *Sharing in Worship* ask the large group pupils to remove the pictures they find under their chairs. The pupils in this group will read their Scriptures, one at a time. After each Scripture, the pupil with the corresponding picture will come forward and show it to the group. The pupils will tell how God proved that he can be trusted.

3. Offering. Pupils will act out two Bible stories about trusting God. Provide Bibles, paper, and pencils. **There are many things that people trust to take care of them. Proverbs 11:28a names one of those things. What is it?** (Pupils read—riches.) **Many people today trust their money, or things money can buy, to take care of them. God wants us to share our money, not keep it all for ourselves. God can take care of us much better than money. You will act out two Bible stories. Jesus told a story about a man who trusted his money and great amount of crops to take care of him. The other story really happened. The other story really happened. A woman trusted God to take care of her.** Assign half the pupils to read and act out Luke 12:16-20. The other half will read and act out 1 Kings 17:7-16. You will need to work with the younger group. If your time is short, only assign the second Bible story. These discussion questions will help the pupils understand the stories. **Who did the man and the woman think of the most? Who or what did they trust? Why is it hard to trust God? Are you trusting God if you don't share your money?** Allow the pupils time to practice their skits. They may choose to say the parts. Another possibility is to have one person read the Scripture, while the actors pantomime.

During *Sharing in Worship* they will present the two plays. Then a pupil will say, "When we give, we are trusting God to take care of us." Another pupil will pray and collect the offering.

4. Devotional. Pupils will write answers to letters asking advice from God. This activity is suitable for older or gifted pupils. Provide Bibles, copies of activity page 9B, pencils, and one "Dear Abby" letter and answer from your local newspaper. **Pretend that you are walking home from school. You notice that a street is blocked off. A man says that there is a gas leak and that you should walk on a different street. What would you do?** (Pupils answer.) **You would do what the man said because you trust him to know what's right. The same principle applies to God. Since we know that we can trust God to be right, we do what He says. Sometimes it isn't easy. What did God tell Abraham to do?** (Refer pupils to Genesis 22:2—sacrifice his son.) **Did Abraham trust God enough to obey?** (Genesis 22:9, 10, yes.) **Abraham trusted God. God made everything work right when He stopped Abraham from killing Isaac. What did God tell the Israelites to do?** (Exodus 12:1-11, how to eat and spread the blood.)

Did they trust God enough to obey? (Exodus 12:28, yes.) **They trusted, and God saved them. What does it mean to trust God?** (To know that what He says is right and to do what He says.) **Have you seen the Dear Abby column in your newspaper?** Read the question and answer you brought. **Many people trust Abby to give them good advice. They do what she says.** Distribute materials. **On this page are some letters to God. They are similar to the letters people write to Dear Abby. You will write advice to these people. However, you won't use your ideas. You'll use God's ideas for the answer. The Scriptures will tell you what God says about it. If we trust God we'll follow His advice, even if it's hard.** Assign each pupil one problem to answer. (For example: Dear Get Even, Don't get even, Forgive your friend.) When pupils are finished ask them to read their letters and God's answers. If time permits, they may write their own letters to God. They can write what God wants them to do.

During *Sharing in Worship* this group will read the letters and answers.

5. Personal Praise. Pupils will present commercials advertising God's trustworthiness. Provide Bibles, pencils, and paper. **I saw a commercial recently on TV where a man was telling about a great diet product. He said that he used it and lost many pounds. The man gave a testimony. A testimony simply tells your personal experience. David gave testimonies about his trust in God. Let's read one of these.** Read Psalm 40:1-3. **Tell about a time when you trusted God. How did God show that He deserved your trust?** (Pupils share.) Emphasize that even when we don't understand why God acted the way He did, God is still always right. **Many times God gives us what we want, but sometimes He doesn't. God always deserves our trust. You will write and perform TV commercials, giving your testimonies about when you trusted God. Write on paper the subject of each commercial. Try to make them different.** Pupils may either use their own personal situations, or ones they had heard.

Suggestions follow:

1. "Are you lonely? Do you sit alone in the cafeteria? When I moved to a new school no one noticed me. The harder I tried, the less people liked me. I trusted God to give me friends. I tried being friendly to everyone. Now I have one good friend. I trust God to give me more. Try it for two weeks. See what happens."

2. "Are you worried? Does everything go wrong for you? I was worried last year when my parents got a divorce. I didn't know how we would live. I decided to trust God to take care of me. He has. We have a great baseball team in our new apartment building. My teacher is cool. Best of all, my mom ad I pray every day. God proved that he deserves my trust."

During *Sharing in Worship* this group will present their commercials.

6. Special Music. Pupils will learn and illustrate a song about trusting God. Pupils may do this activity without adult supervision. Write or tape record the instructions for them. Provide copies of "You Are My Hiding Place" from p. 182, Bibles, paper, tape player, and markers. Before class tape record someone singing and playing the song. **When we know that God can be trusted, we act differently. What did the Israelites do because they trusted God?** Read Exodus 12:28. **What did Abraham do because he trusted God?** Read Genesis 22:2, 9, 10. **Because these people trusted God, they knew that God was right. They didn't worry about the future, because they knew that God would take care of them. We don't have to worry when things are going bad because God will take care of us too. We can trust Him to take care of us. Listen to the song "You Are My Hiding Place" from the tape.** (Pupils do so.) **What does this song say to do when we are afraid.** (Trust in God) **Take paper and markers. Draw a picture of a time you were afraid or another time when you needed to trust God. It could be a time when everything was going wrong in your life. You couldn't understand how things could ever be good again. Even in this situation, you can trust Jesus to protect you. You could draw a picture of a bad time for you. You could draw a picture of a time when your friends dumped you, or a time when you were very sad. When you have finished your pictures, sing along with the tape several times.**

During *Sharing in Worship* the pupils will sing with the tape as they show their pictures.

Sharing in Worship
(20-25 minutes)

Omit any of the following sections if you did not offer the corresponding activities. The offering and devotional may be given without the group presentations.

Call to Worship (Group 1): **David wrote this verse about his experiences with God.** Group 1 shows plaques and quotes verse.

Scripture (Group 2): **Other Bible people also learned that God is worthy of their trust. Group 2 will teach us about some of them.** Group 2 presents activity.

Offering (Group 3): **Group 3 will present two plays. Look for the person who didn't trust God and the person who did. Notice what they did that showed their trust.** Group 3 presents play, prays, and collects the offering.

Lord's Supper: When we think of Jesus on the cross, it is hard to understand how His death could do anything good. Yet we trust what Jesus said. Read John 11:25. We trust that we could be saved because of Jesus' death. Tell God you trust Him as you eat. Pray and serve the Lord's Supper.

Devotional (Group 4)**:** Before class, write these words on white pieces of paper, one per paper: dentist, smartest kid in school, Dad, Mom, teacher, store clerk, older sister, nurse, coach. Write these words on colored pieces of paper, one phrase per paper: toothache, homework, broken doorknob, lost a button, bicycle stolen, problem with a kid at school, can't find your size, hair looks bad, written a report on cancer, can't hit the ball.

What is an expert? (Pupils answer.) **An expert is someone who knows a lot about a certain subject. When we have problems, we trust experts to fix them. I have ten papers. On each paper is the name of an expert.** Give one paper to each of ten pupils. **On these ten papers are different problems that you might have.** Give one paper to each of ten different pupils. **I want you to find the person that has the paper that matches yours. For example: One paper might say "doctor" and the other "broken finger." Those two papers would match. When you find your match, stand by each other.** Give pupils time to find their matches. There are several possible solutions. The pupils may decide who is the best expert for each problem. **Read the problem and then the expert you would trust to fix it.** Pupils do so. **It would be silly to ask advice on baseball from a person who couldn't play the game. You wouldn't ask a four-year-old to help you with your math. When we have problems, we trust people who have proven their knowledge and ability.**

God has proven His knowledge and ability over and over. We should trust Him more than any person. God gives us advice for our problems in the Bible. Sometimes God's advice is different than what we want to do. It's different than what our friends tells us to do. However, when we trust God, we do what He says. Group 4 has answered questions that pretend people wrote to God. They answered with God's advice. Let's see how God answers. Group 4 presents activity.

Personal Praise (Group 5)**: If Abraham and the Israelites were alive today, they would tell us that God deserves our trust. Instead we have Group 5 to present their testimonies of God's worthiness of our trust.** Group 5 presents commercials.

Special Music (Group 6)**: Listen as Group 6 sings about their feelings because they trust God.** Group 6 sings and shows pictures.

Prayer: Let's close in prayer. We will quote David's words. "I trust in your unfailing love," Psalm 13:5a. Prayerfully quote the verse together.

Closing Moments
(10-15 minutes)

Provide pictures of the following: soldiers (guns, bombs), king (rulers of countries), large buildings, friends, idol (Buddha). Also provide a mirror and a dollar bill. Place all in a box. Ask pupils to draw out one picture or thing and tell how some people may trust in this to take care of them. Then ask a pupil to tell how God is more reliable and worthy of trust than the items. For example: **People trust our armies to keep us safe. Armies can lose. God can protect us better. The mirror is to illustrate yourself. God is more reliable than you are. Sometimes people trust money to take care of them. However, on the money itself it tells who we should trust.** Let pupils read it. (In God We Trust.)

Suggested Resources

These materials will help your pupils further understand that God is worthy of their trust.

Books—

The Prodigal Wolf, by Gary Richmond, Word Publishing.

Twister and Shout by Myers, Focus on the Family Publishing.

For Next Week

Gather small empty containers with lids, such as margarine tubs. Use a sharp knife to cut a small rectangle in the top of each container. See Group 4 of Session 9 for more information.

God Is Worthy to Be Obeyed

Worship Focus

Worship God because He is worthy of Honor.

Transition Time
(10-15 minutes)

Honor Badges. To introduce the subject of honoring God, pupils will honor each other by giving badges. Provide copies of badges on activity page 10A, construction paper, markers, scissors, large gold stickers, sequins, glue, ribbon, and straight pins. Before class make one badge for a model. Ask each pupil to name one good thing they have done. Suggestions: helped someone; excelled in a sport, instrument, or school subject; encouraged someone; obeyed someone; overcame a bad habit or behavior; had a good attitude. Ask each pupil to make a badge for another pupil. Every pupil will make and receive a badge. Distribute materials and give instructions for making the badges. Pupils may write on the badges the good thing the pupil did. For example: Best Bedmaker, Most Obedient, Great Pianist. When the pupils are finished they should keep the badges they made for *Launching the Theme.* They will present them then.

Launching the Theme
(10 minutes)

Before class cut out the letters to the word, *Honor,* from construction paper. Hide the letters in the classroom. **There are five paper letters hidden in this room. Leave your badges on your seats and try to find the hidden letters.** When pupils have found the letters, ask them to unscramble the letters to make the word, *Honor.* Attach the letters to the chalkboard. **What does it mean to honor someone?** (Show admiration or respect.) **Whom do we honor?** (Parents, teachers, officials, people who have done something special.) **We'll honor each other now by presenting the badges we made.** Ask the pupils to come forward, one at a time. They should say the name of the person who earned the badge, and the great thing he or she did. The pupils may pin on the badges and wear them today. **Let's clap for each other.** Do so. **Why should we honor God?** (He is greater than any person.) **God deserves our honor, respect, and admiration. Today we will praise God because He is worthy of honor.**

Explain choices of *Building the Theme* activities.

Building the Theme
(30 minutes)

1. Call to Worship. Pupils will write a poem, telling why God is worthy of honor. This is a good activity for older or gifted pupils. Provide Bibles, pencils, paper, poster board, markers, and pushpins. Before class lightly draw lines on the poster board to aid pupils in writing. **People throughout the Bible honored God for the things He did. Why did Abraham's servant honor God?** (Genesis 24:36-38, 42-48. God answered his prayer by showing him the woman that would be Isaac's wife.) **In Revelation we read about John's experience in Heaven. Even there, people honor God. What do they say to God? Read Revelation 4:8, 11 and 15:3, 4.** (Pupils read. They honor God by praising Him for His perfection, the fact that He is eternal, for His decision, for being great, just, and true.) **Today you will write a poem to honor God. First, let's write reasons that God deserves honor and respect.** Do so, as pupils give suggestions. (Possible answers; heals us, powerful, perfect, right, loving.) **From these ideas, we'll write a poem together to honor God. Guide pupils to write one or more poems. It is not necessary that the lines rhyme.** Example:

I will honor You, Lord, in all I do.
The world and everything came from You.
Strength and healing you will provide.
You are a worthy, holy guide.

Ask pupils to copy each poem onto the poster board. Practice saying them together with feeling. They may use any extra time to draw illustrations on the poster.

During *Sharing in Worship* this group will read the poems to honor God.

2. Scripture. Pupils will draw pictures to represent qualities of God. Provide Bibles, paper, markers, and pushpins. **God**

deserves honor because He is great. Why did God deserve honor when the water came from the rock? If necessary, pupils may read Numbers 20:2, 7, 8. (God said the rock would give water when Moses spoke to it.) **Why did God deserve honor when Abraham's servant found a wife for Isaac?** If necessary, pupils may read Genesis 24:42-46. (God answered the servant's prayer, just as he asked.) **These Scriptures give qualities of God. From these Scriptures, describe God.** Genesis 14:19 (creator); Psalm 29:4 (powerful, majestic); Jeremiah 10:10a (true, living, eternal); Romans 16:27 (wise); 1 Thessalonians 1:6a (just); 2 John 4:16 (love). Assign each pupil one quality of God to illustrate. They should draw something to represent the quality of God. (Suggestions: creator—world; powerful—muscular arm; majestic—crown, true—a diagonal line through false; living—a diagonal line through a coffin or gravestone; eternal—a series of calendar pages with years written on them; wise—owl; just—judges; love—heart.) Help the pupils choose their own illustration by asking, "**What do you think of when you hear this quality? What is the opposite of this quality? Could you draw that and cross it out?**" Pupils who do not draw well may write several words that describe the quality. For example: powerful—wind, armies, rulers, huge machines.

During *Sharing in Worship* the pupils will pin the pictures to the wall. A pupil will read one Scripture. Then he or she will ask the large group to choose the picture(s) that illustrate a quality of God that was named in the Scripture. It may be necessary to read the verses more than once. Continue for each Scripture. After all the Scriptures have been read, ask this group to point at the pictures as they name the qualities of God. They should say, "God is worthy of honor because He is ______ (one quality of God)." Continue for each picture.

3. Lord's Supper. Pupils will prepare an insert for their Bibles that tells why Jesus is worthy of honor. They will also sing a song that honors Jesus because of His death for us. Provide copies of the Bible insert on activity page 10A, pencils, hymnals, and Bibles. **Veteran's Day is a holiday in November. Who do we honor on Veteran's Day?** (People who fought for our country.) **On that day we remember what they did for us. We remember the good things that we have because they served our country. The Lord's Supper is also a memorial. It helps us remember what Jesus did for us. What did Jesus do for us?** (Died for us, forgives our sins, came from heaven for us.) **Does it honor Jesus if we are thinking about the fun things we're going to do this afternoon while we are taking the Lord's Supper?** (No.) **What other things could we do during the Lord's Supper that would not honor Jesus?** (Talk, look around, think about other things.) **What should we do during the Lord's Supper that would honor Jesus?** (Think about Jesus, read Bible, pray.) **Today you will make a page to put in your Bibles that will help you honor Jesus.** Distribute materials. **Read the verses to fill in the blanks. Think about the verse in your own words to figure out the answer.** (Answers: love, wrong, died, freed, forever, eternal life.) **On the bottom of the page, write a sentence that tells Jesus how you feel because He died for you. Jesus deserves our honor because He died for us. When you've finished the page, you may keep it in your Bible. You can read it when you want to think about what Jesus did. A good time to read it is during the Lord's Supper.** After pupils have completed the page, ask them to use the hymnals to find familiar songs about Jesus' death for us. The group will choose one song to sing for the large group before the Lord's Supper is served. Practice singing the song.

During *Sharing in Worship* this group will read the sentences from the activity page. Then they will each read the sentences they wrote. They will sing the song, pray, and serve the Lord's Supper.

4. Offering. Pupils will make offering containers. Pupils may do this activity without adult supervision. Copy or tape record the instructions. Provide small margarine tubs with lids (or other small boxes or containers), permanent fine-tip markers, stickers, and other decorations. Before class, use a sharp knife to cut a small rectangle in the top of each container. **Name a gift you received lately.** (Pupils do so.) **How did you feel when you received it?** (Grateful, privileged.) **You probably felt grateful and special. One way people show honor to others is by giving them gifts. Read Proverbs 3:9a. What is one way we can honor God?** (With our wealth.) **Do you have to be rich to honor God?** (No.) **Read a story about a very poor woman who honored God. Read Mark 12:41-44. One of you can read aloud. How did she honor God?** (Gave all she had.) **If you were God, would you feel honored by a person who gave you their last cent?** (Yes.) **When we give to God, we are thinking of Him and others. When we keep all our money, we are thinking of ourselves. Today we will make offering containers. You can take them home and put your offering money in it. It will remind you to "Honor God with your wealth." Take a container. Write Proverbs 3:9a on the lid or side of it. You may decorate the containers any way you want.** Option: If you can gather enough containers and if time permits, they may make containers for the other pupils in the class.

During *Sharing in Worship* pupils will hold their containers and quote Proverbs 3:9a. If they made extra containers, they may distribute them. Pupils from this group will pray and collect the offering.

5. Devotional. Pupils will tell ways they can honor God. Provide Bibles, copies of Activity page 10B, scissors, glue, a paper hole punch, and pencils. Make a model top before class. **How did Abraham's servant show that He honored God? Read Genesis 24:48.** (Bowed down, worshiped, and praised God.) **When you are visiting a friend, you know very soon if they respect and honor their parents. How do you know?** (The way they talk to them, the way they talk about them, the way they listen to them, if they take their advice, if they are considerate and polite to them, if they obey them.) **God deserves our honor. What we do and say shows if we honor Him. It is easy for God and others to know if we honor God. Today we'll tell ways that we can show that we honor God.** Distribute materials. On the activity page, they will cut out the top. They will fold all the broken lines to the inside. Then they will glue the matching sides together. They can use the top you made as a pattern. When the top is assembled, they will push a sharpened pencil through the top with the lead sticking out the bottom. To play the game, they will take turns spinning the top. The pupil will read the words that land on top when it falls. He or she will tell one way he or she can honor God in that place. Give every pupil at least two turns. Encourage pupils not to repeat an answer that was given previously, if they spin the same place. Most of these suggestions are suitable for several places: listening in Sunday School and worship, singing about praying, never swearing, saying good things about God, taking good care of your Bible, giving money to God, helping others, obeying parents and God, wearing clothing with a Christian message, telling people that you love God.

During *Sharing in Worship* pupils will play the game in front of the class. Each pupil should have at least one turn.

6. Prayer. Pupils will personalize prayers from the Psalms. Provide Bibles, pencils, and lined paper. **We honor God when we pray. When God does something for us, we can honor Him by thanking Him. When God caused Abraham's servant to find a wife for Isaac, what did he do? See Genesis 24:48.** (Bowed down, worshiped, and praised God.) **God punished Moses and Aaron for not honoring Him. What did God tell them to do? See Numbers 20:8.** (Speak to the rock to get water.) **Before Moses hit the rock, who did he say would give them water? Numbers 20:10.** (We—Moses and Aaron.) **God said they they did not honor Him. They took the credit for providing water. Today our prayers will thank God for doing things for us. They will honor God.** Give each pupil a paper. Read the following verses with the pupils: Psalm 103:3 (forgiveness, healing); 118:24 (this day); 120:1 (answer); 126:3 (great things); 138:3 (boldness); 139:13, 14 (life); 145:13b (love, kept promises); 145:20a (protection); 146:7b (food); 147:14a (peace); 147:7, 8 (rain, grass). Following each verse, ask, **Has God ever done something like this for you?** The pupils who answer "yes" should write that verse reference on their papers. After you have read all the verses, each pupil should have at least one reference written on his or her paper. **Read your verses again. You will personalize these verses. You will change the Bible words a little, so that they tell the way God has helped you.** Help the pupils copy their verses, changing or adding words to personalize the verses. They will put the verses in the form of prayers. (Examples: Psalm 103:3—God, You forgave me when I took a dollar from Mom's purse. Thank You. Dear God, thank You for healing me when I had pneumonia. 146:7b—Father, You gave food to our family when Dad was out of a job.)

During *Sharing in Worship* pupils will pray their prayers.

Sharing in Worship
(20-25 minutes)

Omit any of the following sections if you did not offer the corresponding activities. The Lord's Supper, offering gifts, and devotional can be given without the group presentations.

Call to Worship (Group 1): **As we begin our worship, Group 1 will tell God why He is worthy of honor.** Group 1 reads poems.

Scripture (Group 2)**: What qualities of God did Group 1 name in their poems?** Pupils answer. Group 2 will help us learn more things about God that make Him worthy of honor. Group 2 presents verses and illustrations.

Lord's Supper (Group 3)**: When we eat the Lord's Supper, we should honor Jesus. Group 3 will help us think about what Jesus did for us.** Group 3 reads sentences, sings, prays, and serves the Lord's Supper. If you did not offer this activity, read the completed sentences from Activity page 10A to the class.

Song: Sing "I Will Sing of the Mercies of the Lord," p. 181.

Offering (Group 4)**: We also honor God during the offering. God is honored by the gifts we give. Group 4 will tell us more about this.** Group 4 quotes verse, prays, and collects the offering.

Devotional (Group 5): Before

class, clip three newspaper articles that honor people for their achievements. Try to find articles that honor children or people your pupils know. Write the alphabet on the chalkboard.

At the beginning of class, we honored each of you for a special thing you did. I brought some newspaper articles that honor people for their special achievements. Show and summarize them. **How were these people honored?** (Pupils answer.) **Name some other ways we honor people.** (Suggestions: name buildings after them, give them medals and trophies, hang their pictures up, write books and movies about them.) **God deserves more honor than any person. We'll think of 26 reasons why God is worthy of honor. We'll try to name one reason for each letter of the alphabet. Point to the letters of the alphabet as pupils give reasons that begin with each letter.** (Suggestions: Always here, Blesses us, Cares for me, Does good, Eternal, Father, Good, Helps, Instructs us, Judges right, and so on.)

In a Bible story, Abraham's servant told many people that God had helped Him find the wife for Isaac. He gave God the honor He deserved. Are you like Abraham's servant? Do you honor God? Listen to these stories and tell if the person honored God. Lindsay promised to ride bikes with Alicia. When it was time, Lindsay said she forgot and didn't want to. Did Lindsay honor God? Why not? (No. It honors God when we obey Him and keep our promises.) **Chad is always picked on by the kids at school. Alex asked Chad to sit with him at lunch. Does this action honor God? Why?** (Yes. When we treat people like God does, He is honored.) **Karen invited Randa to spend the night on Saturday. On Sunday morning, Randa went with Karen's family to church services. Later that day Karen's brother, Jeff, called her names. To get even, Karen and Randa dumped out all of Jeff's drawers. Did Karen's actions honor God? Why?** (No. Even though she was a Christian, she didn't honor God with her actions.) **Group 5 will play a game that describes more things we can do to honor God.** Group 5 presents activity.

Prayer (Group 6)**: The prayers in the Bible show how to honor God. It honors God to thank Him for what He has done for us. Group 6 changed Bible prayers to make them fit their situations. They will honor God now by thanking Him.** Group 6 prays.

Closing Moments
(10-15 minutes)

Play this game to remind the pupils of Bible people that honored God. Before playing the game, review with the pupils the ways a person can honor God. (Suggestions: obeying Him, talking about Him, praying, singing, giving Him the credit.) Ask pupils to stand in a circle. Give one pupil a ball. He will name a Bible person. The pupil to whom he or she throws the ball will tell how that person did or did not honor God. If he or she doesn't know the answer, another pupil may help. Then the pupil will throw the ball to another pupil, who will name a Bible person. Continue with the game. (Suggestions: Noah—preached about God; Abraham's servant—gave God the credit after being saved from lions; Paul—preached; lame man—gave God the credit after being healed; Jonah—didn't want to obey at first, then did; Moses and Aaron—didn't give God the credit.)

God Rewards Those Who Obey Him

Worship Focus

Worship God because He rewards people who obey Him.

Transition Time

(10-15 minutes)

Reward Relay. As pupils play this game, they will focus on times when they have been rewarded. Place many rewards or prizes on a table at one end of the room, such as stickers, candy, money, certificates, ribbons, medals, or trophies. Divide the pupils into relay teams. The teams will line up at the opposite end of the room. The first person in each team will run to the table, take a reward that is similar to a prize he or she has received, then return to the line. The next pupil will take back the item that the first pupil chose and choose another for himself or herself. Continue the game until one team has finished. **We have all received rewards for good things we have done. If we obey God, He will give us the best reward of all.**

Launching the Theme

(10 minutes)

Provide a United States map, map of your city, and pushpins. Before class mount the maps on the wall. (You may also need a world map.) Ask pupils to put pushpins in the places where they have lived. Ask a few pupils to tell about one place they lived. **What was better about living there than here? What was worse?** (Pupils respond.) **The Israelites moved from Egypt to Canaan. God led them to their new home. When we die, God will take us to a new home too. God has made Heaven for us. It is a great reward for everyone who believes in Jesus. Do you know anyone who lives in Heaven now?** (Pupils answer about friends and relatives who have died.) **It will be great to see these people when we move there. There are always good and bad things about any place we live. Heaven is different because it is a perfect place. Today we will praise God because He rewards people who obey Him.**

Explain choices of *Building the Theme* activities.

Building the Theme

(30 minutes)

1. Call to Worship. Pupils will plan actions for Bible verses. Provide Bibles. **Tell us about a time when you received a reward.** (Pupils share.) **It is good to be rewarded when you have worked hard. God also rewards people. What did God give the Israelites? See Joshua 1:2.** (A new home.) **God promised a new land to Abraham, Isaac, Jacob, and Moses. God kept the promise in the verse you read. God has made an even greater promise to us. People who are faithful to God will receive a new home in Heaven when they die. Heaven is a gift from God to us. Psalm 62:12b and Revelation 2:10b talk about the Christian's reward. Let's read them.** Do so. Help pupils plan actions for the verses. They do not need to have one action per word, just one for each thought. (Suggestions: you—point to heaven; reward—crown on head; each person—point at each other in the group; he—point at one person; has done—hold out hands.) To help pupils think of actions, ask them to say the verses in their own words. Clarify the meaning of unknown phrases, such as the crown of life (Living forever in Heaven). Practice presentation.

During *Sharing in Worship* this group will quote the verses while they do the actions.

2. Scripture. Pupils will make a word maze to tell the people whom God rewards. Provide Bibles, posterboard, markers, pencils, pushpins, and paper. With a pencil draw rows of 1 1/2" squares on the posterboard before class. **Have you ever given a reward to someone? Maybe you gave a reward when someone returned something that you lost. When do we give rewards?** (When someone does something good.) **God promises to reward people who obey Him. He blessed Jacob with many good things. He blessed the Israelites with a new home. He rewards us each day. Read these Scriptures. Answer this question: "What kind of person does God**

reward?" Give each pupil at least one Scripture passage. They can write their answers on paper. Psalm 19:7, 11 — Keeps God's laws; Proverbs 9:12a — wise; Proverbs 13:13b — obeys commands; Proverbs 14:14 — is good; Proverbs 19:17 — kind to the poor; Matthew 6:3, 4 — gives secretly; Luke 6:22, 23 — hated because of Christ; Luke 6:35 — loves enemies, gives to enemies; John 3:16 — believes in Jesus; Hebrews 11:6 — seeks God. When pupils have finished, ask them to answer the question above with the answers they wrote. Help them reword their answers as needed to answer the question. **Now you will copy your answers onto the posterboard. Write each letter in a square. You'll write the answers next to each other to form a maze through the posterboard. Don't leave any blank squares between words or answers. Use a pencil so you can make corrections. When all the answers have been written, you can go over the pencil letters with marker. Now fill in any blank spaces with letters of your choice.** Explain the presentation for *Sharing in Worship.* Ask pupils to practice asking the question.

During *Sharing in Worship* hang the poster in front of the class. One pupil will ask, "What kind of person does God reward?" Then he or she will read his or her Bible verse. The large group will give the answer from the verse. The pupils will draw a thick line under the answer on the posterboard. Then another person will ask the same question, read his or her verse, and underline the answer after the large group says it. Continue until all the verses have been read and the path through the maze is complete.

3. Special Music. Pupils will illustrate Heaven according to a song. This activity can be done without adult supervision. Copy or tape record the instructions. Provide Bibles, paper, colored pencils or crayons, pencils, tape player, and "When We All Get to Heaven" from p. 183. Before class tape record a person singing this song. **God blessed Jacob with good things. What did God give the Israelite people? Read Joshua 1:2 to find out. God gave them the new home He promised. God has promised to give every Christian a new home as a reward for trusting in Jesus. Heaven is our reward. Even though we don't deserve it, God has prepared a wonderful place for us to live after we die. Listen to this song and think about heaven. Write down words from the song that describe Heaven. On the paper, put these words into sentences about Heaven. For example: There will be no sadness in Heaven; We will see Jesus, in Heaven. When you are finished writing the sentences, practice singing the song with the tape.** *Option:* If the group is large, divide them into smaller groups. Each group will work on a different hymn. Provide a tape recording of the song, tape player, and copies of the hymn for each group. Suggested songs: "Beyond the Sunset," "We Shall Behold Him," "Soon and Very Soon." Read the words carefully before you assign a hymn. The words should be true facts about Heaven.

During *Sharing in Worship* this group will read their sentences that describe Heaven, then sing the song.

4. Devotional. Pupils will interview each other to tell about Heaven. Provide Bibles, copies of activity page 11A, and pencils. Option: non-working microphone and Bible costumes for the Bible characters. **God rewarded the Israelites by giving them a new home in Canaan. God had promised it to Abraham, Isaac, and Jacob hundreds of years earlier. They didn't deserve it because they made many mistakes. It was a gift from God. Christians get rewards from God everyday. God answers our prayers and takes care of us. God forgives us when we do wrong and lets us try again. When we die, we will get the greatest reward. God will give us a new home in Heaven.** Distribute materials. **We will present an interview of several Bible people. These Bible people either visited Heaven or learned about Heaven. One of you will be the interviewer and ask the questions. The rest of you will answer questions.** Assign parts now. If you have fewer than eight pupils, you may assign pupils to do two Bible parts. **Read the Scriptures that go with your part. Write the answer to your question(s) on the activity page.** The interviewer may help John answer his questions. (Answers: David — God is in Heaven. Matthew — Anyone who does what God wants. Luke — Heaven is our reward. Lazarus — I saw Abraham in Heaven. I was very comfortable in Heaven. It was very different from my life as a beggar on earth. Nicodemus — Jesus told me that people who believe in Him would go to Heaven. Heaven lasts forever. Paul — I know that I'll go to Heaven when I die. John — Some things that happen in Heaven are that angels and people praise God. No one is hungry, thirsty, suffering, or crying in Heaven. There is no night, nothing bad, and no wicked people in Heaven.) When the pupils have finished writing their answers, practice the interview. The interviewer will hold the microphone, if available. He will ask questions of each person. Encourage the Bible characters to memorize their answers. As time allows, pupils may complete their activity page by copying the answers from each other's papers.

For *Sharing in Worship,* pupils

will present the interview.

5. Lord's Supper. Pupils will present a play to show that Jesus' death made Heaven possible for us. Because these concepts are difficult to understand, this activity is good for older or gifted pupils. Provide construction paper, paper, pencils, tape, and copies of the following play.

God's Plan to Save Me

Two pupils, each holding a "mountain," stand in front. They stand about two feet apart from each other. The "man" is taped to one mountain. The other mountain is labeled "God."

Pupil: "At one time you were separated from God. You were God's enemies in your minds because the evil deeds you did were against God." Colossians 1:21, ICB.

Pupil: "There is no one without sin. None!" Romans 3:10, ICB.

Pupil: "God gave Jesus as a way to forgive sin through faith. And all of this is because of the blood of Jesus' death." Romans 3:25a, ICB.

Another pupil holds the "bridge" between the two mountains, connecting them.

Pupil: "Christ has made you God's friends again. He did this by his death. He brings you before God as people who are holy, with no wrong in you. Christ will do this if you continue to believe in the Good News you heard. You must continue strong and sure in your faith." Colossians 1:22, 23, ICB.

When the pupil above reads "Christ will do this . . .," a pupil "walks" the man across the "bridge" to "God." He or she sticks the man there.

Pupil: "You are saved by grace, and you got that grace by believing. You did not save yourselves. It was a gift from God. You cannot brag that you are saved by the work you have done." Ephesians 2:8, 9, ICB.

Pupil: Let's thank God for giving Jesus, so that we can go to Heaven. Pupil prays.

No one deserves the rewards God gives him or her. Even when we try our best, we often sin. The Bible gives us rules for living like God wants. However, we cannot keep them all because we are human. God sent Jesus to die, so that we can be forgiven and go to heaven. God did His part when He sent Jesus. Jesus did His part when He died for us. Our part is to believe in Jesus and continue living for God. You will present a play that explains these ideas to the class. First we'll make the props. Distribute materials and assign pupil pairs to cut from construction paper: a mountain, a mountain labeled "God," a bridge labeled "Jesus," and a man. When pupils have finished, assign parts for the play. **All the reading parts quote God's word. It's written on your papers to make it easier for you to read.** There are ten parts, but pupils may do more than one. Practice the presentation. Discuss the play using these questions: **Why can't we get to God without Jesus?** (We have sinned.) **Do we have any part in our salvation?** (Yes. We must believe. We must continue strong in our faith.) **Why can't we brag that we got to Heaven because we were good?** (Because we have sinned. Heaven is a gift.)

During *Sharing in Worship* this group will present the play.

6. Personal Praise. Pupils will tape record their feelings about Heaven. Provide a blank cassette tape, tape player, Bibles, paper, crayons. Provide at least one *International Children's Bible.* **How do you think Jacob felt when he heard God's blessing for him? The blessing is given in Genesis 27:28, 29.** (The Bible doesn't say, but pupils can guess.) **How do you think the Israelites felt when God gave them a new home? Read Joshua 24:17, 18.** (Grateful, wanted to serve God.) **The greatest reward God will give us is Heaven. We don't deserve to live with God forever because we have all sinned. God says that if we love and obey Jesus, He'll forgive our sins and take us to Heaven. Heaven isn't just a hope for old people. It is something you can look forward too also. From these Bible verses we will discover how we can feel because we will someday live in Heaven.** Give each pupil at least one verse to read. Matthew 5:12 — rejoice, be glad; John 14:1-3 — comforted, peaceful, not worried; Philippians 3:20 — waiting to go home; Colossians 1:5 — hopeful; 2 Peter 3:13 — looking forward; Revelation 5:13 — praising God. **Which one of these Scriptures tells how you feel about Heaven? Tell your feelings about Heaven.** After pupils have expressed their feelings, they will tape record them. When they are finished, ask them to each write one word to summarize their feelings. (Suggestions: peaceful, hopeful, calm, anxious, happy, thankful.) Encourage them to fill an entire piece of paper with each word. They may decorate and color the words as they want. Option: Print the words as banners with a computer. The pupils may each choose a word, color, and decorate it.

During *Sharing in Worship* this group will display their words as the tape is played.

Sharing in Worship
(20-25 minutes)

Omit any of the following sections if you did not offer the corresponding activities. The Lord's Supper and devotional may be given without the group presentations.

Call to Worship (Group 1): Group 1 presents verses.

Scripture (Group 2): **God rewards people everyday. I want**

God to reward me. Group 2 will tell us the kind of people that God rewards. Group 2 presents activity.

Special Music (Group 3): **God's greatest reward for Christians is Heaven. Group 3 will describe Heaven for us and sing a song about it.** Group 3 reads and sings.

Devotional (Group 4): Provide copies of activity page 11B, and red pencils or markers.

That song makes me want to go to Heaven. I'm looking forward to seeing God. As we watch Group 4's interviews, a few Bible people will teach us about Heaven. Group 4 presents interviews.

Even though the Bible tells us many things about Heaven, some people are still mixed up. I think the pupil who did this test might be one of them. Hold up activity page. **I want you to check his or her paper and grade him or her on how well he or she did.** Distribute activity pages and red pencils. Either discuss the sentences as pupils grade the paper, or when they are finished. All the sentences are False. For each sentence, ask the pupils to tell the answer. Then ask them why the statement is false. Help them to use the information they learned in their *Building the Theme* activities. You may ask pupils to read the Scriptures listed if they need help understanding the answer. Suggestions: 1) God sent Jesus so that imperfect people can go to Heaven. Romans 3:22-25, *ICB*. 2) Even though people will be in Heaven, Satan will not. God promises that only good will be in Heaven. Revelation 21:3, 4, 27. 3) Heaven is a real place. Jesus talked about it. Matthew 5:12. 4) Only the people who believe in Jesus will go to Heaven. Matthew 7:13, 14; John 3:16; 14:6. 5) Heaven will not be scary because God and Jesus are there. They will take care of us. Revelation 21:3, 4. 6) When we die, we will be with God. Because of Jesus, He forgives us of the bad things we have done. Colossians 1:22. 7) God forgives us, even after we become Christians. 1 John 1:9. 8) Heaven can't be boring because God planned it. I don't know what we'll do, but it will be wonderful. Revelation 22:3. **If you took this test, I know that you'd get an A+.**

Lord's Supper (Group 5): **God doesn't let us go to Heaven because we deserve it. Heaven is a gift. Only because Jesus died for us can we be saved. People who are saved go to Heaven when they die. Group 5 will present a play that will help us understand this better.** Group 5 presents play, prays, and serves the Lord's Supper. If you did not offer this activity, read the Scriptures listed in Group 5.

Offering: God is generous to us. He rewards us, even when we don't deserve it. Let's give to Him now. Ask for pupil volunteers to pray and collect the offering.

Personal Praise (Group 6): **It is easy to worship God for this wonderful reward. Group 6 will tell us their feelings about Heaven.** Group 6 presents activity.

Prayer: Who wants to thank God for the gift of Heaven? Pupils pray.

Closing Moments
(10-15 minutes)

Play this game to reinforce the concept of behaviors and rewards. Write good behaviors on white slips of paper. Write possible rewards for them on pink paper. Write bad behaviors on two white papers. Write "grace" at the bottom of the paper. Write two ways a person could be shown "grace" on two pink papers. Give half the pupils white papers. Give the other half pink papers. **When you do something good, you usually get rewarded. Some of you have white papers that say a good behavior. Your job is to find the person with a pink paper that tells a reward for you on it. Your white paper might tell a bad behavior, with the word "grace" on it. God gives us chances to try again. That's His grace. If you have a "grace" paper, look for the pupil who has the pink paper that tells a way that someone might give you a second chance.** Suggestions: You return a checkbook you find. / Man gives you $2. You help bake cookies. / You get to eat the first cookie. When your mom sent you to the store, you bought yourself a candy bar with the change. GRACE / Your mom trusted you to go to the store for her again. You lied to your favorite babysitter. You told her you had permission to stay up two hours late. GRACE / Your dad let you stay with that sitter again.

For Next Week

Send notes home about next week's Magic Show.

God Is Omniscient

Worship Focus

Worship God because He knows everything.

Transition Time

(10-15 minutes)

Magic Show. You and your pupils will perform magic tricks for the class. This will introduce today's focus that God knows everything. Your public library has books of simple tricks. Last week you sent home notes with the pupils so they would be prepared. Ask the pupils to present their magic tricks. Option: Before class practice this game with a pupil assistant. You (the magician) and your assistant stand before the class. **When I leave the room, you will choose any object in the room. When I return, I'll be able to tell you what object you chose.** Magician leaves the room. Pupils choose an object. Then the magician returns. The assistant points at different objects in the room. The magician correctly identifies the one that the pupils chose. The secret is that before class the assistant was instructed to point at a white (or nearly white object) before pointing at the correct object. The magician knows that the correct object will be the one following the white object. If there are no white objects in your classroom, choose a different color to be the clue. Play several times, or until a pupil guesses the secret. Option: If a member of your congregation is an amateur magician, ask him or her to perform some tricks for your pupils. **Magicians do tricks that make it look like they know everything. God doesn't need tricks. He truly knows everything. He is omniscient.**

Launching the Theme

(10 minutes)

Before class cut out pictures of the following: babies, children, and adults. Tape the pictures across the chalkboard. After the pictures write "No one." **Name some things that babies know.** Record the pupils' answers under the picture of babies. **Name some things that children know.** Record their responses under the children. Continue in the same manner with "Adults." **Now name things that no one knows.** Suggestions: What will happen tomorrow, what people are thinking, reasons why things happen, many things about space and nature, how to make people do things, how to make life. Record these answers under "no one." **What happens to our knowledge as we get older?** (Pupils answer. We learn more.) **Each of us only knows a very small part of all the things that people can know. As you can see, there are things that no one knows. Do you think we'll ever know these things?** (Pupils respond.) **Maybe someday we will, maybe not. God knows all these things. Today we will praise God because He knows everything.**

Explain choices of *Building the Theme* activities.

Building the Theme

(30 minutes)

1. Call to Worship. Pupils will present a choral reading about God's knowledge. This activity may be done without adult supervision, if you provide written or tape recorded instructions. Pause at the appropriate times to allow the pupils to answer. Provide Bibles, copies of activity page 12A, pastel markers, markers, pushpins, and poster board. **God knows everything. What did God know about Jacob? Read Genesis 28:13, 14 for the answer. God knew the future of Jacob and his descendants. When the Israelites conquered the city of Jericho, God told them not to take anything. We read in the book of Joshua that someone disobeyed God by stealing these things. What did God know about Achan? Read Joshua 7:14, 16-21 for the answer. God knew that Achan was the guilty person. God knows our future and all our secrets. David expressed these ideas in Psalm 139. Let's read these verses together from the activity page. After you read it, you will plan a choral reading. Divide yourselves into two groups. Divide the Scriptures between the groups. Decide which group will read which words. Read the last verse together.** Each pupil should highlight his or her group's part with a pastel marker. **Practice the reading until you can read it smoothly. According to these verses, what specific things does God know about you? You don't**

have to tell any big secrets. God knows what time you fell asleep last night, what you thought when you were at a friend's house, where you are now, what you'll say today at 3:00, and all the good and bad things you've done. On the posterboard write or draw pictures of these things that God knows.

During *Sharing in Worship* this group will display the poster and present the reading.

2. Scripture. Pupils will make books to illustrate God's knowledge. Provide Bibles, copies of activity page 12B (copies on heavy paper), white paper, construction paper, magazines, scissors, stapler, pencils, and glue. **God knows everything. Name some things that God knows, that you do not.** (Pupils respond.) **A hundred years ago man did not know how to make a machine fly. Now we do. God has always known how to make a machine fly. We will never know some of the things that God knows. Today you will make books to show what God knows.** Distribute materials. **First cut out the shape on the activity page. This is the front cover. Use this shape as the pattern as you cut five shapes from the white paper and one from construction paper. The white paper will be the pages of the book. The construction paper will be the back cover. Staple your pages together to make a book.** Assign each pupil one of the following Scriptures to read. **After you read your verses, tell what God knows.** Job 38:19, 20 (where light and darkness live); Job 38:22-24 (where snow, hail, lightning, and wind are stored); Job 38:33 (laws of Heaven); Psalm 50:11 (birds, creatures); Psalm 69:5 (my sin, guilt); Psalm 139:4 (what I will say); Matthew 6:8 (what I need); Revelation 2:2 (my deeds, hard work, perseverance). Write the pupils answers on paper, so they can refer to the list as they work. **Cut out pictures from these magazines to illustrate your answers. You will need to find pictures for five different answers. Glue the pictures in your books. Below each picture write what God knows.** (Example: For a picture of snow, write *God knows where the snow is kept.* For a picture of a person trying hard, write *God knows I try hard.*) Discuss the presentation and practice it.

During *Sharing in Worship,* the pupils from this group will stand before the class. One pupil will ask, "What does God know?" and read a Scripture. The pupils will show their pictures that illustrate that Scripture. Then another pupil will read a Scripture, followed by the pupils showing the pictures for that Scripture. Since there are eight Scriptures and only five pages in each book, not every pupil will have a picture to show for each Scripture.

3. Special Music. Pupils will make stick puppets to illustrate a song about God's knowledge. Provide copies of "My God Is a Great God" from p. 184, construction paper or felt, craft sticks or short dowels, scissors, pencils, markers, and stapler. Before class make one sample puppet and a tape recording of the song. **According to Psalm 139, what does God know?** (Everything about me.) **God knows everything. He knows everything about people. He knows how to do everything. We will sing a song today that worships God for being a great God. Listen to the words of the song.** Play the recording twice. **List things that only God knows how to do.** (Know what we are thinking, turn darkness into light, cause snow, heal blind people, make dew and skies, control the future, and so on.) **We'll make stick puppets to illustrate this song.** Distribute materials and assign each pupil one phrase to illustrate. Pupils will decide on an object to illustrate their phrase. (For example: heal blind people—an eye; make dew and skies—a cloud.) To make a puppet, each pupil will cut out two identical shapes of the object. They will staple the shapes around a craft stick. They can add details with markers. When all the puppets are finished, practice the presentation.

During *Sharing in Worship* use a puppet stage or turn a table on its side. The pupils will show their puppets and tell what God can do. Then they will sing the song for the large group.

4. Devotional. Pupils will write journal (diary) entries. Since this activity involves much reading and writing, it is recommended for older or gifted pupils. Provide Bibles, paper, and pencils. Before class, copy each of these names and Scripture passages on a piece of paper.

1. Pharaoh—Genesis 41:1-7, 15, 16, 25-30. (God knew about the coming famine.)
2. Jacob—Genesis 28:13-15. (God knew Jacob's future, about his descendants, that he would return to this land.)
3. Joshua—Joshua 7:11-21. (God told Joshua that He knew who stole the forbidden objects.)
4. Wisemen—Matthew 2:1-12. (God knew Herod lied.)
5. Joseph—Matthew 2:13-16. (God knew Herod would kill the babies.)
6. Teachers of law—Mark 2:1-12. (Jesus knew what they were thinking.)
7. Women—Luke 24:1-8. (Jesus knew that He would be crucified and raised.)
8. Sailors—Acts 27:1, 2, 13-25. (God knew no one would die.)

Give each pupil a paper. **God always knows more about our situation than we do. He knows**

what everyone thinks. He knows the past and the future. He is omniscient. In these Bible stories, God told people something that He knew. Read your scriptures. Pretend that you are the Bible person. How did you feel before you knew what God knew? How did you feel after you knew what God knew? (Help pupils to answer based on the Bible passages and their imaginations.) **You will write a journal or diary entry to tell how your feelings changed after you knew what God knew.** Example: Pharaoh—Dear diary, Today I'm very tired. I had two dreams last night. I was so upset I asked my magicians to tell me what the dreams meant. No one knew. Finally my cupbearer told me about a prisoner who could tell what dreams meant. His name is Joseph. Joseph told me exactly what the dreams meant. He said his power came from God. God is warning us that we will have seven years of good crops, then seven years of no crops. I should save food for the seven bad years. I gave Joseph the job of collecting the food. Tonight I'll sleep well. Now I know what God knows about our land.

During *Sharing in Worship* this group will read their diary entries.

5. Personal Praise. Pupils will make magnets to proclaim God's knowledge. Provide Bibles, colored index cards, clear adhesive paper, paper, scissors, fine-tip markers, and magnetic tape. **Who is the smartest person you know?** (Pupils respond.) **God knows more than all of these people. He knows everything. In these Bible verses, we'll discover things that God knows. After you read your verse, tell what God knows and how that makes you feel.** Assign each pupil at least one verse. Psalm 94:11 (thoughts—want to keep thoughts pure); Jeremiah 12:3a (knows us—not lonely, secure); Jeremiah 29:11 (His plans for us—secure, not afraid); Amos 5:12 (our sins—want to ask forgiveness and not sin); 2 Timothy 2:19 (people who love Him—joyful, proud); 2 Peter 2:9 (rescue me—secure, hopeful); 1 John 3:20b (everything, honor and trust in a wise God). Distribute materials. **We'll make magnets that praise God for His knowledge. Practice what you will write on your magnet on the paper. When you get it just right, copy it neatly on your index card.** (Suggestions of what to write follow. Copy part of a Bible verse.) "God knows everything." 1 John 3:20; "You know me, Lord Jeremiah 33:3.) Paraphrase verses or describe feelings. (I'm special. God knows me!" "No Secrets with God." "God has big plans for me.") Pupils may also decorate their cards. After pupils have finished writing and drawing, help them cover both sides of the card with clear adhesive paper. Then they can stick a piece of magnetic tape on the back side.

During *Sharing in Worship* they will display and read their magnets.

6. Prayer. Pupils will write and illustrate prayers. Provide Bibles, paper, pencils, black construction paper, and white chalk. **God knows everything. How did Jacob feel when he realized that God knew his future? Read Genesis 28:13-18 to find out.** (Was afraid, worshiped God.) **How did Achan feel when he realized that God knew about his sin? This story is in Joshua 7:11, 20.** (He confessed.) **Jacob was happy because God knew the future. Achan probably wasn't happy that God knew his sin. When we realize that God knows all, we should trust Him and worship Him. Tell us about a time when you felt better because you believed that God knew everything.** (Suggestions follow: when you are wrongfully blamed, afraid, when someone didn't get punished for doing wrong, when you were thinking about doing wrong.) **How do you feel when you realize that God knows everything?** (Suggestions follow: confident about the future, happy because you know God knows the truth, humble because God knows more, afraid to do wrong because God knows.) **Draw with chalk on the black paper about one situation. After you finish your picture, write two or three sentences to praise God for knowing everything.** (Example: Dear God, I'm glad you know everything. You know that I'm trying very hard not to fight with my brothers.)

During *Sharing in Worship* pupils will show and explain their pictures. They will read their prayers in praise of God's knowledge.

Sharing in Worship
(20-25 minutes)

Omit any of the following sections if you did not offer the corresponding activities. The devotional may be given without the group presentation.

Call to Worship (Group 1): **As Group 1 reads the verses, listen to the things that God knows about us.** Group displays poster and presents choral reading.

Scripture (Group 2): **God knows everything. Group 2 will tell us a few of the things that God knows.** Group 2 presents activity.

Special Music (Group 3): **God is greater than any person. He not only knows everything, He also knows how to do everything. You'll notice these things in Group 3's song.** Group 3 presents puppets and song.

Lord's Supper: God knew that we needed Jesus to save us. When Jesus began the Lord's Supper, He told the disciples that He was giving His body and blood for us. Listen as I read. Read Luke 22:17-20. Pray and serve the Lord's Supper.

Offering: **Sometimes I have a hard time buying gifts for people. I just don't know what they need. God gives us perfect gifts everyday because He knows all about us. When we give our money to God, we are thanking Him for giving us what we need.** Ask two pupils to pray and collect the offering.

Devotional (Group 4): Before class prepare and practice the object lesson. Provide a clean glass pane and a glass of soapy water.

When we did our magic tricks this morning, it looked like some of you were mind readers. Of course we know that you were tricking us. Can anyone tell me what I am thinking right now? I'll write it on this glass with water. Turn your back to the pupils, so they cannot see what you write. Dip your finger into the soapy water and write a message on the glass. Show pupils the glass. **You still can't read the message, just like you can't read my mind. There is only one mind reader—God. He always knows what we are thinking, even if no one else does. We can't keep secrets from God. Achan hid stolen goods under his tent, but God knew about it. We can't hide anything from God.** Breathe hard on the message area of the glass, causing moisture to form over the entire message. Hold it up for the pupils to see. **Now you can read what I was thinking. To God, it is as if I wrote all my thoughts on paper for Him to read. Think of the Bible verses you read today. Tell us what the Bible says about God's knowledge of our minds.** Suggestions follow: Psalm 94:11; 139:2, 4, 23—knows thoughts of man; Psalm 69:5—knows sinful thoughts; Mark 2:1-12—Jesus knew the teachers of the law's thoughts. **If you are thinking about something bad, it is scary to remember that God knows everything. Knowing that we can't keep secrets from God should help us do right.**

Sometimes in the Bible God told people some of the things He knew. It helped them know what to do and made them feel better. Group 4 will read diary entries from these people. Group 4 presents activity.

God usually doesn't tell us specific things, like He told Joseph and others. However God tells us much about Himself, the world, Jesus, and ourselves in the Bible. When we read the Bible, God shares His knowledge with us.

Personal Praise (Group 5): **Group 5 will show us the magnets they made that praise God's knowledge.** Group 5 presents activity.

Prayer (Group 6): **I feel very proud of God when I think about all the things He knows. Group 6 will share their feelings and pictures about God's knowledge.** Group 6 presents activity.

Closing Moments
(10-15 minutes)

As pupils do this activity, they will remember qualities of God. They will make signs and/or banners for the classroom and hall. Provide white paper, markers, and pushpins. **If God were to be our guest speaker today, what would He say to us?** Record pupils' answers. (Suggestions: I'm the world's only mind reader. I love you. I'm always right. I don't know the word *impossible.* I heard that thought!) **You'll make signs with these messages from God. Write a sentence from God to us on your paper. Sign the message with God's name. Hang the signs in the classroom, hall, or bathrooms.**

God Helps Us Obey

Worship Focus

Worship God because He guides us through His Word.

Transition Time

(10-15 minutes)

Musical Chairs. As pupils play this version of Musical Chairs, they'll remember people who taught them. Before class set up chairs in a circle. There should be one less chair than pupils. Play Musical Chairs, using music from any Christian tape. When the music stops, the pupil without a chair must tell one thing he or she learned to do and who taught it to him or her. Then repeat the game. Do not remove any chairs. Keep the number of pupils and chairs constant, so all pupils can continue to play. **We all need help in knowing how to do things and how to live right.**

Launching the Theme

(10 minutes)

Before class invite a police officer (or other law enforcement professional) to talk to the pupils. Ask him or her to briefly share how he or she guides children to live by the law. He or she can also tell what steps are taken to rehabilitate children who have broken the law. Following the presentation thank the officer. **It is important to know how to live correctly. Many people guide us as we learn how to live. Most of the rules of our society are based on God's rules. Where do we learn God's rules?** (The Bible.) **God tells us what to do in the Bible. Today we will worship God for guiding us through His Word.**

Option: Ask pupils to name rules they have in their home. Record the pupils answers on the chalkboard. **Let's vote to find out which rule is given in the most homes. How many of you have rule #1 in your home?** Continue with the other rules. As you tell the rule that got the most votes, say, **Most of you have to keep this rule. Why do we need rules in our homes?** (To help us get along better.) **Rules guide us to live correctly. Most of our rules are based on God's rules. God guides us through the Bible. Today we will worship God because He guides us through His Word.**

Explain choices of *Building the Theme* activities.

Building the Theme

(30 minutes)

1. **Call to Worship.** Pupils will tape record Psalm 23 with sound effects. Provide Bibles, blank tape, and tape recorder. **God wants to guide people to help them do right. What guidance did God give Jacob in Genesis 31:3?** (Told him to return to his home.) **What guidance did God give Gideon in Judges 7:4-7?** (Told him how to choose soldiers.) **David compared himself to a lamb in Psalm 23. He said that God was like His shepherd. What does the shepherd do for the lamb?** (Guides him, provides food, protects him.) **David praised God for guiding him. Let's read Psalm 23 together.** Be sure all the pupils have the same version. **Look at Psalm 23 again. In what ways did God guide David?** (Where to eat, drink, rest, good paths, through death, in spite of evil and enemies, to the Lord's house.) **Today God guides us through His Word. In the Bible we find instructions about how to live right, how to go through death, how to act before our enemies, and how to get to God's home. We also can praise God for guiding us. You will tape record a reading of this Psalm. You will add appropriate sound effects to enhance the recording.** Help the pupils plan the sound effects. Guide them as they read the verses with the sounds. The sound effects should help the reading, not distract from it. (Examples: shepherd—sheep sounds, water—make water sounds by rubbing hands over pant legs, walk—footsteps.) Pupils may also hum appropriate music during portions of the reading. Tape the Psalm more than once. Choose the best reading to play during *Sharing in Worship*.

During *Sharing in Worship* the group will play the tape.

2. **Scripture.** Pupils will write God's guidance about various subjects. Provide Bibles, construction paper, scissors, and markers. Before class write each of the following words and corresponding references on a piece of paper. Answers are in parentheses.

Knowledge—Proverbs 1:7 (fearing

God is the beginning of knowledge); alcoholic drinks—Proverbs 23:29, 30 (drinking brings trouble, sorrow, poor health); enemy—Romans 12:17-20 (don't get even, live in peace); needy people—Romans 12:13 (share with them); police and authorities—Romans 13:1 (obey them); your body—1 Corinthians 6:19, 20 (your body is God's house, should honor God with your body); children—Ephesians 6:1 (obey parents); TV and movies—Ephesians 5:12 and Philippians 4:8 (we shouldn't even talk about the bad things people do, we should think of good things); hands—1 Thessalonians 4:11 (work hard); tongue—1 Peter 3:10 (don't say bad things or lies). **If you were writing a report on Japan, where would you look for information?** (Library books on Japan.) **If you wanted to cook lasagna for dinner, where would you look for help?** (Cookbook.) **If you wanted to know the names of your hand bones, where would you look?** (Medical book.) **When we need information there are many places to look. When your parents buy a new washing machine, the manufacturer sends an instruction book. This book tells them how to use the machine, so that it will clean better and last longer. God is our manufacturer. He gave us an instruction book. What is it?** (The Bible.) **God guides us through the Bible. We live happier and better lives when we follow God's guidance. When we have a question about life, we should read God's advice. For example, pretend that a person calls me names. One person might tell me to call them worse names. One person might tell me to ignore them and try to get even. What does God say? That's one question we'll answer today. You will read some of God's instructions.** Give each pupil at least one paper. The pupils will read their verses and decide what God says about the subject. Then they will cut out a shape to represent the subject. The shapes should be large, to allow room for writing on the back. (Examples: knowledge—a brain or owl, enemy—a frowning person.) On the back of the shapes, they will write God's advice from their Scriptures. Explain and prepare the presentation for *Sharing in Worship*. Option: If time allows, pupils may use a concordance to find verses about other subjects.

During *Sharing in Worship* the pupils will place their shapes in their Bibles. One pupil will explain that the Bible is God's instruction book for us. It tells us the best way to live. God guides through His words in the Bible. One pupil will read a verse, show his or her shape, and read what he or she wrote on the back. Continue for each pupil.

3. Offering. Pupils will present skits to demonstrate that God's guidance is good. Provide Bibles and copies of activity page 13A. **God gives us guidance on many subjects. What does God say about our money?** (Pupils share.) **Let's read more of God's guidance about money in these verses.** Assign each pupil at least one verse to read. Psalm 112:5 (good things come to generous people); Ecclesiastes 5:10 (people who love money never have enough); Matthew 6:2-4 (don't give to get praise from people; God rewards people who give); Acts 20:35 (more blessed to give than receive); 2 Corinthians 9:7 (should give happily); 2 Corinthians 9:12 (your giving helps people; they thank God when you give); Hebrews 13:16 (God is happy when we share); James 1:17 (everything we have is from God); 1 John 3:17 (cannot love God if we won't share with others). Divide pupils into groups of 2-3 pupils. **Your groups will each plan a short skit that teaches God's guidance about giving.** **Assign each group one skit from the activity page.** They will use the skit-starters to begin their skits. The principles in the Scriptures they read will help them with the skits. Older pupils may want to write their own skits. Option: If you are leading younger pupils, plan and do the skits as a large group. Prepare as many skits as time allows. Suggestions for skit endings: 1) Giving helps us think of others. God gives good things to generous people. 2) When we give to others, we show that we love God. 3) When we give quietly, we show that we are giving to please God, not others. 4) All our money comes from God. When God has been generous to us, we should share happily.

During *Sharing in Worship* pupils will present their skits, pray, and collect the offering.

4. Devotional. Pupils will name God's rules that people have kept or broken. This activity may be used for older or gifted pupils. Before class, clip *short* newspaper or magazine articles that clearly tell of people who have done something right or wrong. The articles should give the reward or punishment. Don't include articles about graphic, violent crimes. **God guides us so we can live better lives. His instructions and rules are meant to help us. How did God's instruction help Jacob? Read Genesis 31:3; 33:4.** (God told Jacob to go back to his homeland. There he was reunited with his brother, Esau.) **Judges 7:2-7; 8:28 tells how God's instruction helped Gideon. What did Gideon do with God's help?** (Defeated the Midianites.) **God knows how we should live in order to have a life that is pleasing to Him. He guides us in life through His Word, the Bible. When we follow God's guidance we have a life.** Give each pupil one article. **Read your article. Be ready to tell what rule the person**

kept or broke. What happened to him or her as a result? Ask older or gifted pupils to use a Bible concordance to locate Bible verses that tell the rules. Suggestions follow.

1) A person returns lost money and keeps God's rule about loving others as much as yourself (Matthew 22:39). The person gets a cash reward.

2) People repair a house for a widow and keep God's rule about helping widows (James 1:27). They are thanked by the widow.

3) A person steals money from a bank machine and breaks God's rule about stealing (Exodus 20:15). The person is put in prison.

4) A person is paid to do a repair job and doesn't do it. The person breaks God's rule about not lying (Proverbs 19:5). The person must pay a fine.

5) A person breaks the speed limit and breaks God's rule about obeying authorities (Romans 13:1). The person pays a fine.

Sometimes a person breaks God's law and doesn't get punished. We know that God knows everything. He gives each of us the punishment that He thinks is right.

During *Sharing in Worship* pupils will summarize their articles, tell the rules kept or broken (perhaps read them from the Bible), and tell the results.

5. Special Music. Pupils will learn a song and illustrate its application. Provide Bibles, "The Joy of the Lord Is My Strength" from p. 185, copies of activity page 13B, tape player, and pencils. Before the session, record the song on a blank tape. **In the Bible God guided people by His Word. He talked directly to them. What did God tell Jacob? Read Genesis 31:3 for the answer.** (To return to his homeland.) **What did God tell Gideon? The answer is in Judges 7:2-7.** (How to choose the soldiers.) **Today God talks to us through His written Word, the Bible. When we read the Bible, we learn God's plan for us. The Bible tells us how to live correctly. Listen to this verse from Psalm 119. "Your word is like a lamp for my feet and a light for my way." What does it mean that God's Word is a lamp and a light?** (Pupils answer.) **God's Word shows us how to live How does God's Word guide us?** (Pupils answer.) **God's Word tells us what to do and how to act.** Play "The Joy of the Lord Is My Strength." Ask the pupils to sing the song through twice. The first time they will sing, "The Word of the Lord is my lamp." The second time they will sing "The Word of the Lord is my light." **Now look at the activity page. You see several cartoon strips. You will complete the cartoons to illustrate how God's Word can guide these people to make the right choices. The Bible verses will help you.** (Suggested endings: 1) Stealing is wrong! 2) I did it. 3) Here's some for you.)

During *Sharing in Worship* pupils will tell about their cartoons and read the Bible verses that guided the people to do right. Then they'll sing the song.

6. Personal Praise. Pupils will illustrate Scriptures that tell why God's guidance and rules are good. Provide Bibles *(International Children's Bible),* paper, light-colored construction paper, scissors, pencils, markers, and tape. **God guided people in the Bible. What did God tell Jacob to do? Read Genesis 31:3 for the answer.** (Go back to his homeland.) **What did God tell Gideon to do? Read Judges 7:2-8.** (God told Gideon how to choose his soldiers.) **God gives us instruction in His Word, also. His guidance will help us live better lives. Read these Scriptures and tell the reasons why God's guidance and rules are good for us.** Give each pupil one verse to read. They may use the *ICB* Bible to clarify the verses, if needed. Psalm 19:7b (makes us wise); Psalm 19:8 (gives joy, happiness); Psalm 19:11 (gives rewards); Psalm 43:3 (bring us to heaven); Psalm 67:4 (guides justly, fairly); Proverbs 3:13, 14 (worth more than gold); Proverbs 4:4 (gives life); Proverbs 4:11, 12 (keeps us from stumbling or sinning); Isaiah 48:18 (gives peace). You will each draw a picture to show the answer given in your verse. (Suggestions for pictures: Wise—owl or perfect paper; joy—happy face; rewards—trophy; heaven—golden gates and buildings; just—judge; more than gold—price tags on gold and God's rules with God's rules having higher price; life—strong person; no sinning—person thinking about sinning; peace—no worrying.) **When you have finished your pictures, cut frames for the pictures from the construction paper. Write across the top of each frame "I like God's guidance because . . ."** Practice the presentation for *Sharing in Worship.*

During *Sharing in Worship* the pupils will post their pictures on the wall. Leave space between the pictures, so they can be "framed." They will give the frames to pupils in the large group. One pupil will say, "I like God's guidance because . . ." and read a Bible verse. One pupil with a frame will choose the picture that illustrates the Bible verse and tape the frame around it. Continue for all the verses.

Sharing in Worship
(20-25 minutes)

Omit any of the following sections if you did not offer the corresponding activities. The devotional and offering may be given without the group presentations.

Call to Worship (Group 1): **David praised God for guiding**

him in this Psalm. We will worship God as we hear David's words. Group 1 presents activity.

Scripture (Group 2): **God's Word gives us advice on every subject we need. We'll examine some of these subjects now with Group 2.** Group 2 presents activity.

Lord's Supper: God's Word gives us guidance about the Lord's Supper. Listen to it. "So a person should not eat the bread or drink the cup of the Lord in a way that is not worthy of it. . . . Everyone should look into his own heart before he eats the bread and drinks the cup. 1 Corinthians 11:27, 28, ICB. Let's think about Jesus and ourselves as we eat the Lord's Supper. Pray and serve the Lord's Supper.

Offering (Group 3): **God's Word gives us guidance about our money. We'll learn what God says about our money as Group 3 presents their skits.** Group 3 presents skits and collects the offering.

Devotional (Group 4): Before class mount a large map on the wall. Write on paper directions for getting from one city to another on the map. (For example: From Detroit, go West to Route 36 to Route 87. Go North on Route 87 to Springfield.) Provide a light-colored marker.

This is a map of ______. Maps help us get from one place to another. Have you ever used a map to go someplace? Did you follow it correctly, or did you get lost? (Pupils share.) **What might happen if you didn't follow the directions?** (Get there late, reach a dead end, have to turn around.) **I need a volunteer to mark the way from ______ to ______** (the two cities you chose). **Give a pupil the marker. I'll read the directions as you mark the roads.** Do so. **If you followed my directions, you should now be at ______ (final destination). If the pupil didn't end at the correct city, talk about where he or she took a wrong turn. Traveling is much easier when we have directions. If we take just any road, we often get lost. Life is like a trip. We want to live right, but we need directions. God knows this about us. That's why He gave us His word, the Bible. In the Bible we can find the way to please God and live the best life. What are some of God's instructions about how to live?** (Pupils answer from the Scriptures they studied in *Building the Theme* activities. Suggestions follow: think about good things, love enemies, treat people like you want to be treated, love God, obey parents.)

When we follow God's instructions, we live better and happier lives. When we don't follow God's instructions, we make mistakes. We have to face the consequences and punishments for doing wrong. Group 4 read articles about people who did and did not follow God's guidance. They'll tell you what they did and what happened to them. Group 4 presents activity. **If all these people had followed God's guidance, they would not have made some of these mistakes. That's a great reason to praise God for giving us guidance.**

Special Music (Group 5): **God's Word shows us the way to go. Group 5 will sing a song that describes God's Word. They'll also tell us how God's Word can show us what to do.** Group 5 presents activity.

Personal Praise (Group 6): **Group 6 will tell us why they like God's guidance.** Group 6 presents activity.

Closing Moments
(10-15 minutes)

As pupils play this game, they will recognize the difference between God's guidance and wrong guidance. Before class write several situations on paper. The situations should call for a decision on the part of the pupil. (Suggestions follow: sister messed up your room, teacher wrongly accused you, brother broke your airplane, father forgot to take you out for lunch, friend ignored you at the party, friend can't come to your party, mother is grouchy.) Put two colored marbles or buttons in a sack. Ask the pupils to sit in a circle. **God's guidance is often very different from other advice we might hear. If someone told a lie about me, a friend might advise me to get even. That would not be God's advice. I'll read a situation. One of you will draw a marble. If you chose a ______ (one color) marble, you'll tell God's advice. If you draw a ______ (other color) marble, you'll tell the wrong advice.** Continue until each pupil has had a turn.

Suggested Resources

These materials will help your pupils further appreciate the guidance God gives through the Bible.

The Backyard Safari by Gary Richmond, Word Publishing.

Unit Four
Worship God Because He Cares for Us

Session 14

God Cares for the Lonely

Worship Focus

Worship God because He cares for the lonely.

Transition Time

(10-15 minutes)

Send the Juniors in small groups to the rest room and drinking fountain. Welcome the Juniors and involve them in the following activity.

Lonely Search. You will need copies of activity page 14A and pencils. Distribute the activity page to the Juniors as they arrive. Ask them to find and circle as many "lonely people" as they can find in the word search. The words around the border of the page will give them clues. In the box at the bottom of the page, ask them to write any other lonely people they can think of.

Launching the Theme

(10 minutes)

We're conducting an opinion poll today. Raise your hand if you agree with this statement: "It is a bad thing to be lonely." (Write down on the chalkboard how many Juniors agree with this statement and how many disagree.) **Can you think of a reason it might be good to be lonely?** (Let Juniors answer.)

Who are some of the lonely people you found in your word search? (Juniors respond.) **Why are these people lonely?** (Allow Juniors to explain why specific people or groups might be lonely.) **Have you ever been lonely?** (Allow Juniors to share about times when they were lonely. Share with the Juniors a time when you were lonely.)

God is an always God. He always loves. He always forgives. And He always cares. Today we will worship God because He cares for the lonely. We will worship God because He cared for lonely people in the Bible. We will worship God because He cares for lonely people today. We will worship God because He cares for us when we are lonely.

Explain the choices of *Building the Theme* activities. Allow the Juniors to choose in which group to participate.

Building the Theme

(30 minutes)

1. Call to Worship. This group will prepare a tower of praise to God. You will need a large cardboard box (appliance size), markers, construction paper, scissors, glue, scratch paper, pencils, Bibles. Before the session, cut one side out of the card board box. Stand the remaining three sides upright, so that all three sides are visible from the front. Use the cardboard from the cut out side to make braces to help the box stand upright, if needed.

Distribute Bibles. Ask the Juniors to find and read Psalm 68:4-6a. You may want to have Juniors read aloud from several different versions. **We will make a tower of praise from these verses to introduce our worship time.** Show the Juniors the cardboard display. Lay the cardboard on the floor to allow Juniors to work on it more easily. Divide the Juniors into three groups. Assign each group one verse from Psalm 68:4-6a to illustrate. Each group will illustrate one side of the triangular box. Suggestions for illustrations follow: Verse 4—person singing; musical notes; happy faces for *rejoice*, clouds; Verse 5—a father with children, a woman alone, the sky; Verse 6a—a group of lonely people together like a family (could use lonely people listed in *Transition Time*). The Juniors will write the verse on their section of the box and illustrate the verse. Provide scratch paper for them to sketch their ideas. Ask them to draw large figures to completely cover their section of the box.

When the Juniors have completed their illustrations, practice reading Psalm 68:4-6a aloud together.

During *Sharing in Worship*, stand the cardboard display upright. Point to each verse as the group reads it aloud together.

2. Scripture. This group will prepare chains of Scriptures about loneliness. You will need Bibles, construction paper, a poster board, markers or crayons, scissors, and tape. Before the session, print the following Scripture references on a poster board: Psalm 145:18; Isaiah 54:10; Isaiah 61:1; Matthew 18:20; Matthew 28:20; John 8:29; John 14:18; Acts 17:27; Hebrews 13:5.

How does God care for lonely people? (Allow Juniors to suggest ways.) **One way God cares for lonely people is through His Word, the Bible. God has many**

comforting words to say to lonely people. We are going to read some of those words today. Display the poster board with the Scripture references. Assign each Junior a reference to look up and read aloud. Then ask them to cut construction paper into strips, write one Scripture reference on each strips, and tape the strips together to make a construction paper chain. **These chains can help us remember that God cares for the lonely. When you feel lonely, tear off a strip of the chain and read the Bible verse. When someone you know is lonely, give them a strip of the chain with a Bible verse on it.**

During *Sharing in Worship*, ask each Junior to read aloud the Scripture verse he or she read during the small group time.

3. Personal Praise. This group will prepare posters, praising God for caring for them when they are lonely. You will need copies of activity page 14B, scissors, glue, construction paper, and crayons or markers.

How does God care for lonely people? (Allow Juniors to respond.) **One way God cares for lonely people is through His Word, the Bible. In the Bible, God tells us some things we can do when we are lonely.** Distribute activity page 14B. Ask the Juniors to look up the Scriptures at the bottom of the page, cut them out, and glue them next to the matching action at the top of the page. Provide markers or crayons for them to decorate their posters. Then ask them to cut out the posters and glue them to construction paper. **We will take our posters home and put them in our rooms to help us remember to worship God when we are lonely because He cares for us.**

During *Sharing in Worship*, ask the Juniors to display their posters. Ask five Juniors to share the five things God tells us to do when we are lonely. They will say, "God Cares When I Am Lonely. He tells me to (one action from the poster)."

4. Devotional. This group will write diary entries of Bible people who were lonely. You will need writing paper, pencils, Bibles, a poster board, and marker. Before the session, write the following names and Scripture references down the left-hand side of a piece of poster board: Joseph—Genesis 39, 40; Naomi—Ruth 1; Ruth—Ruth 1-4; David—Psalm 31:10-15, 19-21. Leave the center and right-hand side of the poster board blank.

I am going to name some Bible people who were lonely. I want you to tell me why they were lonely. Display the poster board with the Bible names. Record the Junior's answers in the center column of the poster board. Juniors may look in their Bibles if they need help finding answers. Include the following reasons for each Bible character: Joseph—was hated by his brothers, was sold as a slave, was put in prison when he did nothing wrong, was forgotten by the king's butler; Naomi—was living in a foreign country, was left alone when her husband and two sons died; Ruth—was living in a foreign country, was left alone when her husband died; David—was alone in the field when he watched sheep, had to hide when King Saul tried to kill him, had to hide when his son Absalom tried to take over his kingdom. **How did God care for each of these lonely people?** Record the Junior's answers in the right-hand side of the poster board. Answers follow: Joseph—was made ruler in Egypt who was second only to the king of Egypt, brought his brothers and his family to live in Egypt with them; Naomi—returned to her own country, was helped by her daughter-in-law Ruth; Ruth—returned to her own country, married Boaz; David—was made King of Israel when Saul died, returned to his palace after Absalom tried to take over.

Assign each Junior or pair of Juniors one Bible person. Ask them to write a brief paragraph, as if it were a diary entry, for that person, telling why he or she was lonely and how God cared.

During *Sharing in Worship*, ask the Juniors to read their diary entries.

5. Devotional. This group will prepare skits about lonely people. You will need paper and pencils. This activity is for older or gifted Juniors.

We are going to be preparing some skits about lonely people, but we are not going to act out the end of the skit. We are going to let the large group tell us how the skit should end. Read the following situations aloud and ask for volunteers to act out the situation. Juniors may use the paper to write ideas of what to say.

1. A boy misses his older brother who is at college.
2. A grandma wishes her family could come to her home for the holidays.
3. A girl is sad because her Grandma died.
4. A man can't go home for Christmas and misses his family.
5. A family has moved to a new town and has few friends at Christmas.

During *Sharing in Worship*, the Juniors will present the situations for the large group.

6. Prayer. This group will prepare cards for lonely people to introduce the prayer time. You will need Bibles, pencils, markers, scissors, construction paper, used cards to be cut up, envelopes, and a church or telephone directory.

Who are some people you know that might be lonely? These people could be people in

our church or your neighbors or family members. (Allow Juniors to name people.) **One way God cares for lonely people is by sending us, His followers, to care for them. What are some ways we can show these lonely people we care?** (Allow Juniors to respond. Suggestions follow: Visit them; pray for them; send them a card or gift; offer to help in their yard or around the house, and so on.) **Today we are going to make cards to send to people who might be lonely. We will tell these people that God cares for them. We will tell them that we are praying for them.** Distribute the materials to the Juniors and ask them to design a card for a lonely person mentioned earlier. Look up the addresses and ask the Juniors to copy them onto their envelopes.

During *Sharing in Worship*, ask each Junior to say a prayer, asking God to be with the lonely person to whom they wrote.

Sharing in Worship
(20-25 minutes)

Omit any of the following sections if you did not offer the corresponding activity. The devotional may be completed without the presentations of Groups 4 and 5.

Call to Worship (Group 1): **Today we are praising God for caring for the lonely. Group 1 will read us a Scripture that praises God.** Group 1 presents their Scripture.

Song: Sing "The Joy of the Lord Is My Strength" from page 185.

Scripture (Group 2): **One way God cares for us when we are lonely is through His Word, the Bible. Listen to these comforting words for the lonely from the Bible.** Group 2 presents their Scripture verses.

Lord's Supper: When people meet for the first time and want to get better acquainted, one often invites the other for a meal. "Let's go out for a coke," or "Why don't you come over for dinner on Monday night?" Eating together is a special way to conquer loneliness. When Jesus wanted a way for us to remember Him and to get closer to others who know Him, He planned a simple meal for us to eat together. But it's more than a get acquainted time. The Lord's Supper is a reminder that because of Jesus' death on the cross, we don't need to be lonely any more, we can be friends again with God and with others. As we eat together today, let's praise God because He has conquered loneliness. Pray and serve the Lord's Supper.

Offering: God has given so much to us. He loves us. He is always with us—when we are happy, when we are afraid, or when we are lonely. Right now, we have a chance to give to God because He has given us so much. Choose two children to collect the offering.

Personal Praise (Group 3): **God's Word comforts us when we are lonely, and His Word tells us what to do when we are lonely.** Group 3 presents their posters.

Devotional (Groups 4 and 5): **How can we know that God will care for us when we are lonely? We can know because God has always cared for lonely people. Listen to these lonely Bible people who found out that God cares.** Ask Group 4 to share their diary entries. If you did not offer this activity, omit the preceding discussion and begin your devotional talk in the following paragraph.

God cared for lonely people in the Bible like Joseph, Naomi, Ruth, and David. And God cares for lonely people today, especially at Christmastime. You are probably already planning ways to celebrate Christmas. Christmas is such a happy and fun time, it may not seem to have anything to do with loneliness. But Christmas is very much connected to loneliness.

For some, Christmas is the loneliest time of the year. They have no family or close friends to share the season with. As they look around and see others celebrating and buying gifts for loved ones, their own loneliness somehow seems bigger.

Christmas is really about loneliness. God sent Jesus to the world because people were lonely. They were far away from God because of their sins, and far away from each other because of their selfishness and pride. So God sent Jesus to make a way for us to be together again, together with God and together with each other. Jesus is God's Christmas gift to the world, sent to conquer loneliness. Ephesians 2:13 talks about this: "Yes, at one time you were far away from God. But now in Christ Jesus you are brought near to God through the blood of Christ's death."

We can worship God because He has taken away our loneliness by sending Jesus. And we can worship Him for caring for other lonely people. One way we can worship Him is by helping lonely people. Listen as Group 5 tells us about some lonely people. Let's think of ways we could help these lonely people. Ask Group 5 to come forward and share their skits. After each skit, ask the large group to tell ways they could care for that person. If you did not offer this activity, read the situations listed in Group 5 to the large group and ask them how they could care for each person.

Prayer (Group 6): **One thing we can do for any lonely person we know is to pray for them. Group 6 made some cards to send to lonely people they know to tell them they are praying for them. Let's pray and thank God for His care for these lonely people.** Ask Group 6 to pray for the lonely people for whom they made cards. Allow Juniors from the large group to pray for lonely people they know. Close with prayer, thanking God for caring for all of us when we are lonely.

Closing Moments
(10-15 minutes)

Song Match Up. You will need lines from familiar Christmas songs. Divide the Juniors into two teams. Take turns reading a line from a familiar Christmas song to each team. The team must guess the title of the song. If they guess correctly, they get a point. If they guess incorrectly, the other team has a chance to guess. **Variation:** The team must sing the first stanza of the song together to receive a point.

escape. For example, "Sometimes we are tempted to steal. Thank You, God. You help us not to steal because we know Your Word tells us not to steal."

5. Devotional. This group will prepare a puzzle of ways God helped people. You will need Bibles, poster board, scratch paper, pencils, two blank transparencies, markers, and an overhead projector. Before the session, print the following Scripture verses on poster board. Do not print the answers.

Psalm 10:14c—helped fatherless

Psalm 136:24—freed us from enemies

Psalm 145:19—hears and saves

Psalm 145:20—watches over us

Psalm 146:7—gives food

Assign each Junior a verse to find. Ask them to find in the verse a way that God helped someone. Write their answers beside each verse on the poster board. On the transparency, ask the Juniors to print each verse and draw enough blanks for the answer. Then fill in all the vowels. Under each remaining blank, write two consonants, one correct and one wrong. For example for "helped fatherless," the puzzle might read (h, b) e (m, l) (t, p) e (f, d) (f, d) a (m, t) (g, h) e (n, r) (l, c) e (w, s) (p, s).

During *Sharing in Worship*, project the puzzle on the wall. A Junior will read the first Scripture. Then the group will choose the correct consonants to fill in the answer. A Junior will fill in the blanks on the transparency. Continue this procedure with the other verses.

6. Prayer. This group will write a prayer, praising God for ways He rescued people. You will need scratch paper, pencils, Bibles, sheet of newsprint, and markers

For each Bible person mentioned above in *Launching the Theme*, the group should write two sentences, one praising God and explaining how He rescued the person, and the second asking God to help them to follow that person's example. Here is a sample:

Dear God,

When Daniel decided to keep on praying no matter what happened, You kept him safe in the lions' den. Help me, God, to keep on praying no matter what happens.

When Shadrach and his friends decided they would not obey the king and worship the idol, You kept them safe in the fiery furnace. Help me, God, to choose to worship you instead of false gods.

When Jonah disobeyed you and ran away to Nineveh, You rescued him by sending a great fish to save him from drowning. Help me, God, not to run away from doing what is right.

When Joseph was put in prison even though he hadn't done anything wrong, You were with him and rescued him from prison. Help me, God, to remember that you are always with me.

When David was brave enough to face the giant Goliath without armor or sword, You helped him kill Goliath. Help me, God, to trust you when I don't feel brave.

Juniors may wish to include other Bible characters. Don't show the sample to the Juniors. Simply suggest that they fill in the blanks. When (Bible character) did _______, You _______. Help us, God, also to _______. After about ten minutes, ask Juniors to share their ideas. Copy them on the newsprint or transparency. Practice reading aloud. Divide into two groups. Have one group read the first sentence about each Bible character. Have the second group read the response.

During *Sharing in Worship*, the Juniors will read the prayer.

Sharing in Worship
(20-25 minutes)

Omit any of the following sections if you did not offer the corresponding activity. The devotional may be completed without the presentation of Group 5.

Call to Worship (Group 1): **The Bible promises us many times that God will rescue us and help us when we are in trouble. Group 1 will tell us about some of those promises.** Group 1 presents their verses.

Special Music (Group 2): **When do we need God to rescue us? Group 2 thought of some times.** Ask Group 2 to share the times God could rescue us and sing their song.

Scripture (Group 3): **One of the ways God rescues us is through His Word—the Bible. When we store verses away in our hearts and minds by memorizing and applying, the verses can help us in emergencies. We could say the Bible is like a first-aid kit to help us in emergencies.** Ask Group 3 to present their first-aid kit.

Personal Praise (Group 4): **Have you ever been trapped? Maybe you were hiding in a closet during a hide and seek game with no way to get home free. Or perhaps you have waited impatiently with your family in a traffic jam, no way to move. Or maybe you climbed up a tree and couldn't find your way back down. You were trapped. Satan loves for us to feel trapped. He throws a temptation in a person's face and hopes the person will believe that there is no escape. But God has a rescue plan.** Read 1 Corinthians 10:13. **God rescues us by giving us an escape from temptation. Group 4 found some ways that God helps us escape. They will thank God for those ways now.** Group 4 names and thanks God for ways of escape.

Lord's Supper: The most important rescue that God ever

made is the one that happened when Jesus died on the cross. God could have rescued Jesus from that horrible death. But God didn't, because Jesus' death became our rescue. Because He died, we can be rescued from the punishment of our sins.

Offering: Now is our chance to give to God. He gave us Jesus to die for us. He keeps us safe. He rescues us when we face temptation or when we are afraid or sad. One way we can thank God is by giving to Him. Pray and choose two children to collect the offering.

Devotional (Group 5): **Have you ever wanted to be an actor or an actress? A woman named Edith Schaeffer in her book, *Affliction,* says that Christians are always "on stage" for the rest of the world to see. We are living our lives so that nonbelievers can learn about God by our lives. The people who don't believe in God are watching us. Sometimes something bad happens in our lives. The people who don't believe in God can see how God rescues us. God may rescue us by saving us or healing us. Or God may rescue us by giving us strength to deal with our problem.**

When Shadrach, Meshach, and Abednego were standing before Nebuchadnezzar on their way to the fiery furnace because they refused to worship the king's idol, they gave an interesting testimony to the king. Read Daniel 3:16, 17. **These young men were more committed to God than they were to their own rescue. They believed that God could rescue them, but they were more interested in testifying to the king that it would be wrong for them to worship his idol than they were worried about the fire in the furnace.**

We can praise God for every rescue He has done. Group 5 found some other ways God rescues us. Ask Group 5 to present their puzzle for the large group. If you did not offer this activity, you may wish to prepare the puzzle ahead of time. See the instructions in Group 5.

Prayer (Group 6): **Today we have praised God for the way He rescues. Sometimes He does a miracle. Sometimes He gives us what we need to help us through the problem. Sometimes He gives instruction in the Bible about how to handle the problem. Sometimes He provides a way of escape. But no matter what, we can know without a doubt that God truly cares about us. Group 6 will thank God for the ways He rescued Bible people and the ways He rescues us.** Group 6 reads their prayer. Close with prayer, thanking God for rescuing us.

Closing Moments
(10-15 minutes)

You will need index cards or slips of paper and a marker. Before the session, copy one word from 2 Peter 2:9 on each card or paper. "The Lord knows how to rescue godly men from trials." Make one set of cards for each four Juniors. Divide the Juniors into groups of four. Give each group one set of cards. Ask the groups to arrange the words in the correct order. The first group to arrange the words in order wins.

Suggested Resources
Find a local Christian radio station which carries "Stories of Great Christians" by Moody Bible Institute. Tape some of these to use as examples of how God helped courageous Christians.

God Is Merciful to Us

Worship Focus

Worship God because He is merciful.

Transition Time

(10-15 minutes)

Send Juniors in small groups to the rest room and drinking fountain. Welcome the Juniors and involve them in the following activity.

Mercy Movement Game. You will need three pieces of construction paper, markers, Plasti-Tak or tape, three plates, a snack that can be sprinkled with powdered sugar (doughnut holes or cookies), powdered sugar, and baking soda. Before the session, letter the pieces of construction paper *A, B,* and *C*. On the backs of pieces *A* and *B*, write *not merciful*. On the back of piece C, write *merciful*. Post the pieces of construction paper in three different places in your room. For example, post one on the chalkboard, one on the bulletin board, and one over the bookcase. Divide a few of the snacks among the three plates. Sprinkle the snacks on two plates with baking soda. Sprinkle the snacks on the third plate and the remaining snacks with powdered sugar.

Look around the room. You will see three areas labeled A, B, and C. I am going to read some multiple choice questions to you. Choose answer A, B, or C and move to the part of the room that matches your answer.

1. A friend borrowed your new tape of your favorite singing group and lost it. Will you: a) never speak to her again; b) speak to her only when she buys you a new tape; c) tell her that friends are more important than tapes.

2. A weird guy at school just dropped all his books right in front of you. Will you: a) call him "stupid," and kick his papers; b) walk right over his stuff, acting as if you don't see him; c) get down and help him pick up the papers.

3. Your friend told a bunch of other people a secret that you had asked her not to tell. Will you: a) tell your other friends a lot of bad things about her; b) ignore her; c) keep on being her friend.

4. You were supposed to take out the trash. Your little brother said he would do it for you, but he forgot. Now you're in trouble because you were the one who was supposed to take out the trash in the first place. Will you: a) dump all the trash on your brother's bed; b) say, "just wait, I'll get you later!"; c) tell your brother it's okay because you know that he didn't mean to get you in trouble.

5. When someone does something wrong to you, what do you do? a) Get even, no matter what; b) Forgive the person but never forget what they did; c) Forgive and forget.

Distribute the snacks to the Juniors. Give the children in spots A and B the snacks sprinkled with baking soda. Give the children in spot C the snacks sprinkled with powdered sugar.

Launching the Theme

(10 minutes)

Discuss the snacks distributed to groups A and B during *Transition Time*. **What's wrong with the snacks? How do they taste? Bitter? I'm not surprised. I think it has something to do with your attitude about getting even. Proverbs 11:17 tells us why getting even makes us bitter.** Ask children to find the verse in their Bibles. **"A kind man benefits himself, but a cruel man brings himself harm." In other words, when you forgive other people for doing wrong, you are doing something good for yourself. When you try to get even, you are hurting yourself.**

Distribute the remaining plate of sugared snacks to those who tasted the bitter ones.

Today we are focusing on the mercy of God. What is mercy? Let Juniors respond; write their ideas on the chalkboard or a sheet of newsprint. **Mercy means offering forgiveness and kindness to someone who doesn't deserve it, to someone who has hurt you or made you angry. Mercy is different than feeling sorry for someone or being kind to someone because mercy means forgiving someone who has done something wrong to you.**

God is merciful. He forgives us no matter how many wrong things we do to Him. We will worship Him today because He is merciful.

Explain the choices of *Building the Theme* activities. Allow the children to choose an activity.

Building the Theme
(30 minutes)

1. Call to Worship. This group will prepare balloons illustrating God's mercy. You will need Bibles, scratch paper, pencils, one balloon for each Junior in the group, markers, tape or string, and scissors. Before the session, blow up the balloons and store them in a large plastic trash bag.

Assign each Junior or pair of Juniors one of the following verses: Ephesians 2:4; Micah 7:18; Psalm 36:5; 1 Chronicles 16:34; Psalm 100:5; Psalm 117:2; Daniel 9:9; 1 Peter 1:3; Lamentations 3:22. Ask the Juniors to read the verses and think of a picture to illustrate the verse. Provide scratch paper for Juniors to sketch their ideas. Suggestions follow: Ephesians 2:4—bags of coins or stacks of money to illustrate that God is rich in mercy; Micah 7:18—happy faces or banners to illustrate that God delights to show mercy; Psalm 36:5—Clouds in a sky spelling out *mercy* to illustrate that God's mercy extends to the heavens; 1 Chronicles 16:34—a calendar with pages torn off to illustrate that God's mercy endures forever; Psalm 100:5—mountains to illustrate that God's mercy is everlasting; Psalm 117:2—decorated gift boxes to illustrate that God's mercy and kindness is great toward us; Daniel 9:9—people holding spears and swords to illustrate that God is merciful though we have rebelled against Him; 1 Peter 1:3—a baby to illustrate that God has given us a new birth; Lamentations 3:22—a winding river to illustrate that God's mercies never stop.

Distribute the balloons and markers. Ask the Juniors to draw the pictures on the balloon. When the balloons are completed, tape or tie them on a wall where they will be seen during the worship time.

During *Sharing in Worship*, the Juniors will read the verse about mercy and point to the balloon illustrating each verse.

2. Special Music. This group will write new words to a song for the worship time. You will need "I Will Sing of the Mercies of the Lord Forever" from page 181, poster board, markers, and Bibles. Before the session, print the words to the song on the poster board. Leave room for Juniors to add stanzas.

Display the poster board for the Juniors. Sing the song once for them, then ask them to sing it with you. **The Bible explains many things about God's mercy to us. We are going to write some new words for part of this song explaining more about God's mercy.**

Assign each Junior or pair of Juniors one of the following verses: Psalm 86:15, 117:2; Ephesians 2:4; Titus 3:5. Ask them to read the verse, decide what it says about God's mercy, and write new words to replace the words "With my mouth will I make known Thy faithfulness, Thy faithfulness, With my mouth will I make known Thy faithfulness to all generations."

Allow about ten minutes for Juniors to write the new words. Then ask them to share the sentences they have prepared. Select the ones you want to use in the song during large group time. Write these on the poster board. Practice singing the song with the new stanzas.

During *Sharing in Worship*, Juniors will sing the song, using the new stanzas they created.

3. Lord's Supper. This group will prepare a mobile emphasizing God's mercy in sending Jesus to die for us. You will need copies of activity page 16A, markers, scissors, yarn or string, a paper hole punch, and hangers for the mobiles (clothes hangers, cardboard strips with holes punched them, or chenille wire).

What is the greatest way that God showed His mercy for us? (He sent Jesus to die for us.) Ask the Juniors to find Romans 5:8 in their Bibles. Read the verse aloud. **This verse reminds us of God's great mercy. God sent Jesus to die for us while we were still doing wrong things. Jesus died for us before we were even sorry for the wrong things we did.** Ask the Juniors to think of a praise sentence or word for each of the letters in the word *mercy* which worships God for sending Jesus to die for us. An example follows:

Thank You, God, for loving **M**e.
Thank You for sending J**E**sus.
Thank You that Jesus died on the c**R**oss.
Thank You that Jesus **C**ame back alive.
Thank You that You forgive ever**Y**one of the wrong things they do.

Distribute the activity pages. Ask the Juniors to color the mobile pieces, cut them out, and write the sentence about God's mercy on the back. They will then punch holes in the tops of the pieces and use yarn or string to attach the pieces to the hangers. Ask for volunteers to read each of the sentences about mercy during the worship time.

During *Sharing in Worship*, the Juniors will display their mobiles as the Juniors say the sentences about God's mercy.

4. Scripture. This group will prepare a scrambled name puzzle about people to whom God showed mercy. You will need Bibles, a blank transparency, markers, an overhead projector, and scratch paper. **Option:** If an overhead projector is not available, ask the children to write the scrambled names on poster board or a chalkboard.

Distribute Bibles. Ask Juniors to read these verses and find a person to whom God showed mercy: Exodus 2:11, 12; 3:1-10 (Moses, murder); Luke 19:1-10

(Zacchaeus, cheating); Acts 9:1, 2, 17 (Paul, imprisoning Christians); Jonah 1:1-3, 2:10—3:3 (Jonah, disobeying); Isaiah 44:17, 21 (Israelites, idolatry).

Write their answers on scratch paper. Divide the transparency into ten sections. Ask a Junior to scramble the letters of the first name and write it on one section. Underneath the scrambled name, ask him or her to draw a blank for each letter in the name. Repeat with the other answers, scrambling the names and drawing blanks underneath. Assign Juniors to read the verses, or write the answers on the transparency during the worship time.

During *Sharing in Worship*, display the transparency and ask the large group to unscramble the names. When each name is unscrambled, ask a Junior to read the corresponding Scripture, and ask the large group to tell how God showed mercy to that person.

5. Devotional. This group will discuss situations where they can act with mercy. You will need copies of activity page 16B, Bibles, and pencils

Distribute the activity page. Assign Juniors Scriptures to find and read. After each verse is read, ask **What does this verse say about mercy?** Ask Juniors to write what each verse says about mercy on the blank lines. **Read the situations on your activity page. In which two situations is someone showing mercy?** (The girl asking Jenny to go skating; the boy asking Bill to play with him.) **Think about the Bible verses we just read about mercy. How could someone show mercy in the other three situations?** (Allow response. Suggestions follow: The mother could tell her son it's okay he broke the lamp; the girl could tell her sister she forgives her for ruining her sweater; the boy could tell his brother he will teach him how to use the computer.) **When are some other times when we could show mercy?** (Allow Juniors to think of times. Suggestions follow: a teacher forgives a child who lost a special classroom book; mom forgives kid who came home too late for Mom to go to a luncheon with her friend.) Choose two or three situations to share during the worship time. Assign Juniors to tell about the situations and Juniors to read the Scriptures.

During *Sharing in Worship*, ask the Juniors to tell the first part of their situations. Then ask the other Juniors to read the Scriptures telling the merciful solution. Finally, ask the Juniors to tell how the person in their situations showed mercy.

6. Prayer. This group will write a prayer, thanking God for being merciful when we do wrong things. You will need Bibles, scratch paper, pencils, a tape recorder, and a blank tape.

Ask a Junior to read Psalm 130:3, 4a. **Does God keep a record of our sins?** (No.) **What does God do instead?** (He forgives us.) **Let's write a prayer thanking God for being merciful to us when we do wrong things. What are some wrong things we do?** (Allow Juniors to respond. Write their responses on poster board.) Ask Juniors to finish the sentence: "We are wrong when we ________, but You, Lord, forgive us because You are merciful." They may choose from the list of wrong things on the poster board. Ask the Juniors to write their sentences on scratch paper. Practice saying the prayer. Each Junior will say a time we are wrong. Then the group will say together, "You, Lord, forgive us because You are merciful." Record the prayer on the cassette tape.

During *Sharing in Worship*, play the recorded prayer.

Sharing in Worship
(20-25 minutes)

Omit any of the following sections if you did not offer the corresponding activity. The Lord's Supper and devotional may be completed without the presentations of Group 3 and 5.

Call to Worship (Group 1)**: The Bible gives many descriptions of God's mercy. Group 2 illustrated some of these by decorating balloons. Let's have them read some of the Scriptures.** Group 2 will read the Scriptures describing God's mercy.

Special Music (Group 2): **You probably know the song that Group 2 will sing for us, but listen carefully for the new words they wrote that tell us about God's mercy.** Group 2 sings "I Will Sing of the Mercies of the Lord Forever."

Lord's Supper (Group 3): **The greatest way that God showed us His mercy was by sending Jesus to die for us. Group 3 will remind us of reasons to thank God for His mercy in sending Jesus.** Ask Group 3 to share their mobiles and sentences.

Sometimes we hear about a prisoner on death row who receives a pardon and does not have to die. Spiritually, every one of us is like that prisoner: sentenced to death for our sins. But Romans 5:8 says, "Jesus died for us while we were still sinners. In this way God shows his great love for us." That is mercy. The Lord's Supper is a celebration of mercy. Pray and serve the Lord's Supper.

Offering: Sing the following song to the tune of "We Wish You a Merry Christmas": "God showed us mercy at Christmas, He gave us His only Son, We did not deserve forgiveness, But He gave us new life. We wish you a mercy Christmas (repeat twice more) for He gives us new life!" then shout out "Mercy Christmas, Everyone!" Ask two children to collect the offering.

Scripture (Group 4): **We have heard many verses about ways God shows His mercy to us. But the Bible also gives many examples of Bible people to whom God showed mercy. See if you can figure out who these Bible people are.** Ask Group 4 to project their transparency. Allow the large group to guess the scrambled names. After each name is guessed and the corresponding Scripture read, ask, **How did God show mercy to that person?**

Devotional (Group 5): **One way we can understand how God shows us mercy is by showing mercy to other people. What do you feel like doing when someone does something wrong to you?** (Getting mad; hurting them; getting back.) **When someone hurts us, we want to hurt them or get mad at them. But there is a better solution—the merciful solution. The Bible tells us about the merciful solution. Group 5 will tell us some times when we can show mercy.** Ask Group 5 to present their situations, Scriptures, and merciful solutions. If you did not offer this activity, read the situations on activity page 16B and ask the Juniors to suggest merciful solutions. Then read the Scriptures listed on that page.

Sometimes being merciful means saying something kind. "I forgive you." Or "It's okay." And sometimes being merciful means doing something kind, like asking someone to go skating or to play with us.

When we have shown mercy to others, we can ask God for mercy for ourselves and we also thank God for the mercy He has shown us personally.

Prayer (Group 6): Read Psalm 130:3, 4 and play the taped prayer written by Group 6.

Closing Moments
(10-15 minutes)

Divide into groups or 4 or 5. Provide paper and pencils. Ask groups to think of an object that relates to or represents mercy. Draw that object, using the letters in the word mercy as part of the drawing. For example: cross, gift, manger.

Unit Four
Worship God Because He Cares for Us

Session 17

God Gave Us the Gift of Salvation Through Jesus

This session is the Christmas session. Use this session for week 16 or 17, depending on where Christmas falls.

Worship Focus

Worship God because He gave us the gift of salvation through His Son Jesus.

Transition Time

(10-15 minutes)

Send Juniors in small groups to the rest room and drinking fountain. Welcome the Juniors and involve them in the following activity.

Christmas Checklist: You will need copies of activity page 17A and pencils. Distribute the activity page. Juniors are to ask others to sign their names in the squares on the sheet under an activity in which they have participated. Each person may sign another's sheet in two different categories.

Distribute snacks to those who complete their sheets first.

Launching the Theme

(10 minutes)

You will need two puppets and a puppet stage. Before the session, recruit two adult or Junior volunteers to practice the following puppet play and present it during the session.

Puppet 1: Oh, no! It's Christmas Eve, and I still haven't bought my dad a present.

Puppet 2: I think you're too late. But I have an idea. My teacher said that the best presents aren't for sale at a store.

Puppet 1: Good idea. I don't have much money anyway. Let's see, I could give him my old baseball glove. It doesn't fit me right since I left it out in the rain. Or, maybe I'll give him my fishing hat. It's too small for me. Or there's that old. . .

Puppet 2 *(interrupting)***:** Wait a minute! You're talking about trash, not gifts. Miss Steckle read us this story about a couple who didn't have any money for Christmas presents. So the husband sold his gold pocket watch to buy his wife some hair combs. The wife sold her long hair to buy her husband a gold chain for his watch. They were willing to give up the best possession they had for each other. Now those were gifts of love!

Puppet 1: Wow! I'm supposed to give my dad something I really like?

Puppet 2: Right!

Puppet 1: Well. . . my dad's key ring broke last week. I could give him the one I made in my craft club.

Puppet: Now you've got the idea.

The people in the story decided to give up their most important possession in order to buy something special for the most important person in their lives. If we wrote a story like that about you, what possession would you give up, and for whom would you be getting a present? Allow a minute or two for Juniors to form their responses before asking volunteers to share.

God could have given us <u>anything</u> in the world, but He gave us the best gift that He had—His Son, Jesus. God even allowed Jesus to be killed on the cross, so we could be forgiven of our sins. Today we will worship God for the gift of salvation through Jesus.

Explain the choices of *Building the Theme* activities and allow Juniors to choose in which group to participate.

Building the Theme

(30 minutes)

1. Call to Worship. This group will present a Christmas song during the worship time. You will need "Angels From the Realms of Glory" from page 186, a poster board, and a marker. Before the session, write the words to the song on the poster board.

Display the poster board for the Juniors. Ask a volunteer to read the verses for the group. **We need to decide how to present this hymn as a call to worship. Let's divide up the phrases into solo voices, duets, and group parts.** Mark these on the poster board. Rehearse, encouraging Juniors to read: loudly, softly, or emphatically where appropriate.

If time permits, suggest adding another verse, composed by your group, inviting the members of your audience to "come and worship." An example follows: **You who know the Christmas story, come again and hear once more. Come and give your life to Jesus, He will give you so much more.** This part will work smoothly if you draw blanks for each of the beats (or syllables) in the verse. Then the group can start thinking about how to fit their ideas into those spaces, remembering that each blank is a syllable, not a word. Practice the song many times.

During *Sharing in Worship*, the Juniors will sing the song. Close by asking the large group to sing with you, "We will worship, we will worship, worship Christ the newborn King."

2. Prayer. This group will prepare a praise prayer about prophecies God made about Jesus. You will need copies of activity page 17B, Bibles, pencils, a poster board, and markers.

What is a prophecy? (Something that someone says will happen in the future.) **God made many prophecies about Jesus' birth. And every prophecy came true. We are going to find some prophecies in the Bible about Jesus' birth.** Distribute the activity page and Bibles. Assign one Scripture to each Junior. Ask them to read the verse and tell what prophecy it makes. Answers follow: Micah 5:2—Jesus would be born in Bethlehem; Genesis 49:10 and Revelation 5:5—Jesus would be a member of the tribe of Judah; Isaiah 9:7—Jesus would be heir to the throne of David; Jeremiah 31:5—babies in Bethlehem would be killed; Hosea 11:1—Jesus and His family would escape into Egypt; Isaiah 60:3—Wise men would visit Jesus.

Why are these prophecies important to us? (They help us identify Jesus as the true Messiah.) **How do these prophecies help us trust God today?'** When we see that He kept His Old Testament promises, we can trust Him to keep His New Testament promises to us. **We are going to write a prayer, praising God for His true prophecies about Jesus.** Ask each Junior to create a praise sentence about the prophecy he or she read. Write the sentences on the poster board. **Now let's thank God for the ways these true prophecies help us.** Ask Juniors to say praise sentences about why God's prophecies are important to us and how they help us trust God. Write their sentences on the poster board. A sample prayer follows:

"God, You said that Jesus would be born in Bethlehem, and He was. You said Jesus would be a member of the tribe of Judah, and He was. You said He would be descended from King David, and He was. You said that the babies in Bethlehem would be killed, and it happened like You said. But You also promised that Jesus would escape into Egypt, and He did. Thank You. You said that kings or Wise men would visit Jesus, and they did. Thank You, God, that You always keep Your Word. Every plan You make always comes true. We know Jesus is Your Son because everything You said about Him came true. Thank You, God, for Jesus."

Ask each Junior to read the sentence of the prayer he or she created. Ask the group to read the final sentences of the prayer together. Practice reading the prayer.

During *Sharing in Worship*, Juniors will read the praise prayer.

3. Lord's Supper. This group will prepare a responsive reading of the best thing about Christmas. You will need old magazines, scissors, glue, two sheets of poster board cut into fourths, markers, and scratch paper.

Begin by having Juniors brainstorm a list of activities they do at Christmas time: Seeing relatives, wrapping presents, decorating the Christmas tree, making Christmas cookies, singing Christmas carols, receiving presents, sending cards, looking at the Christmas lights. Record their suggestions on chalkboard or a sheet of paper. Choose seven suggestions to illustrate.

What is the most important part of Christmas? (The fact that God sent Jesus as a gift to us.) **The best thing about Christmas is that God gave us His Son. We are going to prepare a responsive reading, thanking God for the best part about Christmas.** Distribute the eight pieces of poster board. On seven of the pieces, Juniors will glue magazine pictures or use markers to illustrate one of the activities they named that they do at Christmastime. On the other poster board, print "But the best thing about Christmas is that God gave His Son."

When the Juniors have completed their illustrations, ask each one to display their poster board and practice saying a sentence which explains their picture. They can write it on the back of the poster, if necessary. After each sentence is said, everyone will repeat together, "But the best thing about Christmas is that God gave us His Son." An example follows: "Decorating the tree is fun at Christmastime. But the best thing about Christmas is that God gave us His Son."

During *Sharing in Worship*, the group will present the responsive reading and ask the large group to join them in saying, "But the best thing about Christmas is that God gave us His Son."

4. Personal Praise. This group will pantomime ways to tell the Christmas story. You will need simple props, such as a telephone, paper, a pen and envelope, a Bible, a child's story book about Jesus, and a song book,

We remember God's greatest gift to us at Christmastime. But there are some gifts we can give to God also. One of the best gifts we can give to God around Christmas is to tell others about Jesus. What are some different ways we could tell others about Jesus at Christmastime? Brainstorm with the Juniors a list of ways to tell the Christmas story: telephone a friend and invite to a special program at church; send a Christmas card with a picture of Jesus instead of Santa Claus, and add a note you have written; invite a friend to watch a Bible story video with you; read a story about Jesus to a little child; sing songs about Jesus' birth when you go caroling; tell a friend the Christmas story from the Bible; give a gift that tells about Jesus, such as a Bible, a Bible-story video, or a Bible-story book.

Ask Juniors to discuss how to pantomime each of these activities during large group time for the rest of the group to guess. Assign specific scenes to pairs or trios of Juniors. Allow them about 5 minutes to rehearse. Then have them "practice" while the other members of your group watch.

During *Sharing in Worship*, the Juniors will present their pantomimes and ask the large group to guess.

5. Devotional. This group will prepare a centerpiece and Christmas Scriptures. You will need five white candles and candle holders, fresh evergreen branches, five cardboard stars, foil or gold wrapping paper, five straws, tape, florist wire, and Bibles,

Ask the Juniors prepare a centerpiece to be used during the worship time. **Set the candle holders, with candles in them, on the table. Arrange the evergreen branches around the candles. Cover the stars with the foil. Tape the stars to the straws. Place the stars among the branches, using the wire to hold them in place, if needed.**

Ask each Junior to find and read one of the following Scriptures: Psalm 119:105; Isaiah 9:2; John 1:5; John 1:9; John 8:12; Isaiah 60:19, 20; Matthew 5:16. **What do these verses have to do with Christmas?** Allow Juniors to share their ideas. **We will discover what these verses have to do with Christmas during the worship time.** Assign each Junior a verse to read during the worship time and ask them to practice reading aloud.

During *Sharing in Worship*, Juniors will read their verses aloud.

6. Offering. This group will prepare gifts to give to Jesus at Christmas. You will need an assortment of boxes, one or two for each Junior in the group (cereal boxes would work); yarn or ribbon; scissors; tape; a roll of newsprint; markers; scratch paper; and pencils. If you do not have a Christmas tree in your room, draw one on newsprint paper before the session and attach it to the wall.

What is something you are hoping to receive for Christmas? (Let volunteers respond.) **What are some gifts you think Jesus might want for Christmas? What attitudes might Jesus want from you? From your family? From our class? What actions might He want? What is the best gift we could give Jesus?** Write the Juniors' suggestions on scratch paper. Then ask each Junior to choose one or two gifts to give to Jesus. They will wrap the boxes with newsprint and write their gift on the outside. Then they will decorate their gifts with markers and yarn or ribbon.

During *Sharing in Worship*, Juniors will tell the gifts they will give to Jesus and place their gifts under the real or newsprint tree.

Sharing in Worship
(20-25 minutes)

Omit any of the following sections if you did not offer the corresponding activity. The Lord's Supper, Offering, and Devotional may be completed without the group presentations.

Call to Worship (Group 1): Ask Group 1 to present their song. Ask the large group to join them on a final chorus by singing, "We will worship, we will worship, worship Christ the newborn King."

Prayer (Group 2): **One of God's gifts to us is the prophecies from the Old Testament. They helped God's people to look for the Messiah, and they help us to know for certain that Jesus is the Messiah.** Group 1 shares their prayer.

Lord's Supper (Group 3): **What is your favorite part of Christmas? This reading will remind us that what is your favorite might not be the most important part.** Group 3 leads responsive reading. If you did not offer this activity, present the following thoughts.

Do you have any special gifts that remind you of the person who gave them to you? Maybe it's a locket with a picture of the giver inside. Maybe it's a special hat or shirt with the name of the place you visited last summer on a trip with some friends or relatives. Whenever you wear it, you remember the wonderful time you had with your friends.

The Lord's Supper is a gift to help us remember the death of Jesus. While it's easy for us to celebrate Jesus' birth, it is more difficult to know how to celebrate His death. The words "celebrate" and "death" just don't seem to go together. So God has given us the instructions: eat the bread and

think about Jesus' body; drink the juice and think about Jesus' blood. When you think about the tremendous gift, Jesus' own life, given just for you, then you can celebrate His death.

When the responsive reading or your Lord's Supper thoughts are completed, pray and serve the Lord's Supper.

Personal Praise (Group 4): **We just heard that the best thing about Christmas is the gift of God's Son, Jesus. And one of the best things we can do for Jesus at Christmastime is to tell others about Him. Group 4 found some ways we can do this for Jesus.** Group 4 will present their pantomimes and ask the large group to guess.

Music: Sing the chorus of "Go Tell It On the Mountain" from page 187. Sing different places to tell it: Go tell it in the city, the shopping mall, the classroom, and so on.

Devotional (Group 5): You will need matches. You may also wish to hand out small mirrors or pieces or reflective tape as reminders. Before you begin, have readers from Group 5 line up around you. Ask another adult to light the candles while you are reading.

If someone asked you what Christmas is all about, you probably wouldn't say, "It's about lights." But close your eyes and check out the pictures of the first Christmas in your mind—Mary and Joseph in a dim stable, proudly examining their new son by lantern light; the shepherds on a dark hillside, standing suddenly and shielding their eyes from the bright light of the glory of the Lord and the angel messenger; The Wise-men, traveling on, night after night, their eyes always focused on a twinkling star. Light and darkness really do help show us the Christmas message.

James 1:17 says God is the Father of lights. And 1 John 1:5 says that in God there is no darkness at all. Christmas was the moment in history when God, who is light, gave us Jesus, the Light of the World.

Let's look at a few Bible verses reminding us about light. Ask a Junior from the small group to read Psalm 119:105. **God is so wonderful that even the words He has written down in His book will help us. His word is like a road map or a direction manual, telling us how to put our lives together.**

Ask a Junior to read Isaiah 9:2, **That's the world without Jesus, hopeless.**

Ask a Junior to read John 1:5. **That's hope and joy: there is escape from the dark way of life.**

Ask a Junior to read John 1:9. **That's hope too, the light is for all of us, no matter who we are or what we've done.**

Ask a Junior to read John 8:12. **Because of Jesus' death and resurrection, we can get rid of the dark, sinful spots on our lives.**

Ask a Junior to read Isaiah 60:19, 20. **This verse described Heaven, a brilliant place, where we need no lamps, or sun, or moon to light our way, because we'll always be in the presence of Jesus.**

Ask a Junior to read Matthew 5:16. **The kind of light described in this verse is like a bike reflector or a mirror. When a light shines on it, it reflects back the light. That is how we are supposed to live: aimed toward Jesus, so that His light will be reflected out of our lives toward others. Let's pray and thank God for the light He brings us through Jesus.**

Father of Lights, we praise you because in you there is no darkness at all. We thank you for the best gift, Jesus, the Light of the World. May all the beautiful lights we see at this season remind us of your gift of life to us. Help us to shine with Your love and truth, so others can find their way in the darkness.

Offering (Group 6): **How many of you have a list of things you are hoping to receive for Christmas? Group 6 thought of some things Jesus would like to receive from us. They will tell us what they will give to Jesus now.** Ask Group 6 to tell about their gifts and place them under the tree. If you did not offer Group 6, ask "What are some attitudes or actions that you think Jesus would like to receive from us this Christmas?" Allow Juniors to respond.

When the presentation is completed, distribute slips of paper and pencils. Ask Juniors to write down a gift they would like to give Jesus. Have them fold their paper in half and write it down twice, one to keep as a reminder and one to place in the offering basket. Then have them tear the halves apart and place one in the offering basket.

Prayer: Choose several slips of paper from the offering baskets and tell God the gifts promised to Him. Close by thanking God for the gift of salvation through His Son, Jesus.

Closing Moments

Use the chalkboard or a sheet of newsprint on the wall. Play a version of "Wheel of Fortune" with names of Jesus. First draw the correct number of blanks on your paper. Let Juniors take turns guessing letters. When someone guesses the answer, have him find the verse in the Bible where this name is mentioned and read it to the group. Suggested names and Scriptures follow: lamb of God—John 1:29; great physician—Luke 4:23; son of David—Matthew 9:27; Yeshua—Luke 1:31; Prince of Peace—Isaiah 9:6; first begotten of the dead—Revelation 1:5; Immanuel—Isaiah 7:14; redeemer—Isaiah 59:20; lion of Judah—Revelation 5:5; dayspring from on high—Luke 1:78

God's Wisdom Protects Us

Worship Focus

Worship God because His wisdom protects us.

Transition Time
(10-15 minutes)

Send the Juniors in small groups to the rest room and drinking fountain. Welcome the Juniors and involve them in the following activity.

Snowflakes. You will need typing paper, scissors, and string. Before the session, make a sample snowflake.

Distribute the supplies to the Juniors. Display the sample snowflake. Give them the following instructions. **Fold your paper in half three times.** (Or fold your paper into eighths.) **Use your scissors to cut designs around the edges of the folded paper. Do not cut all the way across a folded section. Open your paper and see the snowflake design. Tie a string to your snowflake.** Attach the completed snowflakes to the ceiling or to a bulletin board.

Launching the Theme
(10 minutes)

We made some beautiful snowflakes. But what if you hadn't followed one of the instructions for making the snowflakes? They wouldn't have looked right, would they? You had to trust my wisdom about making snowflakes.

God instructs us about many things in the Bible. Even though we can't always see what could happen if we disobey His instructions, we need to trust His wisdom. God's wisdom will protect us from the bad things that can happen when we disobey. Today we will worship God because His wisdom protects us.

Building the Theme
(30 minutes)

1. Call to Worship. This group will prepare a choral reading about God's wisdom. You will need several sheets of newsprint, markers, and Bibles. Before the session, copy the following Bible verses on sheets of newsprint: Isaiah 40:28; Isaiah 55:9; Romans 11:33; 1 Corinthians 1:25; Daniel 2:20; Proverbs 3:19. Cut them apart so each verse is on a separate sheet of paper.

Explain to Juniors that your group will prepare a choral reading of Bible verses about God's wisdom. Distribute the sheets of newsprint and ask the Juniors to find the verses printed on the newsprint in their Bibles and read them aloud. Then ask them to decide which verses they want to include in their choral reading and in what order they want to present the verses. When they have decided on an order, ask them to decide which verses will be read solo, duet, by boys or girls only, or as a group. Write who will say each verse on the sheets of newsprint. When the reading is assembled, ask the group to practice reading it aloud. Practice the reading until the Juniors are comfortable with their parts.

During *Sharing in Worship,* Juniors will present the choral reading.

2. Prayer. This group will prepare a staircase about God's wisdom. You will need a large sheet of poster board or cardboard, markers, Bibles of several different versions, a dictionary, pencils, and scratch paper. Before the session, fold the poster board or cardboard so that it has nine-inch stair steps. (**Option:** draw the stairs on a sheet of newsprint.)

Ask Juniors find and read James 3:13-18. **How does a person show he is truly wise?** (By living right, doing good things.) **What are some of the characteristics of worldly wisdom?** (Jealousy, selfishness, confusion, every kind of evil.) Display the staircase you made. **Write on the steps the characteristics of God's wisdom. Begin at the bottom. Then decide on an explanation or definition of each characteristic.** Provide several Bible versions for Juniors to use to see how the words are explained in James 3:17. Suggested definitions follow: pure—no evil thoughts or words; peace loving—doesn't fight; considerate—thinking of others' needs; submissive—willing to listen to others; full of mercy—forgives other when they do wrong; full of good fruit—good things happen because of this wisdom; impartial—no favorites; sincere—honest motives. Ask the Juniors to write their definitions on scratch paper, then copy them onto the staircase. Ask each Junior to think of a praise sentence to God for one of the characteristics of wisdom. For example, "God, You are wise. Thank You for teaching us that we are wise when we don't fight."

During *Sharing in Worship*, Juniors will display the staircase and praise God for His wisdom.

3. Lord's Supper. This group will prepare posters showing how God protects us. You will need copies of activity page 18A, seven pieces of poster board or lightweight cardboard (cut a poster board into fourths to make the pieces), pencils, markers, and Bibles.

Distribute Bibles, pencils, and activity pages. **Look at the items on your activity page. How does each item protect us? What does it protect us from?** Allow Juniors to respond. **What does God use to protect us? We are going to read some Bible verses that will tell us.** Assign each Junior a verse from the activity page to find and read. Allow about four minutes for Juniors find the verses. **What do these verses say about God's protection?** Answers follow: Psalm 25:21—Goodness and honesty guard me; Psalm 40:11—God's love and truth protect me; Proverbs 2:11—good sense and understanding protect me; Proverbs 4:6—using wisdom and loving wisdom keeps us safe; Proverbs 2:8—when we are fair to others and loyal to God, He protects us; Psalm 73:28—when we are close to God, He protects us.

Assign each Junior an object that protects from the activity page. Ask them to write one sentence about the object's protection and one sentence about God's protection. For example, "A hat protects me from the rain or hot sun. But God says if I am fair to other people and loyal to Him, He will protect me." Distribute the pieces of poster board. Ask the Juniors to draw their protection object on the poster board and write their Scripture verse below it.

During *Sharing in Worship*, Juniors will display their posters and say their sentences about God's protection.

4. Scripture. This group will prepare skits about wisdom. You will need Bibles, pencils, scratch paper, and small sheets of newsprint. Before the session, select 4-6 of the following Scriptures from Proverbs for your Juniors to use to create skits about wisdom: 27:12; 9:12; 2:7; 25:12; 28:16; 28:26; 29:3; 3:7; 8:11; 9:11.

Find and read the verses you have selected. Discuss how to present skits about the verses. Suggestions follow:

Proverbs 27:12: "When a wise person sees danger ahead, he avoids it, but a foolish person keeps going and gets into trouble." Two people labeled *wise* and *foolish* see a person holding a danger sign. The *wise* person turns away, while the *foolish* person keeps going and bumps into the person with the danger sign.

Proverbs 9:12: "The person who makes fun of wisdom suffers for it." One person is labeled *wisdom*. Another person follows *wisdom*, laughing, pointing to him, and making fun. The person making fun of *wisdom* keeps tripping and hurting himself, or experiencing accidents.

Proverbs 2:7: "God stores up wisdom for those who are honest." A person labeled *God* is piling up sheets of paper labeled wisdom for a person who is labeled *honest*. The *honest* person is doing something honest, such as returning too much change.

Assign Juniors to work in pairs or groups of three to prepare and practice their skits. When presenting the skits, one person should read the proverb aloud before the skit is presented. Allow the groups to practice their skits before the small group.

During *Sharing in Worship*, Juniors will present the skits.

5. Devotional. This group will prepare a game showing things or people God protects us from. You will need twenty sheets of construction paper, crayons, markers, scissors, Bibles, scratch paper, pencils, tape or Plasti-Tak, stop watch or egg timer. Before the session, make a copy of the pattern illustrated on this page—the symbol for "not allowed here."

One thing that makes us thankful for God's protection is knowing all the things we need to be protected from. Our job is to prepare a game which will help us all remember why we need God's wise protection.

Distribute Bibles, scratch paper, and pencils. Assign each Junior to look up one or two of the following Bible verses and discover one problem from which we need protection. Answers are in parentheses. Scriptures follow: 1 Peter 5:8 (devil); Ephesians 6:16 (flaming arrows of Satan); 2 Peter 2:1 (false teachers); Proverbs 11:2 (pride); 1 Corinthians 10:13 (temptation); 2 Peter 3:17 (evil people); Proverbs 1:10 (sinners enticing you); Luke 12:15 (greed); Jude 18 (scoffers who follow ungodly desires); 1 Timothy 6:10 (love of money). Have Juniors share their answers. Explain any unfamiliar words or phrases. **Why do we need protection from these things? How will God protect us?**

Give each Junior two pieces of construction paper. On one sheet of construction paper, ask them to draw a simple sketch that represents what we need protection from. They will not write the Scripture reference on the drawing. On the other sheet of construction paper, Juniors will draw the symbol for "not allowed here." Show them the pattern you made before class. On the outline of the circle they will print, "The Lord God is my protection." Psalm 73:28. Ask Juniors to attach their drawings to the wall using tape or Plasti-Tak.

During *Sharing in Worship,* Juniors will read their verses and ask the large group to guess which drawing pictures what God protects us from in that verse. The Junior who answers correctly may use tape or Plasti-Tak to place one of the circle symbols on top of that drawing.

6. Personal Praise. This group will prepare coded words that tell how we feel when God protects us. You will need Bibles, scratch paper, a blank transparency, an overhead projector, a marker, and pencils.

How does a person feel when God protects him? Allow Juniors to respond. Distribute Bibles. Ask the Juniors to find and read aloud the following verses from Psalms: Psalm 4:8 (sleep in peace); 5:11 (sing for joy); 9:10 (trust); 23:4 (no fear); 28:8 (strong). After each verse is read, ask the Juniors to tell how a person feels when God protects him. Write their answers on a piece of paper. **We are going to make a code of our answers for the large group.** Ask the Juniors to prepare a code, using numbers or shapes for letters. Ask a volunteer to write the code at the top of the transparency while other Juniors are writing the answers from their Bible verses in code on their scratch paper. Then Juniors can take turns transferring their coded answer to the transparency.

When the transparency is completed, ask Juniors to draw a picture or write a sentence telling why they are thankful God's protections makes us feel the way mentioned in their verse. For example, for "sleep in peace" a Junior could say, "I am thankful that God protects me because I don't have to be afraid in my dark room at night."

During *Sharing in Worship,* Juniors will project the transparency on the wall and ask the large group to decode the words. After each feeling is decoded, the Junior will say the reason He is thankful for that feeling.

Sharing in Worship
(20-25 minutes)

Omit any of the following sections if you did not offer the corresponding activity. The Lord's Supper and devotional may be completed without the presentations of Groups 3 and 5.

Call to Worship: Group 1 presents their choral reading.

Prayer (Group 2): **God protects us in many ways. One of the ways He protects us is by telling us what is wise. When we know what true wisdom is, we are protected from the bad things that happen when we disobey. I'm thankful that God tells us what true wisdom is. Group 2 will thank God for the true wisdom He tells us about.** Ask Group 2 to present their staircase and praise prayers.

Lord's Supper (Group 3): **Can you think of some things you own or use for your protection?** (Allow response.) **Those things are important, but God's protection is even more important. Group 3 will tell us about God's protection.** Group 3 presents their posters and information about God's protection. Point out or make a list of all the actions that bring God's protection: goodness, honesty, love and truth, good sense, understanding, wisdom, being fair to others, being loyal to God, being close to God.

If you did not offer this activity, choose several of the Scriptures listed in the activity to read to your Juniors. Ask them to tell you what each Scripture says about God's protection.

What is the most important protection a Christian has? It is the protection from the punishment for his sins. When Jesus is your Savior, your sins are gone. Satan can no longer accuse you or confuse you. God planned that the Lord's Supper would be a simple way to remember the great protection He gives through Jesus' blood. Pray and serve the Lord's Supper.

Offering: Many people pay a lot of money to buy things to protect them. They buy expensive clothing to protect them from injury, alarms for their homes or cars to protect them from robbery, and on and on. But the best protection we can receive—God's protection—has been paid for already by Jesus' death. Now is our time to freely give to God to thank Him for the way He cares for us and protects us. Choose two children to collect the offering.

Scripture (Group 4): **The book of Proverbs gives us some specific pictures of how a wise man should and should not act. If we want to praise God by our actions, let's get some ideas from these skits by group 4.** Group 4 presents skits.

Devotional (Group 5): You will need copies of activity page 18B and materials for the game prepared by Group 5.

We have been talking about ways God's wisdom protects us. But what do we need protection from? Group 6 studied some Scriptures and prepared a game to help us find the answer to that

question. Lead the protection game described in Group 6. If you did not offer this activity, choose several of the Scriptures to read to your Juniors. Ask them, "What does this verse say we need protection from."

God is wise enough to give us protection from all these things. He is wiser than any person on earth. Let's think of some ways to complete this sentence: God is like a wise ___________. Distribute the activity page and ask Juniors to think about the people on the page.

When I think of wisdom, I think of a judge. How is God like a judge? (Allow Juniors to respond.) **A judge is the one who can tell when the people in his courtroom are telling the truth. He makes sure that people are treated with justice and fairness. We can praise God today for His fairness.**

Another picture I see is a wise father. How is God like a wise father? (Allow Juniors to respond.) **A wise father takes time to listen carefully to each of his children. He senses their personalities. He plans his discipline and training to fit each individual child. We can praise God today for His compassion.**

And don't forget the wise old trail guide. How is God like a trail guide? (Allow Juniors to respond.) **If you are going camping or headed on a hike through the mountains, a trail guide's advice is the best to follow. He has experience. He knows the safest and easiest trails. We can praise God today for showing us the way to follow Him.**

Of course wisdom makes us think of a teacher or a professor. How is God like a wise teacher? (Allow Juniors to respond.) **A wise teacher does more than just talk. She knows the right questions to ask or the right experiments to show her students so they will want to find the answers. She has stimulated their curiosity. We can praise God today for teaching us.**

Or how about a wise doctor? How is God like a doctor? (Allow Juniors to respond.) **A wise doctor knows more than just the most modern medicines and treatments. He knows his patients, and how to help them get well. We can praise God today for His loving treatment.**

Finally, God is like a wise general. How is God like a general? (Allow Juniors to respond.) **The general always knows what his troops can do. He keeps them well supplied. He knows everything about the enemy and makes careful plans to protect his troops in battle. We can praise God today for His protection.**

Today we praise God for His wise protection with our songs and prayers and skits and games. During the week we can continue our praise. God is praised when we act with fairness and honestly like the wise judge. God is praised when we listen carefully, as though to a wise father. God is praised when we follow His advice, like the advice of a trail guide. God is praised when we are willing to learn, as we would from a wise teacher. God is praised when we obey His plan, the way we would obey a doctor's orders. God is praised when we stay under His protection, the way an army would take orders from their general.

Personal Praise (Group 6): **God's great wisdom includes a plan to take care of you. How does that make you feel? The Bible tells us how God's protection can make us feel. Group 6 will help us praise God for how His protection makes us feel.** Display the transparency prepared by Group 6 and allow the large group to decode each answer. After each answer, a Junior from the small group will say a praise sentence about God's protection.

Closing Moments
(10-15 minutes)

You will need old magazines. Ask Juniors to look in the magazines for pictures of things that either break or don't work when not used according to directions: for example, leaving a wagon or bike out in the weather; never changing the oil in a car; using a hair dryer to heat a room; a camera won't work without film; a flashlight won't work without batteries; plants won't grow without light or water; taking more medicine than prescribed, and so on. Ask each Junior to tell about the pictures he or she found. **When we don't use things according to the directions, they break down or simply won't work. Our lives are the same way. When we don't follow God's wisdom and His directions, our lives will not be right.**

God's Plans Are Best

Worship Focus

Worship God because His plans give us true happiness.

Transition Time
(10-15 minutes)

Send Juniors to the rest room and drinking fountain in small groups. Welcome them and involve them in the following activity.

Treasure Hunt. Before the session wrap some boxes with fancy paper and ribbon. Leave the boxes empty, or put rocks, or broken objects inside. Also prepare several small plain paper bags. Fill these with money from a monopoly game, or with the snacks for the day. Have an equal number of bags and wrapped boxes. Hide them around your room.

Announce a treasure hunt. Tell the group how many objects they are looking for, but don't say "boxes." Explain that the objects are inside the room Divide into teams if you wish. Set a timer.

When the timer goes off, have Juniors show treasures they have found. If none looked inside the paper bags, show them now. If you played in teams, the team who found the most treasures, wins.

Launching the Theme
(10 minutes)

You will need a bruised apple, shiny apple, a dirty sock, new sock, pencil stub, new pencil, broken cookie, whole cookie.

Discuss the game used in Transition Time. **When we look for treasure, we sometimes don't really know what we're looking for. It's the same with happiness. We may think new shoes or new clothes or a new Nintendo™ game will make us happy. But when we get what thought we wanted, it doesn't make us happy. We just want more. Fortunately we have a heavenly Father who does know just what will satisfy us and bring joy to our lives.**

Display the items you brought to the session. **Which of these items would you prefer? Why?** Allow volunteers to come up and choose one item from each pair. **We usually want the best for ourselves. We think we know what will make us happy. We need to remind ourselves that God also wants the very best for us. His plans will truly make us happy. Today we will worship God because His plans give us true happiness.**

Explain the choices of *Building the Theme* activities. Allow the children to choose in which group to participate.

Building the Theme
(30 minutes)

1. Call to Worship. This group will prepare a worship lantern of ways to prepare our hearts for worship. You will need copies of activity page 19B, Bibles, pencils, markers, scissors, and glue.

When you go somewhere, you usually need to prepare. To prepare for school, you collect your homework, lunch money, and school supplies. To prepare for a trip to the supermarket, your mom usually makes a list and sorts out her coupons. To prepare for a trip to the beach or the mountains, you pack your clothes and other items and plan where you will go and what you will do. But how do you prepare to go to church? Our group will investigate some Scriptures so we can share ideas about how to prepare for worship.

Distribute the activity pages, pencils and Bibles. Assign Juniors to find and read aloud the verses on the activity page. Ask everyone to fill in the blanks after each Scripture is read. Then ask Juniors to color and cut out their worship lantern. They will cut around the outside of the lantern. Then they will fold it on the dotted line and cut on the solid lines in the middle.

During *Sharing in Worship*, assign Juniors to read one of the verses from the lantern.

2. Lord's Supper. This group will prepare a rebus of a verse about God's love. You will need a poster board, paper, scissors, glue, and markers. Before the session, write 1 Corinthians 2:9 (*NIV*) in large letters on poster board. "No eye has seen, no ear has heard, no mind has conceived what God has prepared for those who love him."

If you could have your favorite meal, what would it be? Juniors respond. **If you could receive a special gift, what would you want it to be?** Juniors respond. **If I had asked you those same questions when you were four years old, what would you**

have said? Allow for response.

Our ideas about what we want for ourselves—our favorite food, our special desires—change during our lives. If God gave us everything we said we wanted, He'd be making daily deliveries because our lists would change so often. But the Bible says that God really does know what will be best for each of us. And that's what He has planned.

Display the poster board. Ask a Junior to read aloud 1 Corinthians 2:9. **What does this verse tell us that God has in store for us? Something more beautiful than we could visualize, something more wonderful than we could imagine, something more marvelous than we could plan. How should that make us feel? Important to God, special, and cared for!**

Our group will prepare a rebus of this verse to share with the group. When you make a rebus, you replace as many words as possible with pictures. Let's work through the verse together, trying to find pictures and symbols we can use. Jot down ideas on paper. Then assign Juniors to draw the pictures on the paper and glue them over the appropriate words on the poster board.

During *Sharing in Worship*, Juniors will display the poster board and ask the large group to decode the verse. Then they will say the verse together.

3. Prayer. This group will prepare a poster of things the Bible says bring happiness to introduce the prayer time. You will need three pieces of poster board cut into quarters, markers, Bibles, scratch paper, and pencils

Looking for happiness: our treasure hunt showed that it's not easy to do. Christians know that the one place to find a plan for happiness would be the Bible. One particular chapter in Psalms seems to have quite a bit of advice on happiness. Let's look at these verses and see what God says will make a person happy.

Assign Juniors to find and read the verses and tell what is mentioned that brings happiness. Answers are included in the Scripture list. Scriptures follow: Psalm 119: 1—living pure lives; Psalm 119:2—keeping God's rules; Psalm 119:14—living by God's rules; Psalm 119:16—obeying God's demands; Psalm 119:24—God's rules that give good advice; Psalm 119:32—God's commands; Psalm 119:35—obeying God's commands; Psalm 119:47—obeying God's commands; Psalm 119:111—following God's rules; Psalm 119:162—God's promises.

Review the ideas Juniors have found. Discuss how they could illustrate each concept. Assign a verse for each Junior to illustrate. Distribute the poster board sections. Ask Juniors to illustrate their verse on the poster board.

During *Sharing in Worship*, ask the Juniors to display their posters and tell what the Bible verse says will make us happy.

4. Scripture. This group will prepare scrambled words of the wrong ways that Solomon tried to find happiness. You will need Bibles, pencils, scratch paper, a sheet of newsprint, and markers.

Have you ever known someone who took the wrong route to get somewhere? Perhaps he made a wrong turn, or chose a crowded freeway instead of a quiet country road. Perhaps the road he chose was closed for repair or closed because a parade was temporarily marching through the streets. Whatever the reason, he didn't reach his destination. Solomon was an example of a person who took the wrong route. He began his kingship by asking God for wisdom. But instead of following God's "road map," Solomon tried every side road and short cut he came across, just in case it might give him some happiness. As a result, he made many wrong turns and ended his life very unsatisfied.

Our task today is to prepare a list of the various "wrong turns" Solomon tried and found to be unsatisfying. Then we'll make a scrambled word puzzle to share these ideas in large group time.

Distribute Bibles, scratch paper, and pencils. Ask the Juniors look up the Scriptures from Ecclesiastes and find one "wrong turn" that Solomon tried. Answers are included in the Scripture list. Scriptures from Ecclesiastes follow: 1:18—wisdom (this probably refers to man's knowledge, not to following God's wisdom); 3:9—toil or work; 4:16—fame or power; 5:10—money; 7:26—women (explain that Solomon unwisely disobeyed God's plan to take only one wife. He took hundreds of wives, and they were the ones who persuaded him to worship idols.); Proverbs 23:20—drinking or drunkenness. Ask Juniors to jot their answers on the scratch paper. Then ask them to scramble up each word and take turns writing the scrambled words on the sheet of newsprint.

During *Sharing in Worship*, ask the Juniors to read each of the Scriptures aloud and ask the large group to unscramble the words.

5. Devotional. This group will memorize verses about happiness. You will need sixteen sheets of construction paper or lightweight poster board, markers, and Bibles. Before the session write Ecclesiastes 12:13 on the pieces of construction paper, one word to a sheet of paper. The Scripture reference will be on one piece of construction paper. "Honor God and obey his commands. This is the most important thing people can do." Ecclesiastes 12:13. On the other side of the construction paper, write Matthew 6:33, using a different color pen. You will need to put two words together on three of the sheets. "Seek first the kingdom of God and His righteousness and all these things shall be added unto you." Matthew 6:33. Scramble the the sheets with the Ecclesiastes verse showing and arrange them on a table or the floor.

If we took a survey at your school, how do you think most kids would answer this question: What are the ten top things that bring happiness? Jot down their answers and discuss why they think these answers would be important to most kids.

Then ask Juniors to try to arrange the Bible verse in the correct order without looking up the Scripture. After a few minutes have them check their answer by finding the verse in the Bible. Have them say the verse together aloud. Then remove two or three of the pieces of construction paper. Ask the group to repeat the verse again. Remove two or three more pieces of construction paper. Repeat the verse again. Continue removing sheets and reciting the verse until the Juniors can say the verse from memory.

Why is this verse a solution to finding happiness? Let Juniors respond. **Because God made us and knows us and loves us, He has the best plan for making us happy. There is a New Testament verse which gives the same message.** Have Juniors turn over the sheets and place the words to Matthew 6:33 in the correct order. Then ask them to memorize the verse, using the same method as before.

During *Sharing in Worship*, Juniors will quote the two verses.

6. Devotional. This group will write what will make Juniors happy in specific situations. You will need copies of activity page 19A, scratch paper, and pencils

Distribute the activity page. Read Philippians 4:4, 12 together. **The Juniors on this page think some things will make them happy. But these verses in Philippians tell us what will really make them happy.** Assign each Junior or pair of Juniors one situation. Ask them to decide what the person thinks will make them happy. Then ask them to write a letter to the person, telling him or her how to really be happy. Answers follow:
Angelina—friends; Jessica—nice clothes; Brandon—playing sports; Jeff—getting good grades. When Juniors have completed their letters, ask them to share them with the group.

During *Sharing in Worship*, Juniors will read the situations and then read their written responses.

Sharing in Worship
(20-25 minutes)

Omit any of the following sections if you did not offer the corresponding activity. The Lord's Supper and devotional may be completed without the presentations of Groups 2, 5, and 6.

Call to Worship (Group 1): **We prepare for many things. We prepare to go to school by getting dressed and gathering our books and lunch money. We prepare to go on vacation by packing our suitcases. But how do we prepare to worship God? Group 1 will read some Bible verses, telling us how to prepare to worship God.** Group 1 presents their worship lanterns and Scripture verses.

Music: Sing "Come Into His Presence Singing Alleluia" from page 177.

Lord's Supper (Group 2): **Our ideas about what is best for us change during our lives. The things that we think make us happy now are different from the things we thought made us happy when we were three or four years old. If God gave us everything we thought we wanted, He'd have to make daily deliveries because we change our mind so often. But the Bible says that God really does know what is best for us. And He has great things planned for us. See if you can discover what this verse that Group 2 prepared says about what God has planned for us.** Ask Group 2 to present their rebus poster, and allow the large group to guess what the verse says. If you did not offer this activity, read 1 Corinthians 2:9 to the Juniors.

We can't even imagine what wonderful things God has prepared for us. But we can get some idea of how wonderful they will be because we already know the most wonderful thing God has done for us. He sent Jesus, His only Son, to die for us so our sins could be forgiven. Let's remember God's great love now. Pray and serve the Lord's Supper.

Offering: Jesus said "It is more blessed to give than to receive," Acts 20:35. And Paul wrote, "God loves a cheerful giver," 2 Corinthians 9:7. These verses give us a clue that our giving is to be a joyful experience. The blessing we receive when we give is greater than the blessing of getting. Giving to God is not something that we "hafta" do, it's a privilege that brings joy. Choose two children to collect the offering.

Prayer (Group 3): **How does God make us happy? Do we instantly become happy when we know Him? One way God helps us is by telling us in the Bible how we can be happy. In fact, there is a chapter in Psalms that says a lot about how to be happy. Group 3 found out what Psalm 119 says about happiness.** Ask Group 3 to share their posters about happiness. Then pray, asking each Junior to thank God for a way He makes them happy.

Scripture (Group 4): **King Solomon was one person in the Bible who went on an all out**

search for happiness. In fact, Solomon wrote a book of the Bible called Ecclesiastes about the ways He tried to be happy. Ask Group 4 to display their scrambled words and have the large group discover how Solomon looked for happiness.

Devotional (Groups 5 and 6): You will need a camera; several old and faded black and white photographs; bright colorful pictures of Jesus, a church building, and Christians in action.

When I think of someone in the Bible who had just about everything he could want, I think of Solomon. He had money, power, peace, control of his time, possessions. And he looked to all those things for happiness. But in the end of the book of Ecclesiastes, Solomon tells us what he found truly makes us happy. Ask Group 5 to quote Ecclesiastes 12:13. If you did not offer this activity, read the verse from your Bible. **Solomon was right. In fact, Jesus says something similar about our happiness in the New Testament.** Ask Group 5 to quote Matthew 6:33. If you did not offer this activity, read the verse.

Jesus' message is the same as Solomon's, because God's plan never changes. He always wants what it best for us. Display old, faded photographs. **Just for a moment, imagine Solomon with a camera around his neck as he takes his journey through life. His snapshots are all dark shadowy pictures. No color, no real life. He labels each picture, "Empty," "Meaningless," "Vanity," "Nothing." Solomon was miserable because he looked in the wrong places for happiness.**

Sometimes we look in the wrong places for happiness too. But we have the Bible to tell us what we can do. Read Philippians 4:4, 12. **These verses tell us what to do when we think the wrong things can make us happy. Listen to the Juniors in these situations. What do they think will make them happy?** Ask Juniors from Group 6 to read their situations. After each situation is read, ask the large group to tell what the person thinks will make him or her happy. Then ask each Junior to read the letter he or she wrote, telling the person how to truly be happy. If you did not offer this activity, read the situations on activity page 19A and ask your Juniors to say how they would respond to those Juniors.

Display color pictures next to the old, faded pictures. **Imagine that we have a camera around our neck like we imagined Solomon did. But because we are following God's plan for our lives, our pictures are bright and colorful. God's plans bring us true happiness.**

Prayer: Close with prayer, praising God for the happiness His plans give us.

Closing Moments
(10-15 minutes)

Before the session, record (or ask a musician to record) a tape of familiar songs about happiness or joy. Record only the music, not the words. Divide Juniors into two or three teams. The first team to guess each song receives a point. Suggested songs follow: "Happy Am I," "Happiness Is," "I've Got the Joy Down in My Heart," "I've Got Peace like a River," "The Joy of the Lord Is My Strength."

God Is Trustworthy

Worship Focus
Worship God because He is trustworthy.

Transition Time
(10-15 minutes)
Send the Juniors in small groups to the rest room and drinking fountain. Welcome Juniors and involve them in the following activity.

Trust Game. Ask Juniors to sit in a circle. One Junior says to the Junior on his right, "I can _______. Do you trust me?" The statement can be true or false, but it must be something that can be done in the classroom. The person to whom the question was directed says whether or not he or she believes the Junior's claim. If the respondent says "Yes," then it is his turn to say, "I can _______. Do you trust me?" to the person on his right. If the respondent answers, "No," then the first Junior must prove what he or she claimed to be able to do. If the Junior can do it, the doubter must walk around the room once, repeating, "I doubted a trustworthy person." If the Junior cannot carry out his claim, he must walk around the room once, repeating, "I am not trustworthy." Continue playing around the circle. Remind Juniors that God is always trustworthy. Following is a list of possible claims: I can list all the 50 states in two minutes; I can hop on my foot for one minute without putting my other foot down; I can walk across the room blindfolded without stumbling; I can count to ten in Spanish; I can list fifteen presidents in two minutes; I can say all the books of the Old Testament; I can say all the books of the New Testament; I can list ten miracles of Jesus; I can list all ten plagues; I can list the twelve apostles; I can walk across the room with a book on my head without it falling off.

Launching the Theme
(10 minutes)
Distribute slips of paper and pencils. **Imagine that your family is going to live in Africa for one year. You can only take a few clothes with you. No toys, no bike. You have to trust someone to take care of all your stuff while you are gone. Of course, you will want all your things returned in good condition after that year is over. Write down the name of an adult you would trust to take care of your belongings.** Let each Junior write his response on a piece of paper. Collect and tally the answers on the chalkboard. **These must be people whom you feel are very trustworthy. When you trust someone, you believe that the person will keep his word. We praise God today because He is always trustworthy.**

Explain the choices of *Building the Theme* activities

Building the Theme
(30 minutes)
1. Call to Worship. This group will prepare activities to introduce the worship time. You will need copies of activity page 20A, Bibles, and pencils.

Last week, we talked about how we need to prepare to worship God. When we come to worship God, we need to have our hearts or our attitudes ready to worship. What kind of attitude do we need to have to worship? (Humble or not proud, respectful, and so on.) **We also need to have our minds ready to worship. What should we be thinking about and what should we not be thinking about when we come to worship?** (Think about God—how great He is and what He has done; don't think about ourselves or the things we are doing.) **We are going to prepare our hearts and minds to worship God.**

Distribute activity page 20A and ask Juniors to complete the page. Encourage them to work quietly since this is a personal time between God and them. When Juniors are completed, ask them to share some of their answers. Ask one Junior to read Psalm 46:10 during the worship time. Ask several Juniors to share the words they wrote that describe God; ask several to share the things they are thankful with; and ask several to share how they feel about God.

During *Sharing in Worship*, ask Juniors to share from each section of the activity page.

2. Special Music. This group will sing and illustrate a song about God's promises. You will need "God's Promise Is a Promise" from page 179, a sheet of newsprint, markers, scratch paper, and a dictionary. Before the session, write the words to the song on the newsprint.

What does it mean to trust God? (Allow responses.) **We can describe trust in many different ways. Let's look in a dictionary to see how many ways we can describe our trust in God.** Ask Juniors to find the word *trust* in the dictionary and read the definitions. Then ask them to put some of those definitions into a sentence about God. For example: "I depend on God." "I am confident God will do what He says." "I believe in God." "I hope in God." "I know what God says is true." "I rely on God." Record their sentences on the scratch paper.

Display the words of the song for the Juniors. **We are going to sing a song about trusting in God's promises.** Sing the song for the Juniors. Then ask them to sing it with you several times. When the Juniors are comfortable singing the song, assign each Junior one sentence about trust in God from the list they made.

During *Sharing in Worship*, Juniors will say their sentences before the song is sung and during the musical introduction. Then they will sing the song. Practice the presentation during the small-group time.

3. Personal Praise. This group will prepare a responsive reading, praising God for His promises. You will need copies of activity page 20B, Bible, pencils, and markers.

What is a promise that your Mom or Dad made to you and kept? (Allow response.) **Can you think of a promise your Mom or Dad made that they have not kept yet?** (Allow responses, such as my mom promised that I can get my ears pierced when I'm 14; or my dad says he will take me fishing during spring break.)

The Bible is full of promises that God has made. Many of the promises have already been fulfilled. For example, He promised thousands of years before it happened to send Jesus. But many of the promises are ones that relate directly to our lives in the present or the future. Our assignment today is to prepare a responsive reading, mentioning some of these promises and praising God because we know that they will come true. In a responsive reading, we prepare a sentence that the whole group repeats many times, and in between we will fill in with some of the promises we find. Distribute the activity pages. Assign one Scripture to each Junior or pair of Juniors. Ask them to find the promise in the Scripture. Answers follow: 1 John 1:9—to forgive our sins; Acts 2:38—to give us the Holy Spirit; 1 Corinthians 10:13—to provide an escape in temptation; Luke 11:9—to answer prayer; Hebrews 13:5—to always be with us; Revelation 21:4—to deliver from sorrow and pain; 1 John 2:25—to give eternal life.

When Juniors have found their Scriptures, ask them to share the promises with the group. **Why are you thankful for the promise you found?** (Allow response.) **Think of a sentence, telling God why you are thankful for that promise and write it on the lines by your Scripture.**

During *Sharing in Worship*, each Junior or pair will read the sentence, praising God for a promise in Scripture. After each sentence is read, the whole group will say together, "The Lord will do what He says."

4. Devotional. This group will prepare a spider web showing false things in which people trust. You will need a sheet of newspaper, scissors, Bibles, pencils, markers, and scratch paper. Before the session, use the pattern on this page to draw a large "spider's web" on an unfolded sheet of newspaper.

What kinds of things to people trust in if they don't know about trusting in God? Jot down the Juniors' answers on

scratch paper.

Ask a Junior to read Job 8:13-15: "That is what will happen to everyone who forgets God. The hope of the person without God will be gone. What he trust in is easily broken. It is as easily broken as a spider's web. He holds on to it, but it does not hold him up" (*ICB*).

Have you ever walked into a spider's web? It's a bit of a sticky experience, but none of you look any worse for the experience. A spider web is a fragile, frail, temporary construction. It's good for trapping insects. It can be pretty to look at. But it's not very sturdy. Point to the list of things Juniors named in which people trust. **These things are like a spider web. They may look like they can be trusted, but they won't last. The Bible also tells us some things that cannot be trusted. Let's find out what the Bible says.**

Ask each Junior to look up one of the following Scriptures and discover one "fragile thing" not to be trusted. Answers are included for your reference. Scriptures follow: Proverbs 31:30—beauty; Psalm 146:3—men's promises; Proverbs 11:28—riches; Proverbs 27:1—tomorrow; 1 Peter 1:24—earthly glory; Job 19:19—friends; Proverbs 28:26—self; Psalm 44:6, 7—weapons.

Ask each Juniors to write the thing that cannot be trusted on one strand of the spider web you prepared.

During *Sharing in Worship*, Juniors will read the Scriptures about things that cannot be trusted.

5. Devotional. This group will read Scriptures telling why God can be trusted. You will need one large rock for each Junior, tape, markers, paper, Bibles, and pencils.

Imagine that you are preparing to build a house. You must select the proper site. You have a choice between some lovely beachfront property with acres of sandy beach, and an area with no beach, but a solid rock bottom. Which do you choose? Why? Of course you take the rock, because the sand will erode and your house will be washed away.

When we say that God is trustworthy, it means He is like a rock. You can build your life on His promises and plans, and be sure that your life will not be washed away. Ask a Junior to read Psalm 18:2, 3. **What are some reasons we can trust God? How do we know that He is trustworthy?** (The Bible tells us He is; He kept His promises in the Bible; He keeps His promises to us; He sent Jesus like He promised.)

Today our task is to prepare these rocks for a demonstration during the worship time. We'll be looking up some Bible verses that remind us of how trustworthy God is. Then we'll write what the verses tell us about why we can trust God on the rocks.

Assign one of the following Scriptures to each Junior. Answers are included for your reference. Scriptures follow: Romans 4:21—Abraham was fully persuaded that God had the power to do what he promised; Joshua 21:45—Not one of the good promises which the Lord made to the house of Israel failed, all came to pass; Joshua 23:14b—Not one of all the good promises the Lord your God gave you has failed. Every promise has been fulfilled; not one has failed; Deuteronomy 7:9—Know therefore that the Lord your God is God; he is the faithful God, keeping his covenant of love to a thousand generations of those who love him and keep his commands; 1 Corinthians 1:9—God, who has called you into fellowship with his Son Jesus Christ our Lord, is faithful; Hebrews 6:18—These two things cannot change. God cannot lie when he makes a promise, and he cannot lie when he makes an oath.

Ask the Juniors to tell what the verses say about God's trustworthiness and write it on a rock. They may write on paper and tape it to the rocks if the surface is too rough to write on.

During *Sharing in Worship*, Juniors will read about God's trustworthiness from their rocks and place them in a pile.

6. Prayer. This group will illustrate and lead a prayer, thanking God for times He kept His promises in the Bible. You will need a piece of clothesline or twine, twelve clothespins, twelve sheets of construction paper, crayons, markers, Bibles, scratch paper, and old Bible teaching pictures or Sunday-school story papers. Before the session, string a clothesline across the front of your worship area.

One reason we know we can trust God to do what He says is because God always kept His promises to people in the Bible. Can you think of some promises God kept in the Bible? (Allow Juniors to respond.) Assign each Junior or pair of Juniors one of the following Scriptures. Answers are included for your reference. Scriptures follow: Genesis 6:13—God promised to send the flood; Genesis 18:32—God promised to spare Sodom if ten righteous could be found; Genesis 18:10—God promised Abraham a son; Genesis 50:24—God promised to deliver the Israelites out of Egypt Genesis; Exodus 12:12, 13—God promised to kill the firstborn in Egypt and spare the Israelites; Exodus 14:16—God promised to open the Red Sea for the Israelites; Luke 1:13, 14—God promised the birth of John the Baptist; Luke 1:13—God promised the birth of Jesus; Matthew 16:21—God promised to raise Jesus from the dead.

Read your Scripture and tell what promise God made or kept in the Scripture. Distribute construction paper and markers. Ask the Juniors to draw an illustration of the promise God made and kept. Or they may cut pictures from old teaching pictures and Sunday-school papers.

Let's thank God that we can trust Him because He kept His promises to people in the Bible. Think of a praise prayer to say to God about the promise you found. An example follows: "Thank You, God. I know I can trust You because You promised Noah the flood would come, and it did." "You are great, God. I trust you because you said Jesus would come back alive, and He did." Distribute clothespins to the Juniors and decide in which order they will pray.

During *Sharing in Worship*, each Junior will attach his or her drawing to the clothesline and say the praise prayer.

Sharing in Worship
(20-25 minutes)

Omit any of the following sections if you did not offer the corresponding activity. The devotional may be completed without the presentations of Groups 4 and 5.

Call to Worship (Group 1): **When we come to worship God, our hearts and minds need to be prepared to worship. In other words, we need to have an attitude of worship, and we need to be thinking about God, rather than ourselves. Group 1 will help us prepare our hearts and minds for worship now.** Read each section of the activity page, asking the Juniors you assigned during the small-group time to share their responses.

Special Music (Group 2): **What does it mean to trust God? Group 2 will share some different meanings for trust and sing a song about trusting God's promises.** Group 2 shares.

Lord's Supper: 2 Timothy 2:13 says, "If we are not faithful, he will still be faithful." God is always ready for us to turn to Him no matter what. This communion is a reminder of God's faithfulness. Pray and serve the Lord's Supper.

Offering: Choose two children to collect the offering.

Personal Praise (Group 3): **When we trust God, we believe that He will do what He says He will do. Group 3 will lead us in thanking God for doing what He says.** Group 3 presents the responsive reading. Ask the large group to join them in saying, "The Lord will do what He says."

Devotional (Groups 4 and 5): You will need a dishpan half full of water, a cup for pouring, a roll of paper towels for wiping spills, a small electric fan, the spider web made by group 4, the rocks from group 5, two medium-size houses made out of blocks that snap together (or something else that will break up if you place it on top of the newspaper spider web.

This spider web made by group 4, mentions some of the things that we often trust in, forgetting that they are as frail as a spider web. Ask a Junior read Job 8:13-15. Then ask the members of group 4 to read the Scriptures and name the things that can't be trusted.

Now ask the members of group 4 to hold on to the strands of the spider web. Place the web over the dishpan and pour water over it. Remove the dishpan. Turn on the fan and blow the air on the spider web. **Our spider web is beginning to experience some difficulties. I wonder what will happen when we use it as a foundation for our home.** Take one of the block houses and place it in the middle of the spider web. The paper won't support it, and it will crash to the ground.

Let's take a more positive approach. We know what things we can't trust as a foundation for our lives. Members of group 5 have a better idea. Ask Group 5 to bring their rocks and read or summarize the Scripture verse on each rock. Then pile the rocks together. Ask a volunteer to read Psalm 18:2, 3.

We could pour water over these rocks, we could blow them with a huge wind, but that wouldn't change them. They are solid and stable, and trustworthy. Place the second block house on top of the rocks. **The good news is that you choose which support you want for your life: you are not stuck with putting your life upon a fragile and falling apart spider web. You can build your life on the trustworthiness of God. And He is as steady as a rock.**

Prayer (Group 6): **We know God will keep His promises to us because He kept His promises to people in the Bible. Let's thank God now because we know He is trustworthy.** Ask Group 6 to say their prayers to God as they place their illustrations of His promises on the clothesline.

Closing Moments
(10-15 minutes)

Divide Juniors into teams. Ask each team to think of things we can and cannot trust. The other team must try to guess the things by asking questions. The team being questioned may only answer "yes" or "no". The team to guess the most correctly, wins.

God Provides Everything We Need

Note: Today's suggested plan has a long skit and a generous talk by the leader at the beginning. The worship time includes eating foods to remind us of times when God provided food. So you'll probably want to eliminate an earlier snack time and allow extra time during the worship for eating. You may need to adjust your times elsewhere in the session, perhaps making *Building the Theme* 5-10 minutes shorter. The suggested theme is "Celebration," so the worship time will take a different style, having more Junior participation in the events and less talk by the leaders.

Worship Focus

Worship God by celebrating because He provides for us.

Transition Time

(10-15 minutes)

You will need copies of activity page 21A, birthday candles, party hats, a roll of crepe paper, confetti, pom-poms, flags, pennants or banners, noisemakers, and any other party items.

Before the session, contact 4 Juniors and ask them to present the skit on the activity page. If you do not contact Juniors ahead of time, ask four good readers to read the skit.

Show the items you have collected and ask, **What are these items used for?** (Allow Juniors to respond.) **Would you expect to make use of these items at a worship service? Raise your hands if you think yes. Now raise your hands if you think no.**

We're going to begin today with a skit to help answer this question. Ask Juniors to perform the skit.

Launching the Theme

(10 minutes)

Can you think of a tradition that we have inherited from the Pilgrims? (Let Juniors respond.) **That's right, the celebration of Thanksgiving. And today part of our celebration will be like the Pilgrims' tradition of giving thanks by celebrating a meal together.**

You may not know that we have inherited something else from the Pilgrims, not a tradition so much as an attitude. It's the same attitude that Peter had when he heard that there would be a celebration during the worship service. He felt that worship could only mean "holy quietness." You might call his way of thinking a "Pilgrim" complex. What was it like to worship if you were a Pilgrim?

Let's imagine a typical worship service:

Families filed into meeting houses dressed in only somber or "sad" colors, like gray, brown or black. The men sat on wooden benches on one side of the aisle, and the women sat on the other side. This was called, "dignifying the meeting." Beginning at eight in the morning, the congregation stood, sometimes for an hour, while the opening prayer was said. Pilgrims never knelt to pray, it reminded them too much of the Catholic church and the Church of England. Then they sang a Psalm, without any accompaniment by musical instruments. They did not approve of any kind of instrumental music. An organ was the "devil's bagpipes." They used only a psalter—a song book with songs directly taken from the psalms.

Then the preacher gave a sermon, which might last several hours. After the sermon, another song would be sung. The Lord's Supper, offering, and prayer would complete the service.

After a noonday meal, a second service began early in the afternoon. This time the opening prayer and the sermon were shorter. These were followed by a lengthy time of discussion called, "prophesying," when men argued and explained their opinions about various Bible verses. Women had to be silent.

Young pilgrims sat in a special section, under the watchful eye of a deaconess. She boxed their ears if they laughed or talked. Or worse, she whipped them with a birch rod.

So were the Pilgrims right? Should we follow their example?

In some areas, yes. As they read the Bible, they couldn't find much in their church, the Church of England, that matched up with Bible teachings. Church services were filled with all kinds of formal rituals and ceremonies. And they also noticed that in the Bible, the government did not control the church.

So the Separatists, as they were called, set out to be different, or separate, from the Church of England. And while they did get rid of many unbiblical practices and rituals, they overlooked many other parts of the Bible's instruction about worship. Their attitude toward worship was not based totally on what they found in the Scriptures. It was based largely on the things they didn't like in the Church of England.

Today we will check out Scriptures to help us know more about celebrating during worship.

Explain the choices of *Building the Theme* activities. Allow the Juniors to choose in which group to participate.

Building the Theme
(30 minutes)

1. Call to Worship. This group will prepare a song with rhythm accompaniment to sing during the worship time. You will need "I Will Enter His Gates" from page 188, a poster board, markers, two small pie tins for each Junior, two cups of small rocks or dry beans, two or more hole punches, a ball of yarn, and scissors. Before the session, print the words to the song on the poster board.

Ask a Junior to read Psalm 100:4. **We will sing a song that uses these words to introduce the worship time.** Display the poster board. Ask the Juniors to sing the song several times with you.

In Psalm 150, David speaks of praising God with the tambourine, strings, flute, cymbals, and trumpets. Today we are going to praise God with rhythm instruments that we will make. Distribute two pie tins to each Junior. Show them how to punch holes in the edges so the tins can be laced together. Give each Junior a scoop of rocks/beans to place inside. Then have them lace the two tins together with a piece of yarn.

Ask the group to choose a rhythm for their tambourines and mark it on the poster board above the words of the song. Practice singing the song with the tambourines.

During *Sharing in Worship,* Juniors will sing the song with rhythm accompaniment.

2. Call to Worship. This group will prepare praise banners with Scriptures about worship. You will need dowel rods or other sticks to use as flag poles, pieces of felt cut into pennant (long-sided triangle) shapes, felt scraps, ribbon, rick-rack, buttons, stencils for letters, markers or tube paint used for decorating shirts, glue, several pair of sharp scissors, a large container for displaying the completed flags, Bibles, and scratch paper. Before the session, place the container for displaying the flags in the front of the worship area.

Explain that your group will be preparing banners or flags to use during the worship service. Ask Juniors to find Psalm 20:5 and Exodus 17:25 in their Bibles. Read the verses together. **We are going to make banners of praise to God today.** Assign one of the following Scriptures to each pair of Juniors: Nehemiah 12:27; Psalm 97:1; Psalm 149:2; Psalm 145:7; Psalm 42:4b; Psalm 118:24; Psalm 20:5; Psalm 118:27. Ask the Juniors to choose which phrases of the verse to include on their banners. They may also select symbols or simple pictures to include. Have them sketch their ideas on scratch paper and then cut out and glue on letters and other decorations.

During *Sharing in Worship*, the Juniors will march forward carrying their flags while Group 1 sings a song. When the song is completed, the Juniors will say the phrases on their flags and place them in the large container in the front of the worship area.

3. Scripture. This group will prepare pantomimes of worship activities found in the Bible. You will need Bibles and scratch paper.

What kinds of actions are appropriate for worship? Jot down Juniors' answers. **Let's check our answers in the Bible.** Ask each Junior or pair of Juniors to find one of the following Scriptures and discover an action of worship. Answers are included for your reference. Scriptures follow: Psalm 100:1—shout; Psalm 145:4—tell; Psalm 96:6—bow; Psalm 47:1—clap; Psalm 149:3—dance; Psalm 96:1—sing; Psalm 81:2—play instruments; Psalm 63:4—lift hands; 1 Chronicles 16:29—bring offering.

Ask the Juniors to pantomime the actions of worship for the small group.

During *Sharing in Worship,* Juniors will pantomime the actions and allow the large group to guess. After each action is guessed, the Junior will read the corresponding Scripture verse.

4. Personal Praise. This group will prepare an appreciation game of praise for God. You will need two sheets of poster board, a yard stick, markers, scissors, and a bean bag.

We are going to make a praise game to lead the large group in worshiping God. Distribute the materials. Juniors will draw a tic-tac-toe grid on one sheet of poster board. In each square of the grid, they will write one of the following instructions: name an action giving praise to God; praise God for a miracle He did; praise

God for some part of creation you appreciate; praise God for a person He created and tell why you appreciate that person; praise God for a promise He has made; name a word to describe God; tell a name God is called in the Bible; tell a way you enjoy worshiping God; praise God for a way He has helped you. Juniors will cut the other poster board into squares and write *X* or *O* on each square.

Divide your group into two teams and have them play several sample games. In order to claim the square, the team must be able to complete the action mentioned in that square. When they have done so, cover that square with their X or 0.

During *Sharing in Worship*, the large group will play the game.

5. Devotional. This group will prepare a "smorgasboard" of foods that God provided for His people. You will need copies of activity page 21B, Bibles, pencils, food items mentioned below, paper plates, cups, napkins, and a tablecloth.

Can you think of some times in the Bible when God provided food for someone? (Allow Juniors to respond.) Distribute activity page 21B and ask Juniors to find the food in the Scriptures. Explain that your group will prepare a "smorgasbord table" for Juniors to sample some of the foods that God provided in Bible times. Suggestions follow: Exodus 16:31 (manna)—cookies made with coriander seed, or graham crackers with honey; Exodus 16:11- 13 (quail)—chicken wings; 1 Kings 17:7 (bread and meat)—bread and lunch meat; 1 Kings 17:12-16 (flour and oil)—display container of flour and oil and prepare biscuits ahead of time. Matthew 14:20 (bread and fish)—pita bread and sardines or tuna.

Have two Juniors work together to prepare a banner to hang over the table, or to decorate the front of the tablecloth with words from Psalm 34:8, "Taste and See the Lord is Good!"

During *Sharing in Worship*, ask the Juniors to read the Scriptures where God provided food. Then invite everyone to taste the food.

6. Prayer. This group will create a praise mural of things God provides to introduce the prayer time. You will need a large sheet of newsprint, markers or crayons, Bibles, and pencils.

Ask Juniors to find 1 Timothy 6:17b in their Bibles. Read the verse together. ". . . Hope in God, who richly provides us with everything for our enjoyment." **What does this verse say God provides for our enjoyment?** (Everything.) **God knows everything we need, and He provides it for us to enjoy. What are some things God has provided for you that you enjoy?** (Juniors respond—parents, a good friend, a big yard, my own room, and so on.) Ask the Juniors to illustrate some things God has provided that they enjoy on a mural. Encourage to draw large pictures and fill the space.

During *Sharing in Worship*, each Junior will say "Thank You, God, for giving me (things he or she drew) to enjoy."

Sharing in Worship
(20-25 minutes)

Omit any of the following sections if you did not offer the corresponding activity. The devotional may be completed without the presentation of Group 5.

Call to Worship (Groups 1 and 2): Read Psalm 100:4. Ask Group 1 to sing their song as Group 2 marches forward with their flags. When the song is completed, ask Group 2 to share their praise phrases from their banners.

Lord's Supper: Does it seem improper to you for us to be "celebrating" the Lord's Supper? Often you hear us tell you to be solemn and reverent at this special moment. You may think of it as you would a funeral. After all, aren't we remembering Jesus' death? Jesus did die a lonely and painful and unfair death. But that is wonderful news for us. It is cause for celebration. For by that death, we have forgiveness of sin and new life. While it is important to remember how terrible Jesus' death was, it is also important to recognize that the sadness is temporary. Have joy in your heart today as you partake.

Offering: Choose two children to collect the offering.

Scripture (Group 3): **What actions are appropriate to do during worship? Group 3 found Scriptures that tell us. See if you can guess these worship actions.** Ask Group 3 to pantomime their actions and share the Scriptures.

Personal Praise (Group 4): **When the occasion for a celebration is to honor a person for a birthday or for many years of service at a job, friends often honor the person by bringing cards expressing their feelings, or by having a few people give testimonies or speeches of appreciation. We won't be that formal today . Our way of expressing appreciation will come through a game—a new version of tic-tac-toe.** Divide into teams and play the appreciation game made by Group 4.

Devotional (Group 5): **We have sampled a great variety of ways to celebrate today, and most of them would not be found in a Pilgrim church. But at the beginning we did mention their tradition of the Thanksgiving meal. Now we have the opportunity to celebrate and remember the times in the Bible when God fixed the meal.** Ask Group 5 to share their Scriptures of times God provided food for His people. **This is a time to be thankful. Maybe you'll be thankful that you don't have to**

eat some of these items as a part of your regular diet. Remember to give thanks for the way that God provides for His people. Allow Juniors to sample the foods prepared by Group 5. If you did not offer this activity, prepare the foods ahead of time. See Group 5 for instructions.

Prayer (Group 6)**: 1 Timothy 6:17b says that God has given us everything for our enjoyment. Let's pray with Group 6 as they thank God for things He has given them that they enjoy.** Group 6 presents their mural and prays.

Closing Moments

(10-15 minutes)

Before the session, prepare copies of paragraph below. Distribute with pencils. Ask Juniors to complete the paragraph as if it would appear in your church paper next week to report on the worship time. If time permits, have volunteers read their reports aloud. (Check to see if you could possibly print a report in your church's newsletter.)

Celebration was the theme of the worship time last Sunday for Middlers and Juniors at our church. The room was decorated with flags and banners prepared by Juniors. "We shared in some unique experiences that helped us broaden our idea of what it means to worship," said the leader.

"My favorite part of the worship session was _______________," said __________. "One thing I learned about worship was _______________."

God Has Great Power

Worship Focus

Worship God because He has great power.

Transition Time

(10-15 minutes)

Send the Juniors in small groups to the rest room and drinking fountain. Welcome the Juniors and involve them in the following activity.

God's Power in Nature Match-up. You will need paper, a marker, and tape. Before the session, copy the following questions, each on a separate sheet of paper. 1. What animal can run 62 miles per hour? 2. What animal tells you the temperature by the speed of its chirps? 3. What animal catches insects by firing water at them? 4. How many stars are in the universe? 5. What is the average depth of the ocean? 6. What animal's egg could feed twelve people? 7. What plant grows three feet a day? 8. How many hairs does the average blonde have? 9. How many messages can the human eye deal with at the same time? 10. How many sweat glands does a person have? Post the questions around your room. Make copies of an answer sheet. Do not put the answers in order. Answers follow: 1. cheetah; 2. cricket; 3. archer fish; 4. one with twenty-four zeroes; 5. thirteen thousand feet; 6. ostrich; 7. bamboo; 8. one hundred and fifty thousand; 9. one million, five hundred thousand; 10. two million.

Give each Junior an answer sheet and tell them to read the posted questions and write the number of the question beside the matching answer. When questions and answers are matched, ask, **What do these strange collection of facts tell us about God's power?** Everything in nature points to the amazing and complex power behind the universe.

What is your favorite part of nature: something huge and awesome or something tiny and intricate? What does each aspect (huge or tiny) teach us about God's power?

Launching the Theme

(10 minutes)

You will need a sheet of newsprint, lemon juice, a paintbrush, tape, a set of watercolor paints, a paintbrush, a cup of water, a pair of glasses, a pair of binoculars, and a flashlight. Before the session, use lemon juice to paint this message on the sheet of newsprint: "God's Power Is Clearly Seen." The lemon juice should create an invisible message on the paper. Tape the paper on the wall.

Point to the newsprint with the invisible message. **I've written our theme for today on this sheet of paper. May I have a volunteer read it for me?** When Juniors say they cannot read the message, continue. **Well, perhaps the message is there but you just can't see it. Here, try looking through these glasses.** Have volunteers try to read the message using the glasses, the binoculars, and the flashlight. Then ask a volunteer to paint over the paper with the watercolor paints to make the message appear.

The message was there, but you had a good excuse for not being able to see it—it was invisible. Romans 2:20 says, "For since the creation of the world God's invisible qualities—his eternal power and divine nature—have been clearly seen, begin understood from what has been made, so that men are without excuse." People have no excuse for not believing God—His power can be clearly seen by the things He has created. Today we will worship God because of His great power.

Explain the choices of *Building the Theme* activities and ask the Juniors to choose in which group to participate.

Building the Theme

(30 minutes)

1. Call to Worship. This group will prepare a choral reading about God's power. You will need a sheet of newsprint, a marker, and Bibles.

We are going to create a choral reading, praising God for His great power. Distribute Bibles. Ask Juniors to find 1 Chronicles 29:10-13 in their Bibles. Read the verses together. Ask the Juniors to decide who will say each part of the verses and what expression they will use. Print the reading on the newsprint. An example follows:

All *(loudly and joyfully)*: Praise be to you, O Lord,

Group 1: God of our father

Israel,

Group 2: from everlasting to everlasting.

All: Yours, O Lord is the greatness

Person 1: and the power

Person 2: and the glory

Person 3: and the majesty

Person 4: and the splendor

All: for everything in heaven and earth is yours.

Group 1: Yours, O Lord, is the Kingdom;

Group 2: You are exalted as head over all. Wealth and honor come from you;

Group 1: you are the ruler of all things.

Person 1: In your hands are strength

Person 2: and power to exalt

Person 3: and give strength to all.

All (*softly and reverently*): Now, our God, we give you thanks, and praise your glorious name.

Practice the reading several times. If you want to make the activity more challenging, provide concordances and ask Juniors to find verses about God's power and use them to create a choral reading.

During *Sharing in Worship*, Juniors will present the reading.

2. Special Music. This group will illustrate a song about God's power for the worship time. You will need "Song of Moses" from page 190, crayons or markers or colored chalk, sheets of construction paper, and a poster board. Before the session, print the words to the song on the poster board. Before the session, make a tape recording of the words and music to "Song of Moses."

In Old Testament times when people wanted to refer to God's great power, they reminded each other about the time when God opened the Red Sea for Israel to escape from the armies of Egypt. That miracle is the most mentioned one in the Old Testament. In New Testament times, the early Christians had an even greater miracle to look back on: the resurrection of Jesus. Both of these events are combined in the song, "Song of Moses." Display the poster board and read the words of the song. **We are going to illustrate the song to help the large group picture God's great power.**

What are some illustrations we could draw for this song? Write the Juniors' suggestions above the corresponding words on the poster board. Then assign each Junior or pair of Juniors one illustration to draw.

During *Sharing in Worship*, Juniors will show their illustrations at the appropriate times as the song is played.

3. Scripture. You will need pencils, Bibles, a sheet of poster board, a ruler, markers, and scissors. Before the session, write at the top of the poster board **God's Power Is Seen in:** Below the title, write the word *power* vertically on the poster board.

God's Power is Seen in:

His **P**eople Ephesians 3:20, 2 Corinthians 4:7

His S**o**n Ephesians 1:19, Hebrews 1:3

His **W**ord: Isaiah 55:22, 1 Peter 1:23

M**e**: 1 John 4:4, 2 Corinthians 12:9

His c**r**eation: Romans 1:20, Jeremiah 10:12

Display the poster board for the Juniors. **We are going to make an acrostic of places God's power is seen. We are going to find Scriptures that will tell us where we can find God's power.** Assign each Junior or pair of Juniors one letter of the acrostic to complete by looking up the corresponding Scriptures. Scriptures follow: **P**—Ephesians 3:20; 2 Corinthians 4:7; **O**—Ephesians 1:19; Hebrews 1:3; **W**—Isaiah 55:22; 1 Peter 1:23; **E**—1 John 4:4; 2 Corinthians 12:9; **R**—Romans 1:20; Jeremiah 10:12. Answers follow: **P**eople; S**O**n; **W**ord; m**E**; c**R**eation. Do not write the answers to the acrostic on the poster board.

During *Sharing in Worship*, the Juniors will read the Scriptures for each letter and ask the large group to guess the word for the acrostic. Then they will write in the correct word.

4. Devotional. This group will prepare discover Bible people who saw God's power. You will need copies of activity page 22A, pencils, Bibles, sheet of poster board, and markers. This activity may be completed without an adult. Print or tape record the instructions.

We read about many people in the Bible who saw God's power. We are going to read some eyewitness accounts today. Distribute the activity page and ask the Juniors to match each Bible person with the way he or she saw God's power. Ask the Juniors to print the name and Scripture reference for each person on the poster board.

During *Sharing in Worship*, Juniors will display the poster board. Each Junior will read a statement about God's power, and the large group will tell which Bible person is speaking.

5. Personal Praise. This group will prepare a slide show illustrating God's power in nature. This activity is for older or gifted Juniors. You will need "My God Is a Great God" from page 184 or another song about God's power, a poster board, nature slides, a slide projector, a screen, an extension cord, a sheet of scratch paper, a pencil, a marker, and masking tape. Before the session, write the words to the song on poster board, leaving plenty of space between lines. Collect fifty or more slides showing scenes of nature. Juniors will need to work by a window where they can tape up the slides. Or make a light table from a piece of glass or hardened plastic mounted between two tables with a desk lamp beneath it. **Option:** Provide magazine pictures showing scenes from nature. Juniors may mount these on construction paper and display them during the worship time.

Listen to this song about God's power. Display the poster board and play or sing the song for your Juniors. **We are going to create a slide show about God's power in nature to present during this song. You will choose which slides will go with the words of the song.** Distribute the slides to the Juniors. Explain that you have provided more slides than they will need, so they can choose the best ones for the song. Ask the Juniors to begin selecting slides and arranging them in the proper order. Mark on the word sheet when the slides will change. You may want to number the slides with a nonpermanent marker. Arrange slides in the tray for the slide projector. Then preview with your group to make sure the slides are all facing the correct way. Choose a Junior to run the projector and another to start the music. Appoint another person to turn off and on the lights and another person to move the screen if one is necessary.

During *Sharing in Worship*, the Juniors will present the song and slide show.

6. Prayer. This group will prepare a Scripture and a prayer list for the worship time. You will need copies of activity page 22B, one small cardboard tube for each Junior, scissors, markers, construction paper, and tape.

How big is God's power? (Allow Juniors to respond.) **God's power is so big that we can't even imagine it.** Ask Juniors to find Ephesians 3:20 in their Bibles. Read the verse together. **When we pray, we can be certain God will answer our prayers in the best way possible because His power is so great.** Distribute the activity page. Ask the Juniors to color and cut out the tape measure, tape the pieces together, and tape the tape measure to the cardboard tube. Then ask them to cut out a cover for the tape measure and attach it according to the illustration on this page. You may wish to make a sample tape measure before the session.

When the tape measures are completed, ask the Juniors to make a list of prayer requests. Encourage them to include personal requests, requests for our nation and world, and requests for other people. Assign Juniors in the group to pray for each of the requests during the worship time.

During *Sharing in Worship*, the group will pull out their tape measures and read Ephesians 3:20 together. Then they will pray for the items on their list.

Sharing in Worship
(20-25 minutes)

Omit any of the following sections if you did not offer the corresponding activity. The devotional may be completed without the presentation of Group 4.

Call to Worship (Group 1): Group 1 presents their choral reading.

Special Music (Group 2): **One of the greatest examples of God's power in the Old Testament was when God divided the Red Sea to allow Israel to escape the armies of Egypt. In the New Testament, we find an even greater example of God's power—the resurrection of Jesus. Listen to this song that Group 2 illustrated that speaks of both of these great acts of God's power.**

Scripture (Group 3): **We talked about how we see God's power in nature at the beginning of the section. And Group 2 just sang of two great miracles which help us see God's power. What are other ways we see God's power. Group 3 prepared an acrostic to help us discover those ways.** Group 2 presents their acrostic and Scriptures and allows the large group to guess the answers.

Lord's Supper: When Popeye eats his spinach, he becomes incredibly powerful. You've probably read other stories about heroes who become transformed when they eat a magic bean or drink a magic potion.

The Lord's Supper is not a magic meal. The power is not in the bit of bread or the taste of the juice. The food is a reminder that we are already transformed. The food reminds us how this was done: through the death of Jesus. Taking the Lord's Supper doesn't make you powerful. It reminds you that you already have God's power at work in you.

Offering

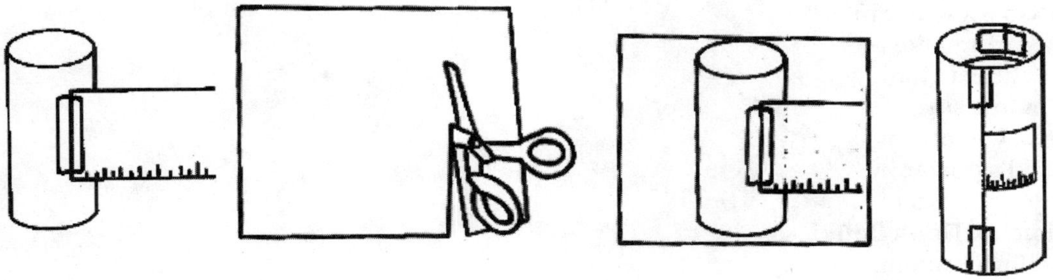

Devotional (Group 4): **Power: it's kind of an exhausting subject. It brings to mind volcanos, and waterfalls and mountains. It makes you think of great machines, or spectacular miracles. Power is awesome!**

But let's look for a moment at another aspect of God's power. 2 Corinthians 19:9 says that God's power is made perfect in weakness. 2 Corinthians 4:7 say that we who have God's power inside of us are only like clay pots: not too attractive and rather breakable. Here's the point. God's power shows up best in small and insignificant people.

A kids' song about that said, "Little is a lot when you're in the right spot." Think of the young David who went to meet nine-foot armored Goliath with only a sling and five smooth stones. Think of the little boy who had only a small lunch in a huge crowd of hungry people. Think of the widow lady who put only two pennies in the offering. See if you can name some other Bible people who saw God's power at work. Ask Group 4 to display their poster, read the statements, and allow the large group to guess which Bible person is speaking. **God's power worked in a mighty way in each of those circumstances because the person was willing to let God work.**

In 1 Kings 19 Elijah had a rare encounter with God's power. God told him to stand on a mountain and watch His presence as He passed by. Then Elijah experienced three great powers of nature: wind, earthquake, and fire. Mountains were torn apart, rocks shattered, fire raged. But God was not in the fire nor the earthquake nor the wind. Elijah heard God speaking to him in a small, gentle whisper.If you are watching for God's power in your life, don't only expect spectacular miracles. Don't think that you must climb a mountain or stand next to a powerful river for God to show His power. You can see His power in people. You can receive His power as you read and obey His Word. God's power can work through you in a mighty way.

Personal Praise (Group 5): **Group 5 has prepared a presentation of God's power in nature. As we watch and listen, let's silently praise God for ways we have seen His power.** Group 5 presents the slide show and song.

Prayer (Group 6): **God's power works directly through our prayers. We can trust that God will answer our prayers in the best way possible, even if we don't understand, because of His great power.** Ask Group 6 to present their tape measure and Scripture verse. Then close with prayers offered by Group 6.

Closing Moments
(10-15 minutes)

Distribute index cards. Ask Juniors to complete these sentences. God's power in my life can help me learn to ________. God's power can help me get rid of _______. God's power can help me reach out to___________. Ask the Juniors to take the cards home with them to remind them of God's power in their lives.

God Cares for Our Physical Needs

Worship Focus
Worship God because He provides for our physical needs.

Transition Time
(10-15 minutes)
Send the Juniors in small groups to the rest room and the drinking fountain. Welcome them and involve them in the following activity.

Newspaper Scavenger Hunt. You will need copies of activity page 23A, old newspapers, scissors, and glue or tape.

Divide the Juniors into teams of two or three. Distribute an activity page to each team. Ask them to find in the newspapers the words indicated on the activity page. They are to cut out the words and glue them in the correct space. The first team to finish wins.

What is the title of our activity page? (God Provides.) **Does God provide all these things we found?** (Yes.) **God provides all of our needs.**

Launching the Theme
(10 minutes)
If someone in your church is familiar with sheep, ask him or her to speak to the children for several minutes about the characteristics of sheep and what a shepherd does.

Why do you think sheep need a shepherd? (They need someone to lead them, to provide shelter, to take them to food and water, to protect them.) **Why do we need God?** (God guides us; He provides for our physical needs, such as food and shelter; He protects us; He gives us Salvation.) **Jesus calls Himself our shepherd many times in the Bible. Jesus is our shepherd because He provides for our needs like a shepherd provides for the needs of his sheep. Today we will worship God because He provides for our needs.**

Explain the choices of *Building the Theme* activities and allow the Juniors to choose in which group to participate.

Building the Theme
(30 minutes)
1. **Call to Worship.** This group will name ways God cares for us like a shepherd to introduce the worship time. You will need index cards, and pencils or pens, and a children's encyclopedia (optional).

We just talked about how Jesus cares for us like a shepherd. What were some of the things we learned that a shepherd does for his sheep? List Juniors' ideas on a chalkboard. You may wish to provide a children's encyclopedia and ask Juniors to find the article for *shepherd* or *sheep*. Include these ideas in your list. Distribute index cards. Ask each Junior to choose one way a shepherd cares for his sheep and write it on one side of the index card. On the other side, they will write a way Jesus cares for us. For example, "A shepherd protects his sheep from lions and bears. God protects us from bad things."

During *Sharing in Worship*, each Junior will read how a shepherd cares for his sheep and how Jesus cares for us.

2. **Special Music.** This group will prepare a song for the worship time. You will need "Like a Good Shepherd" from page 191, shelf paper, and markers. Before the session, print the words to the song on shelf paper. Make the letters large and leave plenty of space between lines.

"Like a good Shepherd,
Christ cares for His sheep.
Each night He watches
His lambs while they sleep.
Then with the dawn,
He sees to the needs
Of each single sheep.
Gently He cradles
The lambs in His arms.
Bravely He keeps the sheep
Safe from all harm.
Beaming with love
And a smile on His face,
Christ comforts and cares
for His own."

To what did we compare God's care for us? (A shepherd caring for his sheep.) **We are going to sing a song about how God cares for us like a shepherd cares for his sheep.** Display the words to the song. Sing the song once for the Juniors. Then ask them to sing it with you several times. **What does the first line of the song mean? Say the line, using different words.** (Allow Juniors to respond.) Write the Juniors' paraphrase in a different color of marker below the first line of the song. Continue with the other phrases of the song, writing the Juniors' paraphrases below each phrase. A sample paraphrase follows: "We are like Jesus' sheep. Jesus gives us what we need like a shepherd gives his sheep what they need. Jesus cares for us all the time just like a shepherd watches his sheep even at night when they are sleeping. Jesus cares for each of our needs individually just like a shepherd cares for each sheep's needs. A shepherd loves and holds his lambs close. Jesus loves us. Jesus protects us from bad things like a shepherd protects his sheep. Jesus is happy that He made us. He likes to take care of us and provide our needs."

Assign each Junior a part of the paraphrase to read.

During *Sharing in Worship*, Juniors will read the paraphrase of the song. Then they will sing the song.

3. Scripture Study. This group will prepare a rebus of Psalm 23. You will need shelf paper, markers, old magazines, construction paper, scissors, glue, and a Bible. Before the session, print the words to Psalm 23 on a large piece of shelf paper. Make the letters large and leave plenty of space between the words.

Display the words to Psalm 23 for the Juniors. **This Psalm talks about how Jesus cares for us like a shepherd cares for his sheep.** Ask a Junior to read the Psalm aloud. **We are going to make a rebus of this Psalm. We will replace some of the words with pictures.** Ask the Juniors to think of pictures for some of the words of the Psalm. Suggestions of words to be pictured follow: shepherd, green pastures, quiet waters, paths, walk, valley, shadow, rod and staff, table, enemies, head, oil, cup overflows, love, house.

Assign each Junior a word or words to illustrate. They may draw pictures on the construction paper or cut pictures out of magazines. They will glue the pictures on top of the appropriate word on the shelf paper. When the rebus is complete, practice saying Psalm 23 together several times.

During *Sharing in Worship*, children will display their rebus and read Psalm 23 for the large group.

4. Personal Praise. This group will name things they are thankful God provides for us. You will need construction paper, scissors, glue or tape, scratch paper, and markers or crayons.

What are some things God provides for us? (Allow Juniors to respond. List their responses on a chalkboard.) **What one thing on this list are you especially thankful that God provides?** Ask each Junior to choose one thing from the list. **How do you know God provided that thing for you?** Ask Juniors to name all the different ways God helped in providing each thing. Ask them to write their ideas on scratch paper. For example, "I am thankful that God provides ice cream. God created the people who make the ice cream. God created the metals used in the machines that make the ice cream. God created cows that make milk. God created sugar cane so we could make sugar. Without God's creation, we would not have ice cream."

Ask the Juniors cut the construction paper into strips to make paper chains. On each strip of the chain, they should write a way God helped provide the thing for which they are thankful.

During *Sharing in Worship*, Juniors will display their chains, name the things they are thankful for, and tell the ways God helped provide those things.

5. Devotional. This group will discover Scriptures that tell how Jesus cares for us like a shepherd cares for his sheep. You will need copies of activity page 23B, Bibles, and pencils.

What did we say Jesus' care for us is like? (A shepherd caring for his sheep.) **The Bible mentions many ways that Jesus is like a shepherd. We are going to find some of those ways.** Distribute the activity page and ask the Juniors to find the Scriptures and match each thing that Jesus does with something a shepherd does for his sheep. When Juniors are completed, discuss the answers as a group. **Option:** If you have younger Juniors, assign each Junior one Scripture to find and read aloud to the group. Decide on matches as a group.

When the page is completed, assign each Junior one Scripture to share during the worship time. They will read the Scriptures, tell what Jesus does for us, and then tell what the shepherd does for his sheep. Allow them to practice reading their Scriptures during the small-group time.

During *Sharing in Worship*, Juniors will share their Scriptures and information about Jesus being a shepherd.

6. Prayer. This group will make a montage to show the different ways God provides for us. You will need old magazines, construction paper, scissors, glue or tape, markers, and poster board.

What are some things God provides for us? Encourage the Juniors to name as many different things as possible. List their ideas on a chalkboard. **We are going to make a montage of many of the things that God provides.** Ask Juniors to find or draw pictures of things God provides and glue them on the poster board. Ask them to cover the poster board with the pictures.

When the montage is completed, ask each Junior to choose one thing he or she is thankful for to thank God for during the worship time.

During *Sharing in Worship*, display the montage and ask Juniors to offer sentence prayer, thanking God for one thing for which they are thankful.

Sharing in Worship
(20-25 minutes)

Omit any of the following sections if you did not offer the corresponding activity. The devotional may be completed without the presentation of Group 5.

Call to Worship (Group 1): **How does a shepherd care for his sheep? And how does Jesus care for us? Group 1 will help us begin to think about God's care now.** Ask Group 1 to come forward and share their sentences about Jesus' care.

Special Music (Group 2): **Jesus cares for us a like a good shepherd cares for his sheep. Group 2 prepared a song about how Jesus cares called "Like a Good Shepherd."** Ask Group 2 to present their song and paraphrase.

Lord's Supper: We have been talking about ways God provides for our needs. God knows everything we need. And He knew our greatest need. Our greatest need was to be saved from the punishment for all the wrong things we do. God provided for that need. He sent Jesus to die and take our punishment. Now we can be saved because Jesus died for us. Let's thank Jesus now. Pray and serve the Lord's Supper.

Offering: Sometimes God provides our needs through other people. We can be a person that God uses to provide other people's needs. When we give our money to the church, we are helping to provide for people's needs. We are helping people learn about Jesus. We are helping people worship Jesus. Our money helps God provide people's needs. Choose two children to collect the offering.

Scripture (Group 3): **One Psalm in the Bible talks about Jesus being a shepherd. Does anyone know the number of that Psalm?** (Allow response.) **Psalm 23 tell us about God's great care. Listen as Group 3 shares this Scripture with us.** Ask Group 3 to present their rebus of Psalm 23.

Personal Praise (Group 4): **We have named many things that God provides. But how does God provide us with these things? Group 4 found some ways God provides us with things they are thankful for.** Ask Group 4 to share their chains of ways God provides.

Devotional (Group 5): **How does the Bible say Jesus cares for us like a shepherd? Group 5 found some ways.** Ask Group 5 to share. If you did not offer this activity, read the Scriptures from activity page 23B and tell the ways Jesus cares for us like a shepherd.

The Bible promises that Jesus will take care of us and that He will give us everything we need. And God keeps His promise. Listen to this story about how God kept His promise to provide.

Amy Carmichael was a missionary who spent fifty-three years serving God in India. Many times God provided for their mission in miraculous ways. If they had a need, they would ask God to supply it. And He did. Many times God provided food, money, and workers in mysterious ways. One time when they had no money to buy food, they prayed. The mail came. Someone wrote them, "I was taking a nap, and God woke me up and told me to send you some money." The person included a check to buy several weeks' worth of food. Another time they were building a house and needed some money to complete it. A letter arrived from the United States with a check for one hundred dollars. They finished their house.

We know God will provide our needs because He tells us in the Bible, because we see the way He provides for other people today, and because we see the way He provided for His people in the Bible.

When God led the Israelites out of Egypt, He provided for their needs, but not in the way they expected. Who can tell me what God provided? (Manna and quail.) **The Israelites had never seen manna before and didn't know what it was, but Moses explained, "It is the bread the Lord has given you to eat." Sometimes God provides for us in unusual ways.**

Have you ever asked God for something, but He didn't answer your prayers in the way you wanted? (Have one or two persons share.) **God knows our needs far better than we do.** (Have one Junior look up and read Exodus 16:21.)

How much does this verse say everyone gathered? (Everyone gathered as much as he needed). **God provided exactly as much as each person needed. Sometimes when we pray we ask for much more than we need. Let us remember that God knows what we need better than we do and to thank Him for everything He provides.**

Prayer (Group 6): **Let's close by thanking God for the many things He provides. Look at the montage made by Group 6 and think of some things you are thankful for.** Ask Group 6 to display their montage and say their prayers. When they are finished, have a few minutes of thanksgiving and ask Juniors to call out things they are thankful God provides. Close with prayer, thanking God for providing our needs.

Closing Moments
(10-15 minutes)

What are some ways we can help provide others' needs? Listen to these situations and tell me what you could do?

A new kid begins attending your school. (Invite him or her to your home or to church; eat lunch with him or her; introduce him or her to your friends.)

Your mom and dad are tired after a long day of work. (Volunteer to help with the dishes; volunteer to watch your little sister or brother; obey without complaining.)

Your grandma just moved to a nursing home. (Visit the home with your parents or with your Sunday-school class.)

God Gives Us Rules to Make Us Happy

Worship Focus

Worship God because obeying His rules makes us happy.

Transition Time
(10-15 minutes)

Send the Juniors in small groups to the rest room and the drinking fountain. Welcome them to the Worship time and involve them in the following activity.

Simon Says.

Play this game to emphasize the necessity of following rules. Have the students line up at one end of the room. Choose one student to be Simon. Simon will issue commands, such as "Hop on one foot," "Touch your toes," and so on. The children are to do what Simon says only when the command is preceded by the words "Simon says." Explain that "Simon" will try to trick them by giving a command without saying, "Simon says." They will be out if they move any time other than when Simon says, "Simon says."

Give several Juniors a turn at being "Simon." Be very strict with the rules at the beginning of the game, but then begin to ignore when Juniors disobey the rules, even when the other Juniors protest.

Launching the Theme
(10 minutes)

How did you like the game? Did you think I played fairly? (No.) **I didn't obey the rules of the game. The game does not work if we don't follow the rules. We can have a good time playing a game only when we follow the rules.**

Today we are going to be talking about rules. Do you have any rules to follow at your house? What is the most important rule at your house? Can you think of other rules we have to obey? Why are they important? What happens if we don't obey the rules? What happens if we do follow the rules? Let the Juniors respond. **Just as games have rules and your parents have made rules for you to follow at home, God has given us rules to follow in our lives. They are found in the Bible. These rules are for our protection and for our benefit. If we obey God's rules, we will be happy. But if we disobey them, we will be as mixed up as when we try to play a game without following the rules. Today we will worship God because obeying His rules makes us happy.**

Explain the choices of activities for *Building the Theme*. Ask the Juniors to count off by six and go to the activity whose number corresponds with their number. Or allow Juniors to choose the activities in which they will participate.

Building the Theme
(30 minutes)

1. Call to Worship. This group will read verses about God's rules and prepare a call to worship. You will need Bibles, shelf paper or poster board, and markers.

How does following God's rules make us feel? We are going to read some verses from Psalms that tell how the writer felt about God's rules. Assign each Junior one of the following Scripture passages to find and read aloud. Verses follow: Psalm 119:97-104; Psalm 119:1-3; Psalm 119:9-11; Psalm 119:14-16; Psalm 119:129, 130. When the Juniors have completed reading their verses, ask them to name as many words as they can think of describing God's rules and how we feel when we obey God's rules. Suggestions follow: love, wise, sweet, pure, joy, delight, wonderful, light, understanding. Ask the Juniors to use the words to make a graffiti poster. They will use markers to cover the poster board or shelf paper with the words describing God's rules.

When the Juniors have completed the poster, ask them to practice reading their Scriptures for the worship time.

During *Sharing in Worship,* Juniors will display their poster and read the Scriptures.

2. Scripture. This group will memorize Psalm 119:9-11. You will need Bibles, a chalkboard, and chalk.

Ask the Juniors to find Psalm 119:9-11 in their Bibles. Read the verses aloud. **What does it mean to *keep your way pure?*** (Allow response. It means to keep from doing wrong things in our lives.) **How do these verses say we can keep from doing wrong things?** (By obeying God's Word.) **What does *stray from your commands* mean?** (To disobey God's commands.) **What does it mean to hide God's word in our hearts?** (To memorize God's Word.) **We are going to hide some of God's Word in our hearts this morning. We are going to memorize these verses and say them for the large group during the worship time.** Read the verses aloud together several times. Then ask the Juniors to say the first sentence without looking at their Bibles and so on. Snap your fingers or clap your hands and say the verses in a rhythm to make it easier for Juniors to memorize the words. Practice the verses until everyone is comfortable saying them from memory.

During *Sharing in Worship*, Juniors will say the verses for the large group.

3. Lord's Supper. This group will prepare pictures to remind the group of some of God's rules. You will need construction paper, markers, old magazines, scissors, and glue.

What are ten rules that God gave us in the Old Testament? (The Ten Commandments.) **Obeying the Ten Commandments will make us happy. We are going to make a game to help the large group remember each of the Ten Commandments.** List the commandments on a chalkboard. Ask the Juniors to think of pictures or words to describe each commandment. For example, for "You shall not make an idol," they could draw a picture of an idol. For "Honor your Father and Mother," they could draw a picture of a husband and wife. For "Remember the Sabbath day," they could draw a picture of a church. Assign each Junior one or two commandments to illustrate. They can draw pictures or cut pictures out of magazines and glue them to construction paper. On the back of their construction paper, they should write the commandment they are picturing.

During *Sharing in Worship*, Juniors will display their pictures and allow the large group to guess which commandment each picture illustrates.

4. Personal Praise. This group will discover benefits of obeying God. You will need copies of activity page 24B, Bibles, paper, and pencils.

Obeying God's rules makes us happy. But what does that mean? What are the benefits of obeying God's rules? We are going to read some verses from Psalm 119 that tell us the benefits of obeying God's rules. Distribute activity page 24B. Ask Juniors to find the verses and fill in the words of the acrostic. **Option:** If you have younger Juniors, assign each Junior a verse to find and read aloud. Complete the acrostic as a group. Answers to the acrostic follow: joy, blessed, mercy, understanding, wiser, peace, strength, comfort, love.

When the acrostic is completed, assign each Junior a word or words to praise God for. Juniors will write a praise sentence, telling why they are thankful to God for that benefit. Discuss any unfamiliar words, and encourage the Juniors to say the benefit in their own words. For example, "When I obey God's rules, He has mercy. He will show me kindness and forgive the things I do wrong." Ask Juniors to write their sentences on scratch paper.

During *Sharing in Worship*, Juniors will share their praise sentences.

5. Devotional. This group will prepare a story game about obeying God's rules for the worship time. You will need activity page 24A, scissors, and four lunch-sized paper bags. Before the session, cut the activity page into four sections, so that each section has five matching cards in it.

How does obeying God's rules makes us happy? (Allow response.) **We are going to make a story game to help us learn how obeying God's rules makes us happy.** Distribute the materials. Ask Juniors to cut apart the story cards and place them in the four paper bags. Five matching cards will go in each bag. They will label the paper bags **person, place, commandment, and obey/disobey.** Check to be sure that the correct cards are in each bag.

We are going to play a game to help us see how obeying makes us happy. I want you to draw one card from each of the bags and make up a story. Allow Juniors to work in pairs or groups of three. Each group will draw a card from each bag and tell how that person obeyed or disobeyed the commandment they drew at the place they drew. For example, a group draws *Nate, store, Honor your father and mother, and disobey.* A sample story follows: Nate's mom gave him some money and asked him to ride his bike to the store, buy a gallon of milk, and bring her back the change. Nate bought a gallon of milk. But when he gave his mom the change, he kept $.75 for himself.

After each group's story, ask how obeying or disobeying the commandment could make the person happy or unhappy. For example, Nate's mom could find out he didn't give her all the change. Then she wouldn't trust him to go to the store anymore. She might not give him any money to spend.

When each group has had a chance to make up a story, place all the cards back in the bags.

During *Sharing in Worship*, the large group will play the game.

6. Prayer. This group will record a prayer, thanking God for His rules. You will need Bibles, scratch paper, pencils, a tape player, and a blank cassette tape.

What are some of the rules God has given us? List the Juniors' answers on the chalkboard. Suggestions follow: Do not steal; obey your parents; do not lie; worship only God; love everyone. **Why are you thankful for these rules? How would it hurt you if God had not made these rules?** Allow Juniors to respond. Suggestions follow: We might have possessions stolen all the time; we would not learn from our parents; we couldn't know if other people were telling us the truth; we would not know for sure that God was the best God and only God; other people would not treat us with love.

Ask each Junior to choose one rule for which he or she is thankful and compose a sentence prayer, telling God why he or she is thankful for that rule and how it would hurt him or her if God had not made the rule. Ask the Juniors to write their sentences on the scratch paper. Decide on an order for saying the prayers and practice saying them. Then turn on the tape recorder and record the prayers for the worship time. Pause the recorder between each prayer so no one feels rushed. When the Juniors have finished the prayer, rewind the tape and let them listen.

During *Sharing in Worship*, play the taped prayers.

Sharing in Worship
(20-25 minutes)

Omit any of the following sections if you did not offer the corresponding activities. The Lord's Supper and devotional may be completed without the presentations of Groups 3 and 5.

Call to Worship (Group 1): **Let's listen to Group 1 as they prepare us to worship God by sharing ways obeying His Word makes us feel.** Ask Group 1 to share their poster and Scriptures.

Scripture (Group 2): **What does it mean to hide God's Word in our hearts?** (To memorize His Word.) **The Bible tells us that memorizing God's Word helps us obey Him. Group 2 hid some of God's Word in their hearts this morning.** Ask Group 2 to say their memorized Scripture.

Lord's Supper (Group 3): **Who can tell me the name of ten rules that God gave in the Old Testament?** (The Ten Commandments.) **Group 3 prepared some pictures to help us name some of those commandments. See if you can guess which picture illustrates which commandment.** Ask Group 3 to come forward and display their illustrations. Allow the large group to guess the commandments. If you did not offer this activity, ask the Juniors to name as many of the Ten Commandments as they can.

In the Old Testament, the way to be perfect was to obey every one of those Ten Commandments. If you messed up just once, you weren't perfect anymore. Can you imagine how hard obeying them would be? If you lied once or talked back to your mom once or stole something once, you were no longer perfect. In fact, the only perfect person was Jesus. And because of Jesus, we can be perfect even though we mess up and do wrong things sometimes. God sent Jesus to die for all the times we break God's commandments. Because of Jesus, God forgives all the wrong things we do. Let's thank God now for sending His perfect Son, Jesus. Pray and serve the Lord's Supper.

Offering: God doesn't give us a rule in the Bible about how much money we should give to Him. But He does tell us how we should give. He says we should be happy when we give. We shouldn't give money to God because we think we have to, or because someone else tells us to. We should give to God because we are thankful for all He has given us. Ask two children to collect the offering.

Personal Praise (Group 4): **Group 1 told us how obeying God's rules makes us feel. Group 4 discovered some benefits of obeying God's rules. The Bible tells us it is good for us to obey God's rules.** Ask Group 4 to share their praise sentences.

Devotional (Group 5): You will need several examples of projects which have not been started, and one or two completed projects. Examples might include a completed model (car or airplane) and the parts of one which has not been started; a sample of thread and cloth and a finished needlepoint project; yarn and knitting needles and a sweater; flour, sugar, and yeast, and a loaf of bread; lumber and plans and a birdhouse.

Display projects for the Juniors. **What do people need in order to start and finish projects like these?** (Allow answers.) **Instructions, of course. You can try to do a project without directions or bake a cake without a recipe, but there is no guarantee it will turn out right. Most likely, you'll end up with a mess.**

The same is true for a coach and his team. If the players don't obey the coach's directions and follow the prearranged signals, the team will end up as confused losers.

There is a saying, "If all else fails, read the instructions." A smarter piece of advice would be, "Before everything fails, follow the directions." Instructions are written and given by those who know the answers or who have

had the experience first. If you want to make a German chocolate cake, you must read and follow a recipe. In order to sew a dress you must have a pattern. (If you have any personal experience about failed projects that you can share, do so at this point.)

In 2 Kings 5, the Bible tells how the Syrian captain, Naaman, almost failed to find healing for his leprosy because he didn't like the instructions Elisha gave him. Elisha had simply told Naaman to dip seven times in the muddy, Jordan River. When Naaman followed Elisha's instructions, God healed him.

There are other instructions in the Bible that probably seemed strange to those who were asked to obey. Can you think of any? (Encourage Juniors to make suggestions.)

Abraham was told to move, but God didn't tell him where. Noah was told to build a boat, but it had never rained and he had no place to float it. Samson was told not to cut his hair, and as long as he obeyed those instructions, he had his strength. Joshua was told to march around Jericho seven times. When he followed the instructions exactly, the city was conquered. Ezekiel was told to build a miniature replica of Jerusalem and lie down in front of it for many days.

When these Bible people obeyed God's commands, no matter what they were, they were happy. We will be happy too if we obey God's commands.

Can you think of a time when you obeyed God's commands? How did that make you feel? Can you think of a time when obeying God made you feel happy? Could you share what you did and what happened? (Let Juniors answer.)

Group 5 prepared a game to help us discover ways obeying or disobeying God can make us happy or unhappy. Let's play their game now. Ask volunteers to come to the front and draw a card from each of the paper bags. Then ask the large group to make up a story using the cards. After each story is completed, ask **How did obeying make (person's name) happy? How did disobeying make (person's name) unhappy?** If you did not offer this activity, follow the instructions in Group 5 for making the game yourself.

Sometimes it's hard for us to see the end results of our actions. But we can see that obeying God will make us happy. And disobeying will make us unhappy.

Today we will worship God and thank Him because He has made rules for us which help us and make us happy.

Prayer (Group 6): Play the praise prayer recorded by Group 6.

Closing Moments
(10-15 minutes)

You will need envelopes, stamps, pencils, and index cards.

What rule of God do you have trouble obeying? How could you obey that rule this week? Ask Juniors to write how they will obey a rule of God on an index card. Then ask them to address the envelope to themselves and place the index card inside. Tell them you will mail the envelopes to them later in the week to remind them to obey. **Option:** Rather than mailing the envelopes, distribute them to the Juniors next week.

God Is the Only God

Worship Focus

Worship God because He is the only God.

Transition Time

(10-15 minutes)

Send the Juniors in small groups to the rest room and the drinking fountain. Welcome the Juniors to the worship time and involve them in the following activity.

Desert Wandering Relay. Divide the Juniors into four teams. Plan a course for the "wandering" in either a large square or rectangle shape. Assign a team to stand at each corner. Have each team choose a member and blindfold that person carefully so they can't see.

The blindfolded person must go around the square or rectangle and return to his own team. The first person to return from "wandering" wins. Allow each team member a turn. In the first two rounds, the team members are allowed to shout directions but are not allowed to leave their corner.

In the second and subsequent "wanderings," allow each team to choose a "guide" to walk with the blindfolded person (they may not touch the person) to give them careful directions. Play until each person has had a chance to do a "wandering."

Launching the Theme

(10 minutes)

You will need copies of activity page 25A and pencils.

Was it easier to find your way during the game when you were alone or with someone else? (With someone else.) **It's easier to find our way around when someone tells us which way to go.**

Distribute activity page 25A. **In life, we can listen to many voices that tell us what to do. Look at the people on this page. How do these people influence your choices?** Ask Juniors to fill in the speech balloons with what those people might say.

Sometimes different influencers tell us different things to do. A movie we watch may say that it's OK to use bad language. But we know that the Bible tells us it's not OK. How do we know which voice to listen to? Allow Juniors to discuss.

Why is God's advice for our lives always the best advice? Because He is the only God. Sometimes people can give you good advice for your life. But God *always* knows what is best for you! He is the only One who knows everything about you. Today we will worship God because He is the only God!

Explain the choices for *Building the Theme.* Allow Juniors to choose in which group to participate.

Building the Theme

(30 minutes)

1. Call to Worship. This group will read Scripture verses with motions. You will need Bibles, shelf paper, and markers. Before the session, write the words to Psalm 104:1-5 (*NIV*) on the shelf paper.

Ask the Juniors to find Psalm 104:1-5 in their Bibles. Read the verses aloud. Display the shelf paper. Assign each Junior or group of Juniors a verse. Ask them to make up motions for the verse. Each group will demonstrate the motions for their verse to the rest of the Juniors. Practice reading all the verses without motions first; then add the motions. Suggested motions follow: praise the Lord—hands waving over head; Lord, my God—point up; you are very great—clap on last two words; clothed—act like pulling on a shirt; majesty—act like putting a crown on head; wraps—act like wrapping a blanket around; stretches—stretch arms up toward ceiling; tent—hold fingertips together to form a tent shape; waters—ripple fingers; chariot—act like flicking horses' reins; wings—flap arms; set the earth—hold arms in large circle and act like setting something down.

Option: If someone in your church is familiar with sign language, ask them to teach Juniors signs for some of the words of the verses.

During *Sharing in Worship*, Juniors will read the verses using the motions.

2. Special Music. This group will prepare a praise song for the worship time. You will need "My God Is a Great God" from page 184, a poster board, and markers. Before the session, print the words to the song on poster board.

"My God is a great God,
A great God is He.
Who made the heavens
and the earth
Then the deep blue sea.

"My God is a great God,
A great God is He.
Who placed the moon and
stars for night,
Day's sun to shine upon me.

"My God is a great God,
A great God is He.
He sent His Son from
Heav'n above,
That I from my sins
might be free.

"A great big wonderful,
marvelous God,
Oh, my God is a great God,
A great God is He."

What are some things that only God can do? (Allow response.) **Today we will sing a song about things that only our great God can do.** Display the poster board for the Juniors. Sing the song once for them. Then ask them to sing with you. Sing the song several times until Juniors are comfortable singing it. Then ask them to illustrate the things only God can do around the edges of the poster board.

During *Sharing in Worship*, the Juniors will display the poster board and sing the song. Then they will name the things only God can do that they illustrated while the music of the song is played through again.

3. Scripture. This group will prepare commercials illustrating attributes of God found in the Bible. You will need copies of activity page 25B. Before the session, gather the props for the commercials found on the activity page.

The Bible contains many verses which tell us about God. We are going to be reading a few of those verses today. Distribute the activity page. Ask the Juniors to find the Scriptures listed on the page. Read them aloud together. **What do these verses tell us about God?** (Allow response.) **Today we will present commercials, which will tell things about God.** Assign each Junior or pair of Juniors a commercial from the activity page to practice and present. **Option:** If you have older Juniors, provide them a list of the following Scriptures and ask them to create their own commercials about God. Scriptures follow: Jeremiah 32:17; Psalm 11:7; Psalm 86:15; 1 John 3:1; John 17:3; Leviticus 11:45.

When the Juniors have practiced their commercials, ask them to present them for the small group. After each commercial is presented, ask a Junior to read the corresponding Scripture verse.

During *Sharing in Worship*, Juniors will present their commercials and Scripture verses for the large group.

4. Personal Praise. This group will create mobiles, praising God for things only He could create. You will need paper plates, yarn or string, construction paper, old magazines, scissor, glue, and a paper hole punch.

What are some things only God can do? (Allow response.) **One of the greatest things that only God can do is create. Humans can invent new things. But we cannot make something from nothing. God can make something from nothing. Today we will praise Him for things He has created.** Distribute the materials to the Juniors. Ask them to write **Only God can create** on both sides of their plates. Then ask them to draw or cut out magazines picture of things God created. Punch holes in their pictures and in the paper plate and ask them to use yarn or string to tie the objects to the plate, so that they hang down in a variety of lengths and shapes. Punch one hole in the top of each paper plate and tie a length of yarn in it for hanging.

Ask each Junior to choose one or two things from their mobile to tell about during the worship time.

During *Sharing in Worship*, Juniors will display their mobiles and name things God has created for which they are thankful.

5. Devotional. This group will prepare a guessing game about things only God can do. You will need pencils, paper, and Bibles.

Ask the Juniors to find Psalm 104 in their Bibles and list things only God can do. Write their suggestions on a chalkboard. Assign each Junior one or two items. Ask them to make up clues about the items. Each clue should begin with the phrase, "Only God could." Examples follow: Verse 5—It is very large and round. It is covered with water and land. Nothing can fall off this thing. Only God could make this thing from nothing. (Earth.); Verse 14—This is food and a carpet. It is also a home for many small creatures. Only God can make this grow. (Grass.); Verse 11—We usually like this cold in the summer and hot in the winter. We couldn't live without it. The world would be like a desert without it. Only God could create this thing. (Water.)

During *Sharing in Worship*, Juniors will present their clues for the large group.

6. Prayer. This group will write prayer poems to God. You will need Bibles, pencils, and paper.

Ask the Juniors to find Psalm 104 in their Bibles. Ask them to spend a few minutes looking through the Psalm. **This Psalm names many reasons God is great and many things that only He can do. We are going to write praise poems to God about some of the things mentioned in this Psalm.**

Ask the Juniors to write a poem or psalm to God in one of the following forms. Cinquain: (SIN-kane) a five-line poem in which the first line states a subject in one word; the second line describes the subject in two words; the third line is three action words (verbs) about the subject; the fourth line is a sentence about how one feels about the subject; and the fifth line is one word that means the same as the subject or a repeat of the word in the first line. Haiku: (HI-ku) a three-line poem in which the first line has five syllables, the second line has seven syllables, and the third line has five syllables. Psalm: Have the Juniors read Psalm 100. Using Psalm 100 as an example, have the Juniors write a similar psalm of praise to God. They need to include thanks to God for His special blessings.

During *Sharing in Worship*, the Juniors will read their praise poems as prayers to God.

Sharing in Worship

(20-25 minutes)

Omit any of the following sections if you did not offer the corresponding activity. The devotional may be completed without the presentation of Group 5.

Call to Worship (Group 1): Group 1 presents their verse with motions.

Special Music (Group 2): Ask Group 2 to sing their song and tell the things only God can do. Then ask the large group to join them in singing the song again.

Scripture (Group 3): **The Bible tells us many things about our great God. Group 3 found some of those things and prepared commercials to help us understand. See if you can guess what thing about God each commercial is telling us.** Group 3 presents commercials. After each commercial, ask the large group to tell the attribute of God. Then ask the Junior to read the Scripture that corresponds with the commercial.

Lord's Supper: God is the only God, and Jesus is His only Son. Jesus is also the only way that we can come to God. Jesus died for us, so that we would be able to talk to and know the great God who created the earth! Let's thank Jesus for what He did for us now. Pray and serve the Lord's Supper.

Offering: Sometimes it seems like there are so many important things to spend our money on that we can never get enough. Maybe we need new tennis shoes or a new outfit or a new game. Giving money to God may not seem very important. Maybe we put it off or forget. There are many, many tennis shoes and outfits and games in the world. But there is only one God! He is the most important thing in the world. Giving our lives and our money to Him is the best choice we can make. Choose two children to collect the offering.

Personal Praise (Group 4): **We have named many things that only God can do. But one of the greatest things that only God can do is create. Man can invent many wonderful things. But we cannot make something from nothing. Only God can do that. Let's join Group 4 in praising God for making so many wonderful things from nothing.** Group 4 presents their mobiles.

Devotional (Group 5): You will need a table and chair set up in front of the large group.

What if I started out our worship time this way? Oh, great chair, how great you are. Please bless this day. Wonderful table, please guide my thoughts today. Praying to a table or chair seems silly, doesn't it.

In the Old Testament we learned how Aaron made a golden calf for the Israelites. When Moses came down from Mount Sinai, Moses was very angry with Aaron and the Israelites. Moses knew the Ten Commandments said, "You shall not make for yourself an idol in the form of anything in heaven above or on the earth beneath or in the waters below. You shall not bow down to them or worship them; for I, the Lord your God, am a jealous God."

Many religions around the world worship animals or statues. God calls those things idols.

We can also have idols in our lives. An idol can be anything which takes our attention away from God. Can you think of anything which might be an idol in your life? (Let the Juniors respond; then explain that any thing we treat as more important than God is an idol.)

We have been talking today about the many ways we know that God is the only God. He is more important than anything in the world. Group 5 found some more reasons why God is the only God. Let's see if we can guess what they are. Ask Group 5 to present their clues and allow the large group to guess. If you did not offer this activity, omit this section and continue with the following conversation.

When we think of how great God is, it seems silly to treat anything else as more important than God. It seems almost as silly as praying to a chair or a table. God is great! He is greater than anything we know or see. He is the only God!

Prayer (Group 6): Ask Group 6 to read their prayer poems. Then ask several volunteers to say sentence praise prayers, thanking God for being the only God.

Closing Moments

(10-15 minutes)

Divide the Juniors into two teams. Ask each team to think of a list of things that we are tempted to think are more important than God. Teams will take turns answering "yes" or "no" questions about a thing on their list. For each thing guessed correctly, the team who guessed gets a point.

God Gives Us Everything We Need

Worship Focus

Worship God because He gives us everything we need.

Transition Time

(10-15 minutes)

Send the students in small groups to the rest room and the drinking fountain. Welcome them to the Worship time and involve them in the following activity.

Wants and Needs. You will need old magazines, two pieces of poster board, scissors, markers, and glue. Before the session, title one poster board **Wants.** Title the other poster board **Needs.**

Ask the Juniors to cut pictures out of magazines and glue them on the posters. Encourage them to find as many pictures as possible to cover the poster boards.

Launching the Theme

(10 minutes)

You will need copies of activity page 25B and pencils.

Distribute the activity page. **Look at the things on this page. What things do you want? What things do you need? Cross out the things you don't need. Put a star by your two most important needs.** Allow Juniors time to do so.

When we really think about it, we don't need nearly as many things as we think we do—things like new clothes or a new bike. Just a couple of weeks ago, we talked about how God provides our physical needs, like food, and clothes, and a place to live. But our most important needs aren't even things we can see. Our important needs are things like love, and peace, and salvation. No amount of money or work or time can get rid of those needs. The only One who can meet every one of those needs is God. He knows everything we need, and He gives it to us. Today we will worship God because He gives us everything we need.

Explain the choices for *Building the Theme* and allow the Juniors to choose in which group to participate.

Building the Theme

(30 minutes)

1. Call to Worship. This group will create a choral reading about our wants and needs. You will need the posters made during *Transition Time*, paper, and pencils.

Display the posters for the Juniors. **Does God always give us what we want?** (No.) **Does God always give us what we need?** (Yes.) **Let's use these posters to thank God for giving us everything we need.** Ask the Juniors to write sentences about what God gives us. They may use the things pictured on the posters. The first part of the sentence should name something we want. The second part should name something God gives us that we need. For example, "God, we want new clothes. But we need love. You give us love." "God, we want great bikes. But we need Jesus to die for us. You sent Jesus to die for us."

When the sentences are completed, ask the Juniors to share them with the large group.

During *Sharing in Worship*, each Junior will say his or her sentences. After each Junior speaks, the group will say together, "You give us everything we need." Practice the presentation during the small-group time.

2. Special Music. This group will prepare a paraphrase of a hymn to share during the worship time. You will need "We Give Thee But Thine Own" from page 192, a dictionary, shelf paper, and markers. Before the session, write the words to the hymn on a large piece of shelf paper. Leave room between each stanza for the Juniors to write.

"We give Thee but Thine own,
Whate'er the gift may be,
All that we have is Thine alone,
A trust, O Lord, from Thee.

"May we Thy bounties thus
As stewards true receive,
And gladly, as Thou blessest
us,
To Thee our firstfruits give.

"To comfort and to bless,
To find a balm for woe,
To tend the lone and fatherless,
Is angels' work below.

"The captive to release,
To God the lost to bring,
To teach the way of life
and peace,
That is a Christlike thing.

"And we believe Thy word,
Though dim our faith may be,
Whate'er for Thine we do,
O Lord,
We do it unto Thee."

What do you own that belongs to God? (Allow response.) **Everything we own belongs to God because He made it. Today we will look at the words to a hymn about God's ownership.** Display the shelf paper for the Juniors. Read through the stanzas for them. Assign each Junior or pair of Juniors one stanza of the song. Ask them to write the stanza in their own words. They may use the dictionary to look up any unfamiliar words. An example follows for Stanza 1: When we give You anything we own, God, we are just giving You something that is already Yours. Everything we have belongs to You. You have given it to us to care for."

Assist Juniors as needed. When Juniors have completed the paraphrases, ask them to share them with the small group.

During *Sharing in Worship*, Juniors will read their paraphrases as the music to the song is played softly in the background.

3. Scripture. This group will read a Scripture about giving and tell what they will give to God. You will need Bibles, pencils, and paper.

Ask the Juniors to find and read Psalm 116:12-14 (ICB). **What does the Psalm writer want to do to God for all the good God has done to him?** (Repay God.) **What does he mean when he says he will lift up the cup of salvation?** (Let other people see what God has done; tell them about God.) **What do you think he means when he says he will fulfill his vows to the Lord?** (He will do what he told God he would do?) **What is a vow?** (A promise.) **We can worship God like the Psalm writer did. We can worship Him by promising what we will give Him.**

Ask the Juniors to write a sentence modeled after verse 13 which tells what they will give to God. Encourage them to write about what they can give to God.

When Juniors have completed their sentences, ask them to practice reciting verse 12, followed by their sentence, followed by verse 14. An example follows:

What can I give the Lord
for all the good things he Has
given to me?

I will give him my talent to talk.
And I will talk about the Lord.

In front of all His people,
I will give the Lord what I
promised.

You may wish to write out verses 12 and 14 on poster board and display it for the Juniors to aid them in their recitation.

During *Sharing in Worship*, Juniors will share their verses and promises.

4. Offering. This group will make bookmarks to give to each Junior during the worship time. You will need copies of activity page 26A, markers, scissors, and glue.

Ask the Juniors to find Psalm 116:12 in their Bibles. Read the verse aloud together. **What can we give to God for all He has given us?** (Allow Juniors to respond.) **Today we will make bookmarks for the large group to remind us to give to God.** Distribute the activity pages. Ask Juniors to color and cut out the bookmarks and glue them together. Make enough bookmarks for each person in the large group.

During *Sharing in Worship*, Juniors will distribute the bookmarks to the large group.

5. Devotional. This group will make "ME" posters that will include their talents, hobbies, and personalities. You will need poster board cut into half sheets (one half sheet for each Junior in your group), construction paper, markers, pencils, scissors, glue, and old magazines.

Distribute materials to the Juniors. Ask them to make a poster showing their talents, hobbies, and personalities. They may draw pictures on construction paper or cut pictures out of magazines.

When the posters are completed, ask the Juniors to look at their posters and decide what they can give to God or how they can give to God. Some examples follow: helping people know about Jesus; singing or playing an instrument in the worship time; using hobbies to influence others for God; being kind to younger children; helping their parents at home; being kind and obedient.

On the bottom of their "ME" poster, have the Juniors write what they can give to God.

During *Sharing in Worship*, Juniors will show their posters and tell what they can give to God.

6. Prayer. This group will prepare a prayer about what God has given and ways to give to God. You will need paper, pencils, a poster board, and markers. Before the session, divide the poster board into four columns. Title the columns **Praise, Thanksgiving, Requests for others, Personal requests.**

What are the four parts of prayer? (Allow response. Display the poster board.) **One part of prayer is praise to God—telling God things we know about Him and that we love Him. Another**

part of prayer is thanksgiving—thanking God for things He made and things He has given us. A third part of prayer is requests for other people—praying for sick or hurting people we know. The fourth part of prayer is personal request—praying that God will help us. We are going to write a prayer to God about the things He gives us and the things we can give others, using these four things.

First, what can we praise God for? What is it about God that makes Him able to give us everything we need? (He has all power; He has all knowledge; He created all people.) **One way to praise God is to give to Him. What are some things we can give to Him?** Write the Juniors' responses in the **Praise** column.

God has given us everything we need. What are some things He has given us that we can thank Him for? Record the Juniors' responses in the **Thanksgiving** column.

What are some things that some other people you know need? Write responses in the **Requests for others** column.

What are some things that you need? Write responses in the **Personal requests** column.

Ask four Juniors to pray for things in the four columns during the worship time.

During *Sharing in Worship*, the Juniors will lead the large group in prayer.

Sharing in Worship
(20-25 minutes)

Omit any of the following sections if you did not offer the corresponding activity. The offering and devotional may be completed without the presentations of Groups 4 and 5.

Call to Worship (Group 1): **Does God give us everything we want?** (No.) **Does God give us everything we need?** (Yes.) **Let's praise God for giving us everything we need.** Ask Group 1 to come and present their sentences.

Special Music (Group 2): **What do you own that belongs to God?** (Allow response.) **Everything we own comes from God because He made it. Listen to the thoughts of this song by Group 2.** Ask Group 2 to share their paraphrases as the music to the song is playing.

Scripture (Group 3): **The writer of Psalm 116 knew that God had given him everything. He wanted to give some things back to God. Group 3 read that Psalm and thought of some things they could give to God.** Group 3 says the verses and names things they will give to God.

Lord's Supper: We talked earlier about how our greatest needs were things we couldn't see. One of those needs is for a Savior. We needed Jesus to die for us, so we could live forever with God. We needed Jesus to die, so we wouldn't have to suffer the terrible punishment for our sins. Let's thank God for His great love in sending Jesus for us. Pray and serve the Lord's Supper.

Offering (Group 4): **Group 3 talked about things they could give to God. Now everyone will have a chance to choose something to give to God. Group 4 made some bookmarks which will remind us to give to God.** Ask Group 4 to distribute the bookmarks and pencils. Ask the Juniors to write on the backs of their bookmarks what they will give to God. If you did not offer this activity, distribute index cards and ask Juniors to write what they will give to God and place the cards in their Bibles.

Pray and choose two children to collect the offering.

Devotional (Group 5): You will need slips of paper, pencils, small boxes, scissors, wrapping paper, and tape. Before the session choose several of the following Scriptures to write on slips of paper. Place each paper in a small box and wrap the box with wrapping paper. Scriptures follow: Philippians 4:7; Philippians 4:19; Romans 10:9, 10; John 10:28; Matthew 6:33; John 10:10; Galatians 5:22, 23; John 2:29; 2 Timothy 3:16, 17; Colossians 1:13, 14.

Ask Juniors to find Psalm 139:13-17 in their Bibles. Read the verses to the Juniors.

God has created you to be a unique, one-of-a-kind creation. He has made you special. What are some ways God creates each person to be special? How has God made you different from other people? Group 5 made some posters telling how they are special. They will share their posters with us now. Ask Group 5 to share their posters and tell what they will give to God. If you did not offer this activity, omit this part and continue with the following discussion.

What are some special ways you can give to God? Allow response.

God has made each person unique and special. And He has a plan for each one of you. And God's plan is not only for your future; His plan is for right now as well. God gives you everything you need right now, and He will continue to give to you in the future. Let's look at some things God gives us right now. Distribute the gift-wrapped boxes to the Juniors. Ask them to open the boxes and read the Scripture inside to the large group. After each Scripture is read, ask the large group to tell what God gives us.

God is so great! He knows everything we need! And we see that the Bible tells us that He will give it to us!

Prayer (Group 6): Ask Group 6 to share their four-part prayer.

Closing Moments
(10-15 minutes)

You will need a poster board and markers. Before the session, title the poster board **God Gives Us Everything We Need.**

Lay the poster board on a table or on the floor. Ask Juniors to write what they will do to give to God this week and sign their name.

ACTIVITY PAGES

1
3
6
5

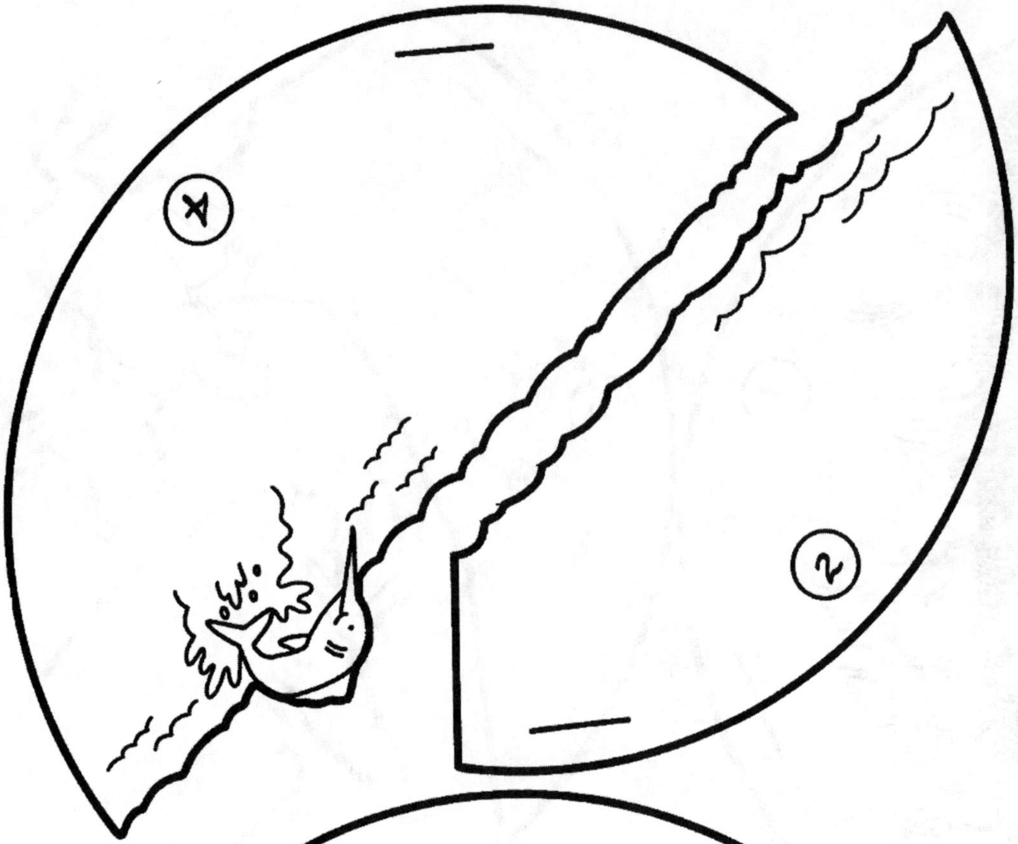
4
2

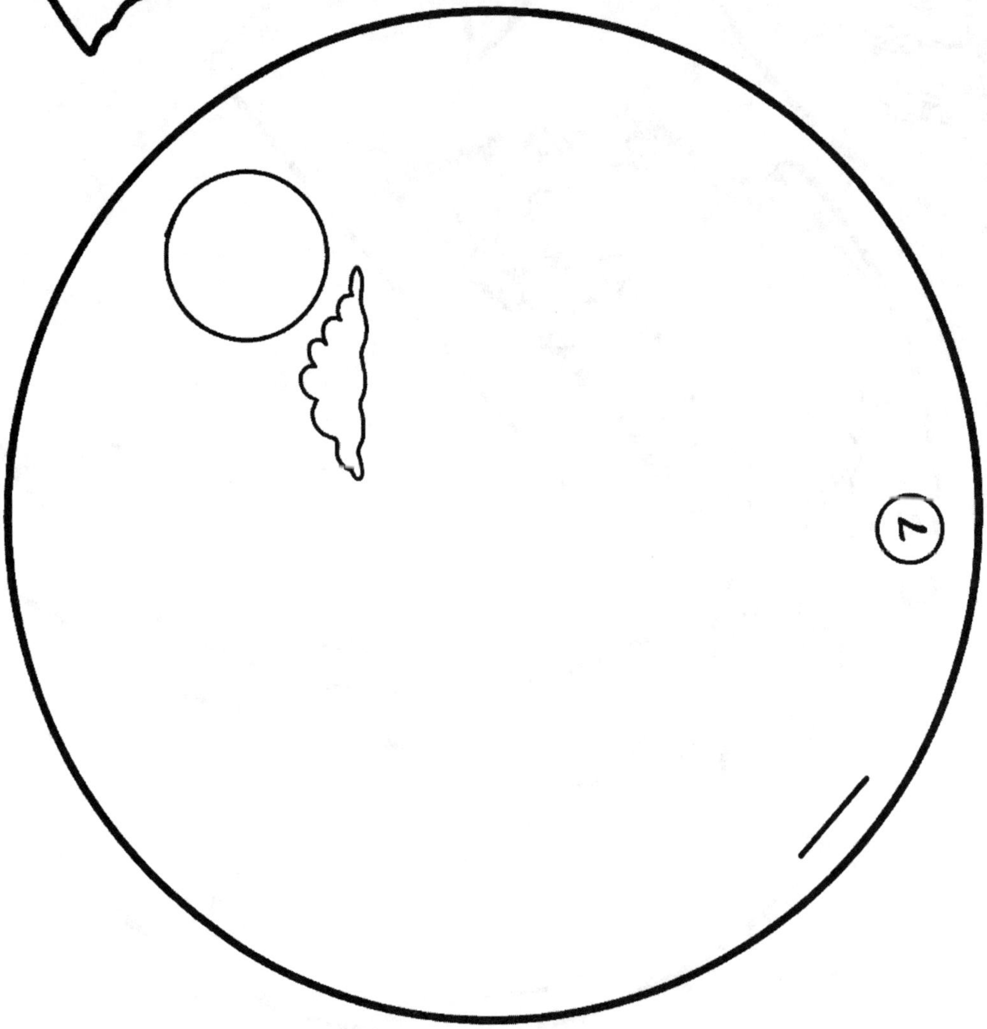
1

What's the Difference?

Draw a stick figure beside the sentences that only describe people.

1. God wants them to reproduce.
2. Are born knowing how to do some things.
3. God wants them to take care of the world.
4. Are made by God.
5. Can think and reason.
6. Can feel pain.
7. Can decide to do good or bad.
8. Can be taught to do things.
9. Parts of the body can fix themselves when broken.
10. Can speak a language.
11. Can communicate their needs.
12. Can love God.
13. Are made in God's image.

I praise you because you made me in an amazing and wonderful way (Psalm 139:14, *ICB*).

Verses	Who sinned?	What did they do?	What was their punishment?
1. Genesis 2:16, 17; 3:6, 16, 17, <u>23</u>			
2. Exodus 32:7, 8, <u>35</u>			
3. Numbers 20:2-<u>12b</u>			
4. 1 Samuel 15:2, 3, 9, <u>26</u>			
5. Jonah 1:1-3, <u>17</u>			
6. Luke 22:55-<u>61</u>			
7. Acts 9:1-7, <u>8</u>, <u>9</u>			

What You Will Need
200 used kitchen matches
cross pattern from this page
9" x 6" piece of cardboard
a marker or crayon
white glue

What To Do
1. Cut out the cross on this page and trace it onto the cardboard.
2. Cut out the cardboard cross.
3. Write the words from Isaiah 53:5 on the cross.
4. Turn the cross over. Glue four matches in the center of the cross as shown picture 1.
5. Glue the other matches to the cross as shown in picture 2. Place the matches on the cardboard so that the burned ends point outward. You will glue ten groups of matches to the cross. There will be about 20 matches in each group.

Picture 1

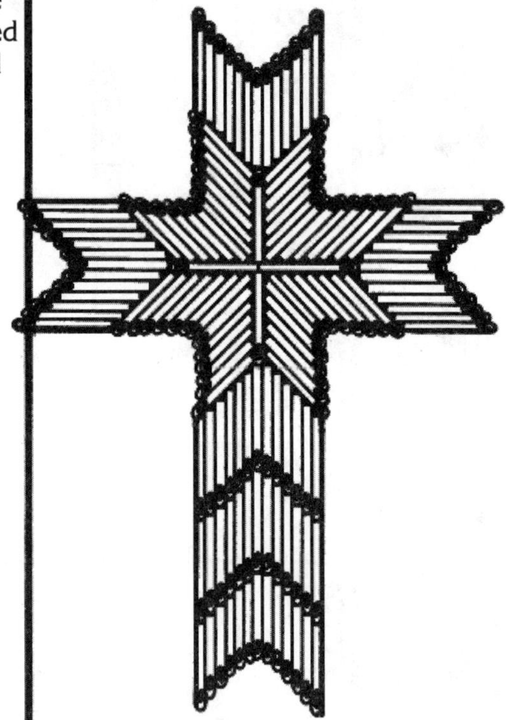

Picture 2

1. Your mother is sick. Because she is in the hospital, you have to stay with a baby-sitter that you don't like. Everything is different without your mother home. You know that God keeps His promises. What will you do? (1 John 5:14)

2. One night you remember that you are having a Science test the next day. You forgot to take your book home to study. The next day your best friend says that she'll put her paper close to you, so you can see the answers. You usually get good grades and study hard. You know that God keeps His promises. What will you do?

3. You go to your friend's house to spend the night. At midnight, you are both bored and flip through the channels on his TV. You start watching a movie. Soon you begin to feel uncomfortable because this movie has many bad words and scenes. You ask him to turn the channel. He turns the TV off and yells at you for being too good. You know that God keeps His promises. What will you do? (Psalm 62:12)

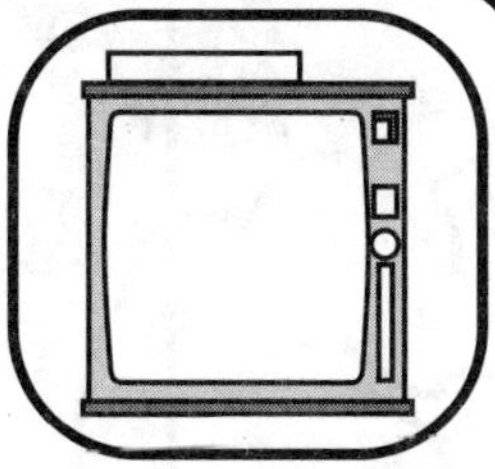

4. Your big brother's friend comes to your house often. He always teases you. He calls you names and makes fun of the way you dress. You are very angry with him. Sometimes you think of ways to get even. You know that God keeps His promises. What will you do? (Romans 12:17-19; 2 Thessalonians 1:6-8)

5. Your grandfather died this morning. You are sad and know that you will miss him. He took walks with you and sat by you in church. You know that God keeps His promises. What will you do? (John 3:16)

6. In the lunchroom, your table was doing "the wave." You were the only person who did not do it. The teacher made everyone at your table miss recess. You were innocent, but were punished. You know that God keeps His promises. What will you do? (Proverbs 2:8)

Fulfilled Promises

Read the verses. Find the promises God made about Jesus. Write the promises on the blank lines below the verses.

1. Micah 5:2

____

____

2. Matthew 2:14, 15

____

____

3. Matthew 8:16, 17

____

____

4. Matthew 13:34, 35

____

____

5. John 12:12-15

____

____

6. Isaiah 53:5, 9

____

____

7. Matthew 1:21

____

____

Anywhere With Jesus
Anywhere with Jesus I can safely go;
Anywhere He leads me in this world below,
Anywhere without Him dearest joys would fade.
Anywhere with Jesus, I am not afraid.

I Never Walk Alone
I never walk alone in stormy weather,
When winds of trouble sweep about my head;
I know I'm safe, because we are together,
And 'round me his protecting love is spread.

O Worship the King
O worship the King, all-glorious above,
and gratefully sing His wonderful love:
Our Shield and Defender, the ancient of days,
Pavilioned in splendor and girded with praise.

Tis the Blessed Hour of Prayer
Tis the blessed hour of prayer when our hearts lowly bend.
And we gather to Jesus, our Saviour and Friend.
If we come to Him in faith, His protection to share
What a balm for the weary, O how sweet to be there.

SUNDAY	MONDAY	TUESDAY	WEDNESDAY	THURSDAY	FRIDAY	SATURDAY
		1	2	3	4	5
6	7	8	9	10	11	12
13	14	15	16	17	18	19
20	21	22	23	24	25	26
27	28	29	30			

Wonderful Peace
I am resting tonight in this wonderful peace,
Resting sweetly in Jesus' control;
for I'm kept from all danger by night and by day,
and his glory is flooding my soul.

Safely Through Another Week
Safely through another week
God has brought us on our way;
Let us now a blessing seek,
waiting in His courts today.

SCENE 1

Teacher and Carl stand in front of the class. Class is seated.

Teacher: Good morning, class. I want to introduce a new student, Carl.
Holly *(to David)*: Look at those shoes! They look like my dad's.
David: I'd die if I had to wear them.
Justin *(to David and Holly)*: He's blind too. His glasses are an inch thick.
Carl takes a seat close to Holly, Justin, and David.
Teacher: It's time for math. Do all the problems on page 34.
Students begin writing. Carl breaks his pencil lead.
Carl: *(to David)* Where's the pencil sharpener?
David: Right in front of you. *(to Holly and Justin)* He is blind!
Holly, Justin, and David laugh.
Justin *(to Carl)*: Where did you get those shoes?
Carl: My tennis shoes are too small. I have to wear these until I get a new pair.
Holly *(to Justin and David)*: He won't be playing baseball with us—not in those shoes!
Justin *(to Holly and David)*: He couldn't see the ball anyway.
Holly, Justin, and David laugh. Carl hears them and is embarassed.

SCENE 2

The next day at Carl's home. Father and mother are on stage. Carl is off stage. Carl has on tennis shoes and no glasses.

Mother: Carl, are you ready for school?
Carl *(in a grumpy voice)*: I guess so.
Carl tries to sneak across the stage. He walks slowly because his shoes are too small.
Father: Carl, you're walking funny, and where are your glasses?
Carl *(still sneaking out)*: I'm OK.
Mother: Carl, come here. Those shoes are too small. You know we're buying new ones as soon as we get settled.
Carl: I know, but the kids at school laughed at the other shoes. They look stupid!
Father: I suppose that's also why you aren't wearing your glasses.
Carl: Yeah.
Mother: Doing what the kids want is not good protection against getting teased. Suppose today they decide that your hair is the wrong color. Are you going to change that?
Carl: Could I?
Father: No. We have to trust God to give us protection. He can do it much better than we can. Let's pray right now that He'll protect you and help you do what's right.
Mother: And maybe they would like to come over next week. By then you'll have your tennis shoes, and you can all play baseball.

·····Family Facts·····

Lives on a farm 	Was not born in the United States 	Has a large dog 	Has more than one cat 
Is over eighty years old **80**	Is under one year old 	Has a pet that is <u>not</u> a dog or cat 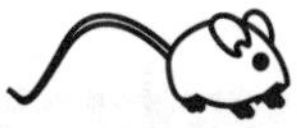	Drives a motorcycle 
Has white hair 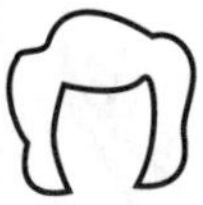	Drives a truck 	Bakes cookies 	Has more than three sisters or brothers 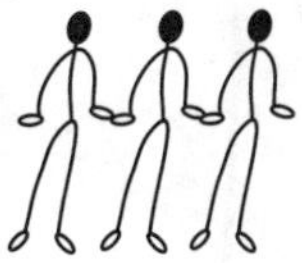
Plays a musical instrument 	Sends you a birthday card through the mail 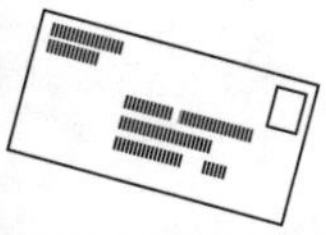	Is the same age as you 	Lives in a different state than you 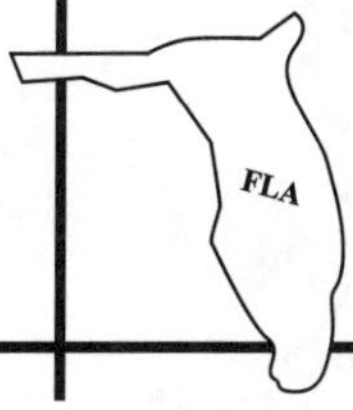

1
The Lord's faithfulness continues through all generations. (Psalm 100:5)
2
Our ancestors ______ what you did in their days. (Psalm 44:1)
3
The Lord is ______ in all he does. (Psalm 33:4)
4
I will make your faithfulness known through all ______. (Psalm 89:1)

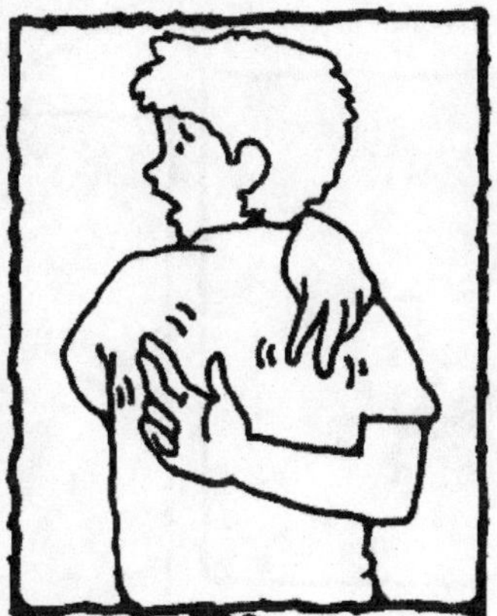

Christ died for us while we were still weak. We were living against God, but at the right time, Christ died for us. Christ died for us while we were still sinners. In this way God shows his great love for us. We have been made right with God by the blood of Christ's death. So through Christ we will surely be saved from God's anger. I mean that while we were God's enemies, God made friends with us through the death of his son. Surely now that we are God's friends, God will save us through his son's life. And not only that, but now we are also very happy in God through our Lord Jesus Christ. Through Jesus we are now God's friends again. (Romans 5:6, 8-11, ICB)

I need Jesus because . . .

God provided Jesus to . . .

Write the name of one part of your house.

What is it made of?

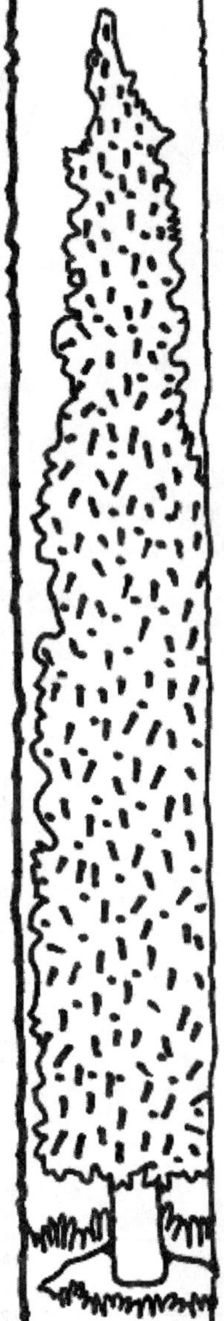

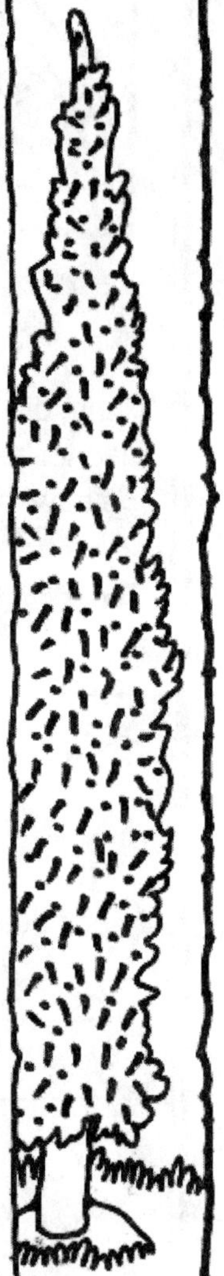

What raw materials make up that part?

What did God provide to furnish those raw materials?

God Always Hears Prayers

Scripture	Person	Prayer
Exodus 3:7	Manoah	freedom from suffering
Numbers 11:18	Cornelius	a son
Judges 13:8, 9	David	life for Lazarus
1 Kings 17:17-22	Israelites	how to raise the boy
Psalm 18:6	Elijah	someone to teach him about God
Luke 1:13	Zechariah	safety from Saul
John 11:41-44	Israelites	meat
Acts 10:30, 31	Jesus	life for the boy

The Lord listens when I pray to him.

(Psalm 4:3b, *ICB*)

Family	Friends	Me

BILL BROWN
'a man
you can
trust'
RESCUE
123
STOP
BURGERYUM
ENTER

Dear God,
My best friend told lies about me. What should I do?
Ready to get even
Matthew 6:14

Dear Get even,

____

____

God

Dear God,
I get $3 a week allowance. What should I do with it?
Rich in Iowa
2 Corinthians 9:7

Dear Rich,

____

____

God

Dear God,
My brother wants to borrow my new bike. Should I let him?
Just Wondering
Matthew 5:42

Dear Wondering,

____

____

God

Dear God,
I hate the boy who sits beside me in school. What should I do?
Mad
Matthew 5:44

Dear Mad,

____

____

God

Dear God,
I'm worried about the chance of war.
Worried
Matthew 6:34

Dear Worried,

____

____

God

Dear God,
My parents argue a lot. What should I do?
Afraid
Philippians 4:6

Dear Afraid,

____

____

God

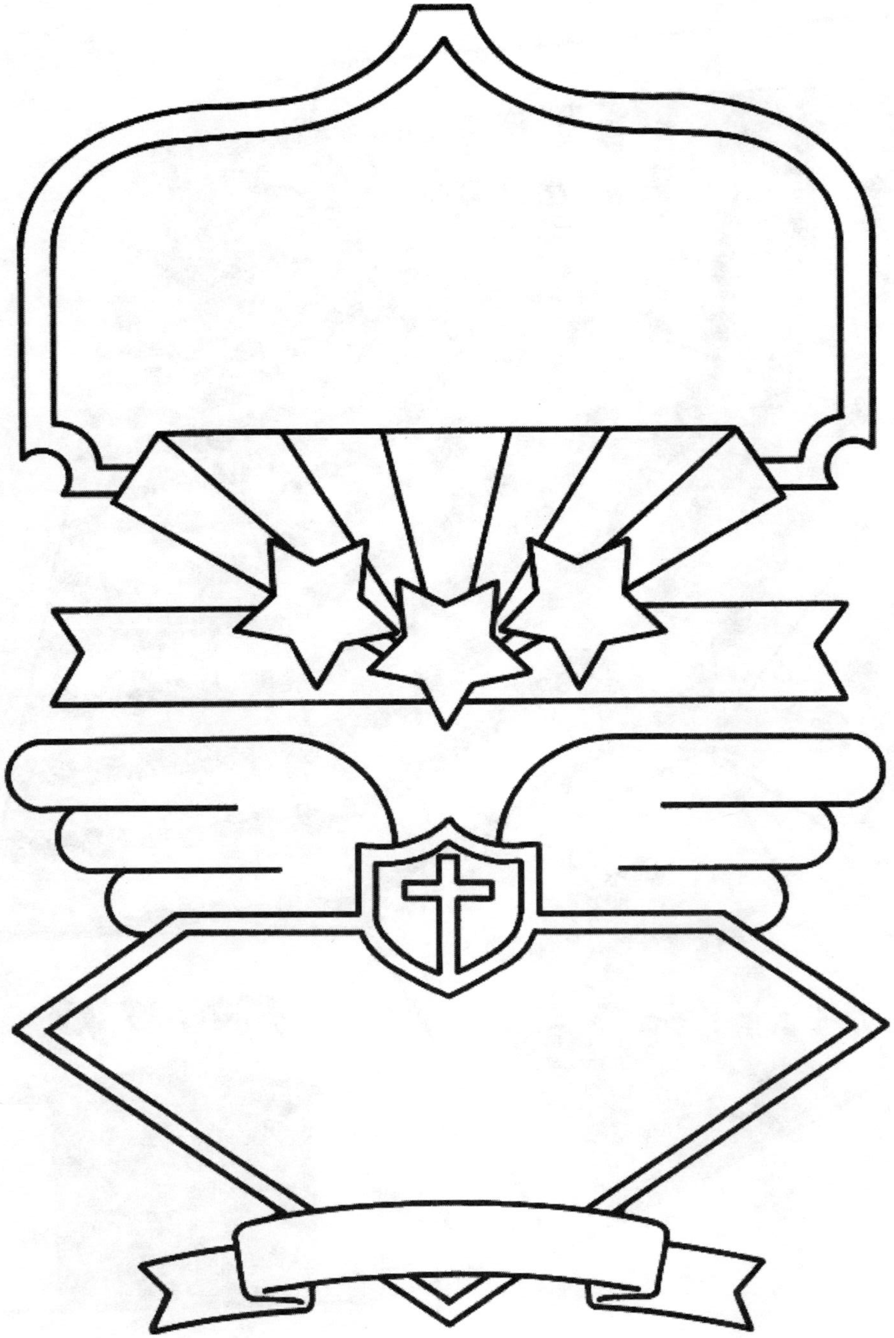

I Honor You, Jesus

You ________ me. (Revelation 1:5b)

You were wounded for the ___________ things I did. (Isaiah 53:5a)

You __________ for me while I was a sinner. (Romans 5:8)

You have __________ me from my sins. (Revelation 1:5b)

You will rule __________ and ever. (Revelation 11:15 b)

Because I believe in you, you will give me _________ _________. (John 3:16)

____

____

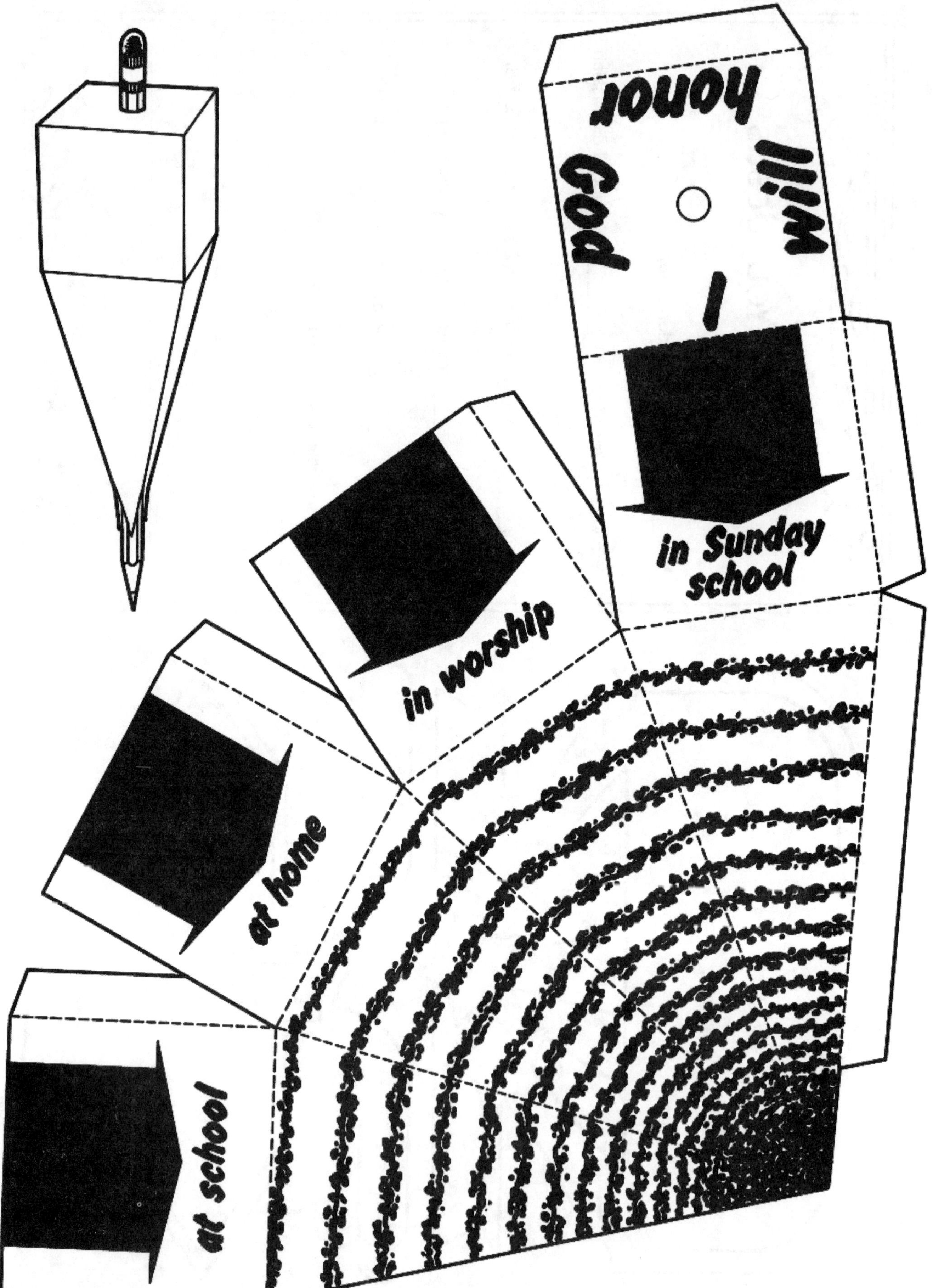
I
will
honor
God
in Sunday school
in worship
at home
at school

Reporter: Good morning. This is ________________ reporting live from ________________ .
(your name) (your city)

Today's topic is Heaven. What is it like? Our panel includes some of the world's top experts on Heaven. First we have David, former king of Israel. *(As panel members are introduced, they bow.)* He is the noted author of the book, *Psalms*. Next we have Matthew, apostle of Jesus and author of *Matthew*. Luke is the author of the book of *Luke*. Both of these men learned from the Holy Spirit about Heaven. Lazarus actually went to Heaven. He'll share his experience with us. Nicodemus was taught about Heaven by Jesus. Paul was an apostle and wrote about Heaven. And finally, John was taken by God to Heaven. You can read of his experience in the book of *Revelation*. We are honored to have you gentlemen with us tonight.

David, who lives in Heaven?

David: (Psalm 33:13)____

Reporter: Matthew, who can go to Heaven?

Matthew: (Matthew 7:21)____

Reporter: Luke, why does God let Christians go to Heaven?

Luke: (Luke 6:23)____

Reporter: Lazarus, who did you see in Heaven?

Lazarus: (Luke 16:22)____

Reporter: Lazarus, how did you feel in Heaven? How was it different from your life on earth?

Lazarus: (Luke 16:19-22, 25)____

Reporter: Nicodemus, according to Jesus, who can go to Heaven?

Nicodemus: (John 3:16)____

Reporter: Paul, where will you go when you die?

Paul: (1 Corinthians 5:1)____

Reporter: John, what did you see happening in Heaven?

John: (Revelation 7:9-12)____

Reporter: John, how is Heaven different from earth? What things are not in Heaven that are on earth?

John: (Revelation 7:16, 17; 21:25-27)____

Reporter: Thank you to our special guests. I'm looking forward to Heaven. I hope to see you there.

Read Jarrod's test. Decide which answers are right and which are wrong. Write Jarrod's grade at the top of his paper.

Name Jarrod Reeves

Heaven Test

Write True or False by each sentence.

T 1. Only perfect people can go to Heaven.

T 2. Since so many people will be in Heaven, it will be just like it is on earth.

T 3. Heaven is an imaginary place.

T 4. Everybody will go to Heaven.

T 5. Heaven is a scary place.

T 6. After God has punished me for the bad things I've done, I can go to Heaven.

T 7. If I sin when I'm a Christian, I can't go to Heaven.

T 8. Heaven will be boring.

Lord, you have examined me.
    You know all about me.
You know when I sit down and when I get up.
    You know my thoughts before I think them.
You know where I go and where I lie down.
    You know well everything I do.
Lord, even before I say a word,
    you already know what I am going to say.
You are all around me—in front and in back.
    You have put your hand on me.
You knowledge is amazing to me.
    It is more than I can understand.
God, examine me and know my heart.
    Test me and know my thoughts.
See if there is any bad thing in me.
    Lead me in the way you set long ago.

Psalm 139:1-6, 23, 24 (ICB)

God's
Knowledge

1. *(Pupils are talking together before Sunday school.)*
Dan: My dad made me bring a dollar for the offering! He says it's good to give. Giving my money away sure isn't good for me!
(From God's guidance, explain to Dan why giving is good for him.)

2. **Teacher** *(to class)*: We will take a special offering next week for the Christmas baskets for needy people. Please bring extra money for the offering.
(Pupils talk to each other.)
Laura: I can't give any money! I just saved enough to buy a t-shirt. It says "God is Number 1." Besides, I don't even know any poor people.
(From God's guidance, explain to Laura that if we love God we must share with God's people who are in need.)

3. *(Pupils are passing the offering basket. One pupil pulls out his wallet and slowly puts five dollar bills into the basket, making sure that the others see him. The other pupils look impressed.)*
Jonathan: I gave five dollars. Since God rewards people who give, I'll get a great big prize.
(From God's guidance, explain to Jonathan that God wants people to give quietly. We should give to please God, not to impress people.)

4. *(A family is talking.)*
Father: The family of a man at work is having a hard time this year. I think our family can help them by buying the children new shoes. We can all help pay.
Holly: That's not fair. You already make me give at church. Now I have to give more? I earned this money all by myself. It's mine.
(From God's guidance, explain to Holly that God wants us to give cheerfully. All our money comes from God.)

This is hard!
Jamie is done!

COOKIES
How did this happen?

This is all for me.
Next Day
Do you want some of my candy bar?
GOO-BAR

ELDERLY • WIDOW • SINGLE PARENT • TEEN • CHILD

• WIFE • POLICE • NURSE • ORPHAN • SOLDIER • MISSIONARY • PRISONER • HUSBAND

• SINGLE PARENT • WIDOW • ELDERLY • NURSE • HUSBAND

• POLICE • ORPHAN • SOLDIER • MISSIONARY • PRISONER • HUSBAND • WIFE •

Lonely People

M	A	B	E	P	R	I	S	O	N	E	R	S
W	I	D	O	W	C	W	I	F	E	S	O	U
L	A	S	J	I	N	O	N	A	T	E	R	M
F	E	O	S	I	N	G	G	O	E	L	D	O
C	A	L	O	I	B	E	L	D	E	R	L	Y
O	H	D	P	M	O	T	E	A	N	A	P	E
B	U	I	O	X	R	N	P	A	S	Y	X	R
D	S	E	L	M	P	P	A	T	I	E	N	T
X	B	R	I	D	H	A	R	R	T	I	O	N
G	A	S	C	H	A	I	E	N	Y	K	I	L
A	N	D	E	O	N	O	N	U	R	S	E	S
N	D	O	W	I	S	T	T	H	E	T	I	M

God Cares When I Am Lonely

Listen to God.

Rest.

Help others.

Pray.

Think about God.

Matthew 14:13, 14

I Samuel 3:10

Mark 6:31

Luke 5:16

Psalm 63:6

God gives us _______ by His love so we can _______ His rules. Psalm 119:88

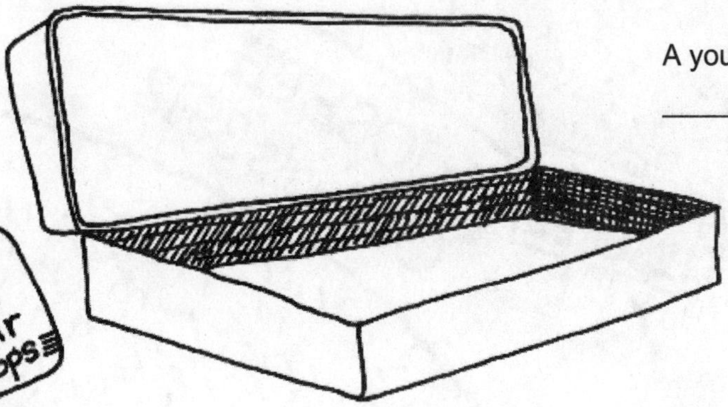

A young person can live a pure ________ by obeying God's _______.
Psalm 119:9

God's word is like a ________ for our feet and a ________ for our way.
Psalm 119:105

God will give us life by His _______.
Psalm 119:107

God's word is like a ________ for our feet and a ________ for our way.
Psalm 119:105

God will comfort us with His _______.
Psalm 119:76

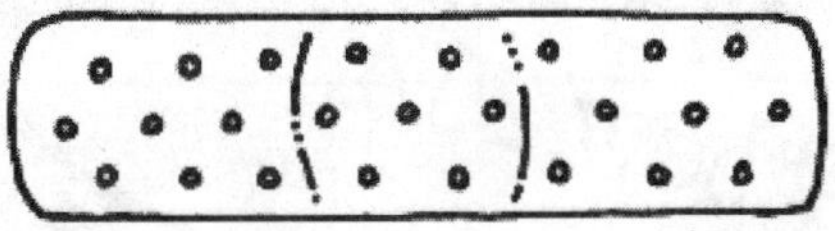

God can open our ________ to see wonderful things in His _________.
Psalm 119:18

TEMPTATION MAP

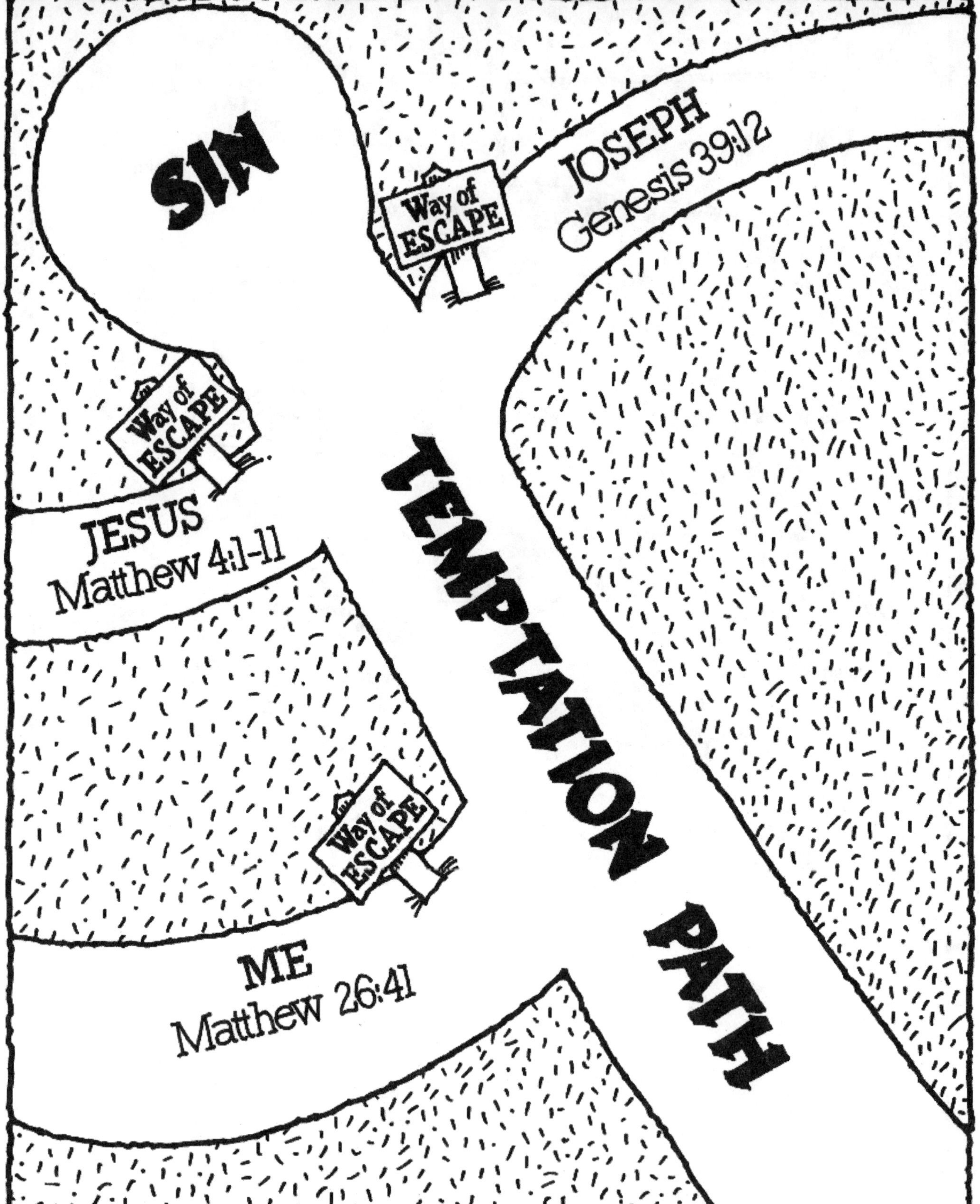

E
M
Y
C
R

The Merciful Solution

Micah 6:8

____

Matthew 5:7

____

Luke 6:36

____

James 2:13

____

Christmas Checklist

I helped put up Christmas lights outside.

I helped decorate the Christmas tree.

I helped make Christmas cookies or candy.

My family has a nativity scene.

I have wrapped my gifts.

I have gone Christmas caroling.

I have sung or listened to a Christmas music program.

I have bought or made gifts for my family.

I have sent Christmas cards.

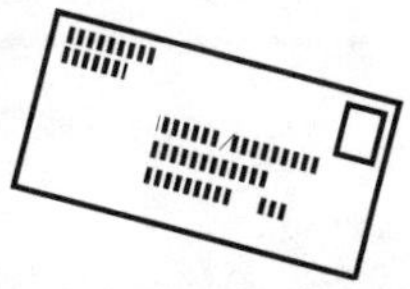

I have helped eat Christmas cookies or candy.

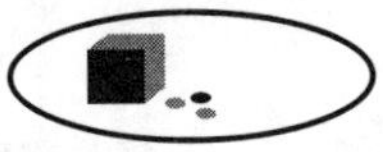

I have watched a Christmas special on TV.

My family has an Advent calendar.

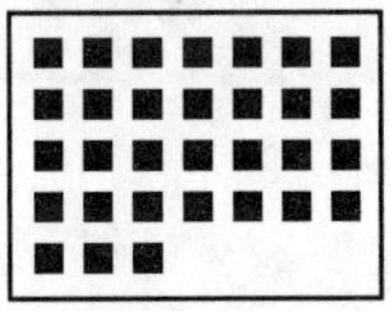

I have read or listened to the Christmas story from the Bible.

My family has purchased food or gifts for a poor family.

My family will visit relatives for Christmas.

I have memorized some of the Christmas story from the Bible.

Micah 5:2

Genesis 49:10; Revelation 5:5

Isaiah 9:7

Jeremiah 31:5

Hosea 11:1

Isaiah 60:3

Proverbs 2:8b

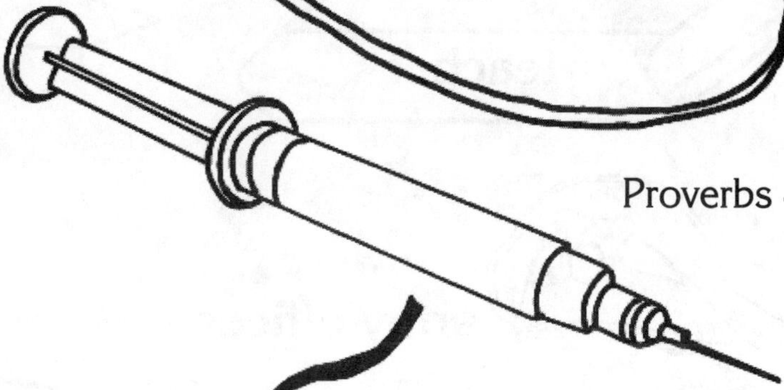

Proverbs 4:6

Psalm 73:28

Proverbs 2:11

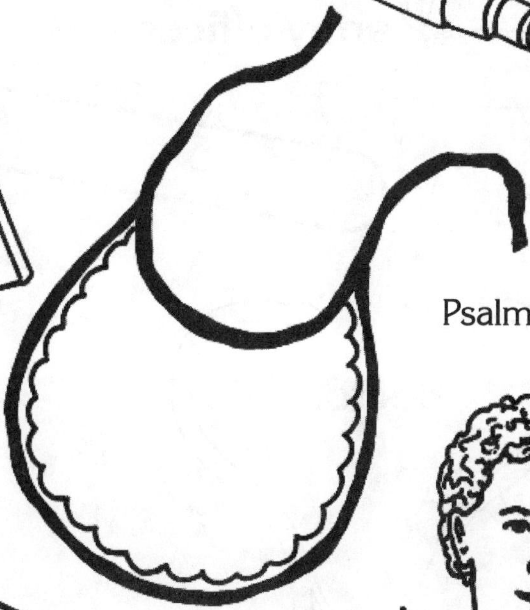

Psalm 40:11

Proverbs 2:8

Psalm 25:21

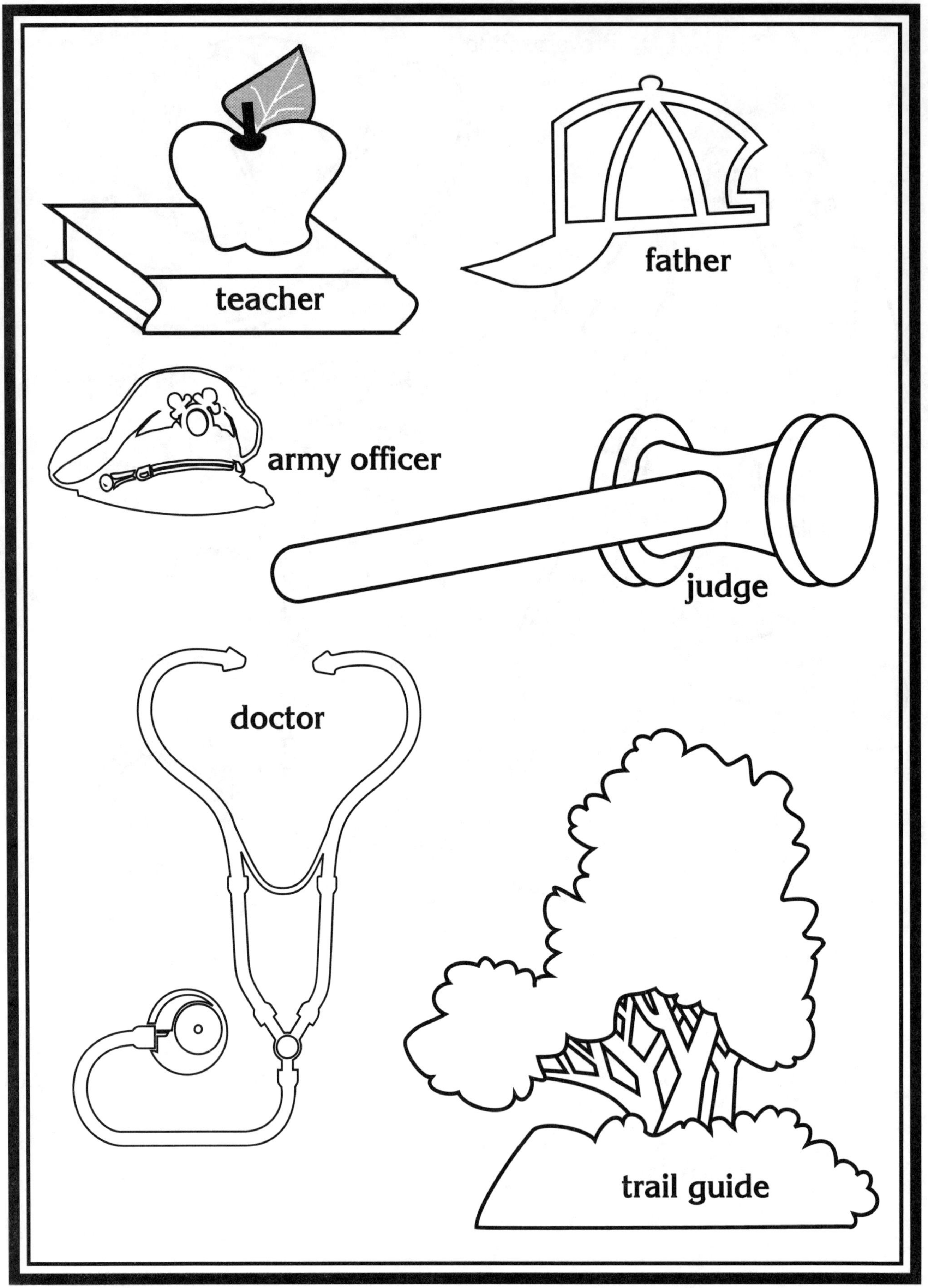
teacher
father
army officer
judge
doctor
trail guide

Read about Angelina, Jessica, Brandon, and Jeff. What do they think will make them happy? What will make them happy? Read Philippians 4:4, 12 to find the answer.

1. Angelina's best friend, Marcie, just moved away. Her other friends, Tina and Lisa, don't include her anymore. There are no other kids in her neighborhood. She doesn't have many friends at school. "I'll never be happy if I don't have any friends," says Angelina.

2. Jessica hates going to school because she doesn't have nice clothes to wear. She has one or two new outfits, but most of her clothes are hand-me-downs from her older sister. "I'll never be happy if I don't have nice clothes," says Jessica.

3. Brandon is not very good at any sport! He always drops the basketball or misses hitting the softball. The other kids make fun of him in gym class, and nobody wants him on their team. "I'll never be happy if I can't play sports," says Brandon.

4. Jeff has trouble getting good grades. No matter how hard he studies, he always gets B's and C's on his report card. "I 'll never be happy if I can't get good grades," says Jeff.

God says, "Be _____ and _____ that I am God. Psalm 46:10

Come before Him with _______. Psalm 100:2

Let's come to Him with ___________. Psalm 95:2

We should worship God in a way that pleases Him. So let us worship Him with _________ and _________. Hebrews 12:28

Let those who worship Him _________. Psalm 149:5

Be still

and know

that I am

God.

Psalm 46:10.

Write your name

d
o
w
n

this side of the page.
Write words that describe God that begin with the letters in your name.

Write your name

d
o
w
n

this side of the page again. Now write things you are thankful for that begin with the letters in your name.

Imagine that God is right beside you. Tell Him how you feel about Him.

____

_____________________________________ (1 John 1:9)

The Lord will do what He says.

____

_____________________________________ (Acts 2:38)

The Lord will do what He says.

____

_____________________________________ (1 Corinthians 10:13)

The Lord will do what He says.

____

_____________________________________ (Hebrews 13:15)

The Lord will do what He says.

____

_____________________________________ (Luke 11:9)

The Lord will do what He says.

____

_____________________________________ (Revelation 21:4)

The Lord will do what He says.

____

_____________________________________ (1 John 2:25)

The Lord will do what He says.

A Celebration Party

Joel, Janine, and Steve walk by carrying a banner, drum, tambourine, or other musical instrument. Peter stops them.

Peter: Where are you guys going?

Janine: We're on our way to church?

Peter: You're kidding! What are you going to do with that stuff *(he nods at the banner and musical instruments)* at church?

Joel: We're planning a celebration party?

Peter: A party? I thought church was a place to be quiet and think about God.

Steve: Well, church is a place to think about God. But we're not always quiet!

Peter: What's the party for? Is it your minister's birthday or something?

Janine: No, it's not a birthday party.

Peter: Well, then is it some kind of church holiday or something?

Steve: No, it's not a holiday. We're celebrating God.

Peter: I don't get it.

Joel: We think God is great, and we want to thank Him.

Peter: Oh, yeah. Well, I already do that—once a year at Thanksgiving. What are you guys going to do with those instruments anyway?

Janine: We're going to play them. And it's going to be loud. And it's going to sound happy!

Peter: What about the banner? Do you have a bunch of people waving flags while you play?

Steve: The banner is for the procession.

Peter: What is a procession?

Joel: It's kind of a like a march or a parade, where a few guys come in with these banners while someone plays or sings music that praises God.

Janine: The procession gets us in the mood to celebrate!

Steve: It sounds like you don't have much experience at celebrating at church. What about coming with us?

Peter: Oh, I don't know. Would I have to do anything? I mean, like would I have to get up in front of everyone.

Joel: No. You can just come and watch.

Janine: Don't just watch. Celebrate with us!

Bible Smorgasboard

Read the verses below. Write the foods that God provided on the blank lines

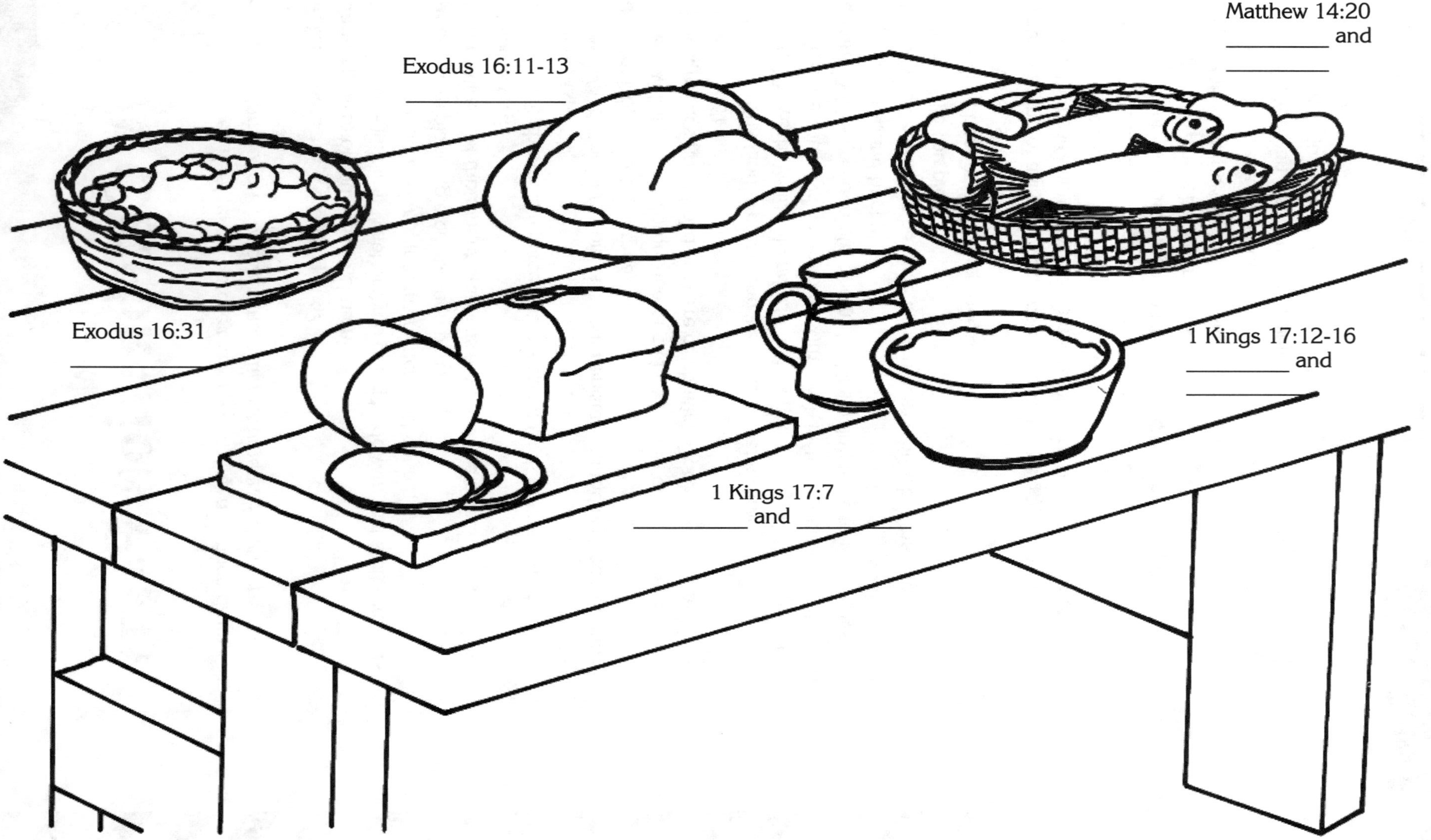

I saw God's power bring my brother back to life.

Moses
Exodus 14:21

John
John 20:5

I saw God's power in a bright light
on the road to Damascus.

Martha
John 11:38-44

I saw God's power burn up an altar drenched with water.

I saw God's power open up the Red Sea so
my people could escape the Egyptians.

Elijah
1Kings 18:38

I saw God's power at the empty tomb.

I saw God's power
shut the mouths of lions.

Daniel
Daniel 6:22

Saul
Acts 9:3-5

"He is able to do
according

IMMEASURABLY more than
to His power" Ephesians

all we ask or think
3:20

1. attach to tube

2. attach to piece 1

3. attach to piece 2

God Provides

Food

Find four kinds of food and glue them here.

Shelter

Find four kinds or names of buildings and glue them here.

Clothing

Find four kinds of clothing and glue them here.

Family

Find four names of family members and glue them here.

A Good Shepherd

Jesus takes care of us like a good shepherd cares for his sheep. Read what Jesus does for us in the verses. Then match each verse with the sentence that tells what a shepherd does for his sheep.

Jesus died for us.
John 10:11

Jesus takes care of us.
Isaiah 40:11

Jesus gives us everything we need.
Psalm 23:1, 2

Jesus calls us each by name.
John 10:3

Jesus is always with us.
Psalm 23:4

A shepherd never leaves his sheep alone.

A shepherd gives his sheep food,water, and rest.

A shepherd will carry small lambs in his arms when they are tired.

A shepherd knows each sheep in his flock by name.

A shepherd will risk his own life to rescue a lost sheep.

Sarah	home	Do not steal.	Obey
Nate	school	Honor your father and mother.	Disobey
Rebecca	store	Do not use God's name thoughtlessly.	Obey
Jeff	yard	Remember the Sabbath day as a holy day.	Disobey
Chris	church	Do not lie about your neighbor.	Obey

The Key to Happiness

Read the verses from Psalm 119 and finish the acrostic puzzle.

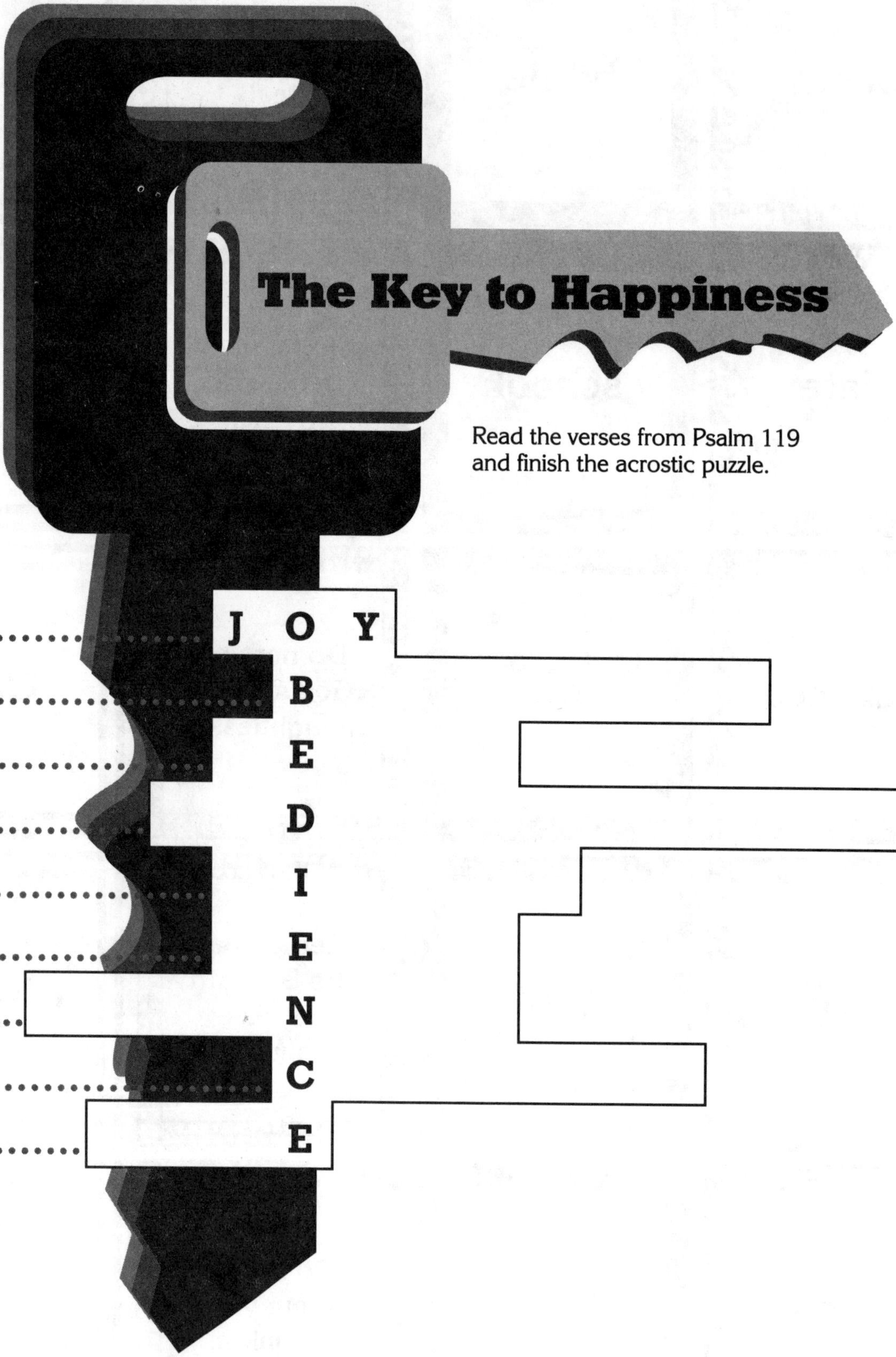

verse 111 .... J O Y

verse 1 .... B

verse 132 .... E

verse 104 .... D

verse 98 I

verse 165 .... E

verse 28 .... N

verse 50 C

verse 76 .... E

Who Tells You What To Do?

What do each of these people say to influence you. Fill in the empty speech balloons.

Friend

Parent

Movie

Music

Bible

Teacher

Suggested Props: A crown, an empty hamburger box, a picture of a snake or a rubber snake.

King Tut was a famous Pharaoh or Egyptian king who was buried in a tomb full of precious gold and jewels. A king cobra is a very poisonous snake. But God is a king who is different from any other kind of king. All other kings will be gone someday. But God will be king forever.

Psalm 10:16

Suggested Props: A globe or map.

Japan is so far away that when it is the middle of the day here, it is the middle of the night there. It takes one day of flying in an airplane to get to Japan because it is almost halfway around the world. But God can be here and in Japan and anywhere else in the world at exactly the same time. God is everywhere! He is so big that He fills the heaven and the earth.

Jeremiah 23:23, 24

Suggested Props: A banana, a piece of cloth with a small flaw.

A flaw is something very small that is wrong with something. A tiny little scratch on our skin is a flaw. Or a soft spot in a banana that looked okay with the peel on it. A bumpy uneven part of the material in our clothes is also a flaw. But God has no flaws. Not even the tiniest thing is wrong with God. He is perfect!

Psalm 18:30

What can
I give the
LORD
for ALL the
GOOD
THINGS
he has
GIVEN me?
Psalm 116:12

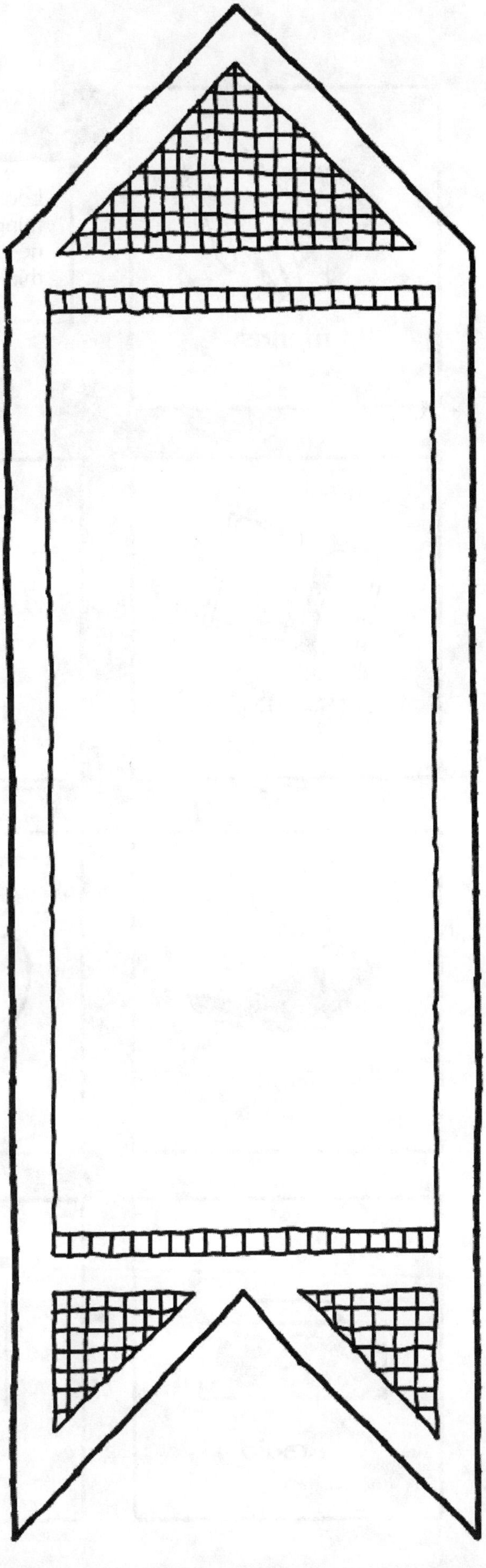

Look at the things below. What things do you need? What things can you do without? Cross out the things you don't need. Put a star ★ by the two things you need that you think are most important.

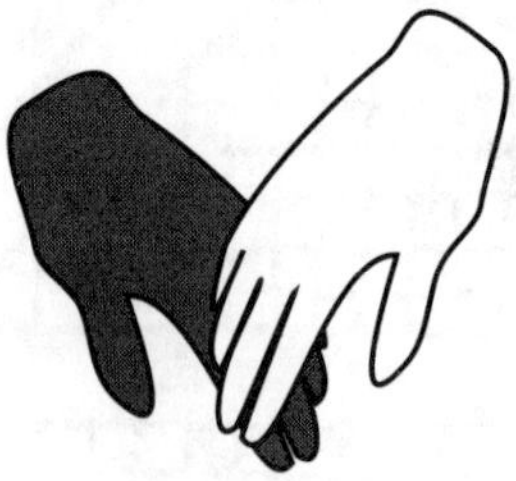

friends

the Bible

new clothes

food

a bike

a place to live

a radio

a television

family

WORSHIP SONGS

He's Got the Whole World in His Hands

Spiritual

Come Into His Presence

UNKNOWN

God Is the Great Creator

L. KARNS | L. KARNS

Verse 2:
Next day He made the firmament, With water way up high
And water also down below. The heaven we call sky.

Verse 3:
The third day dry land did appear, When God made all the seas.
On this same day He made the grass, The flow'rs, the plants, and trees.

Verse 4:
The fourth day God did place in heav'n, The sun to give earth light,
The stars for signs and seasons, And the moon to rule the night.

God's Promise Is a Promise

M.K.B. Gently

Mary Kay Bottens

Anywhere With Jesus

1,2 - JESSIE B. POUNDS
3 - HELEN G. ALEXANDER

DANIEL B. TOWNER

I Will Sing of the Mercies of the Lord Forever

PSALM 89:1

J. H. FULLMORE

Joyfully

You Are My Hiding Place

To sing as a round in two parts, Group 2 should begin singing when Group 1 arrives at measure 9.

When We All Get to Heaven

Eliza E. Hewitt — Emily D. Wilson

My God Is a Great God

S.B.S. STELLA B. STACK

The Joy of the Lord Is My Strength

SOURCE UNKNOWN

Angels From the Realms of Glory

James Montgomery | Henry Smart

Go, Tell It on the Mountain

Traditional
Arr. by Todd Tyler

I Will Enter His Gates

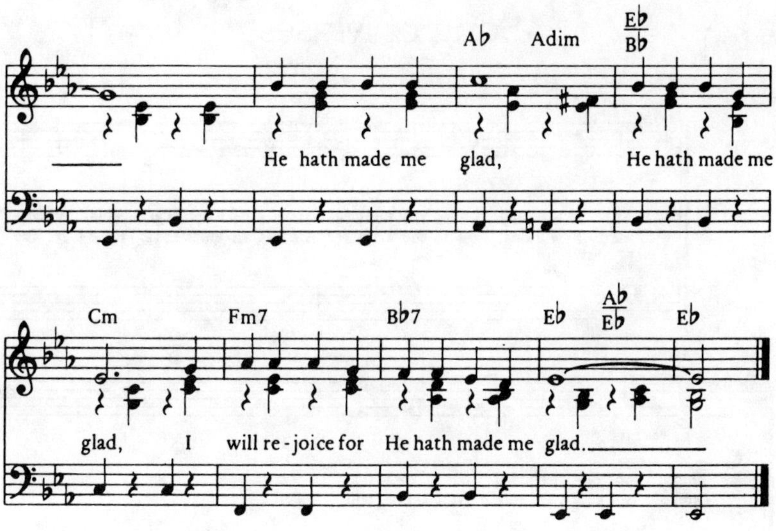

The Peace of God

ELEANOR PANKOW

Song of Moses

JEWISH SONG

God Is So Good

Like a Good Shepherd

M.K.B.

MARY KAY BOTTENS

Let Us Thank the Lord

MARY KAY BOTTENS

We Give Thee But Thine Own

William W. How | Ascribed to Robert Schumann

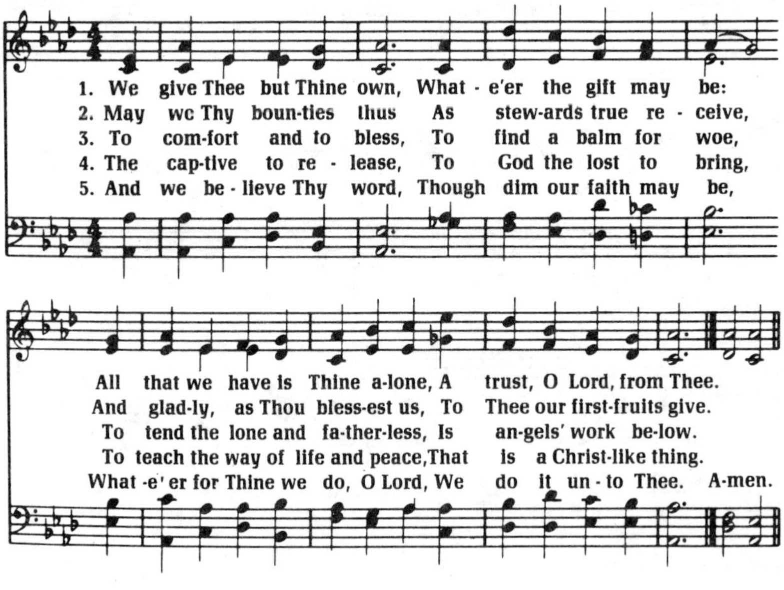